A visitor glanced at his thin, pale face, high receding forehead, pointed nose, and piercing, close-set eyes. "It is useless to say Jerry McAuley is an honest man," she said. "He cannot be. He was born to be bad. How can he help it with that type of head?"

He was a river thief, con man, and drunk. Then he had a vision of God and was transformed. He blazed a path that many others have followed. Because of Jerry McAuley, millions have been fed, many wounds have been healed, and many hearts mended.

JERRY McAULEY

and his mission

Revised Edition

By ARTHUR BONNER

LOIZEAUX BROTHERS

Neptune, New Jersey

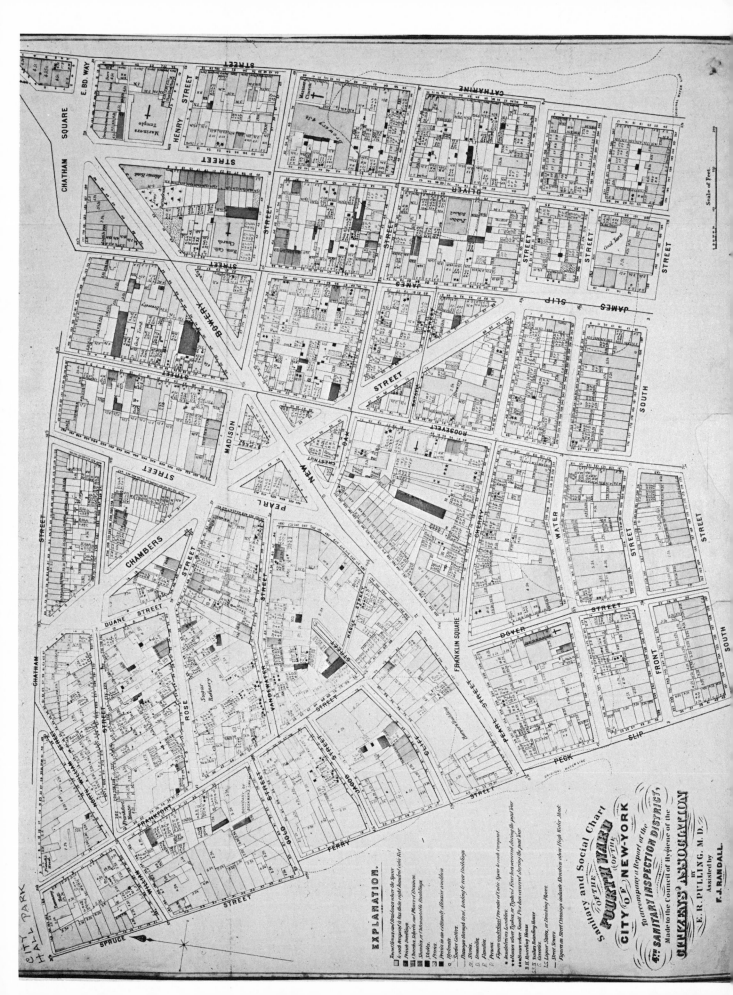

EXPLANATION.

Tenant Houses and Residences where the Space

- occupied or required is less than one hundred cubic feet.
- Private Distilleries
- Breweries, Sugar, and Places of Steam.
- Slaughter, or Manufactories Buildings
- Stables.
- Privies.
- Privies in an extremely offensive condition
- ○ Hydrants.
- Sunken Gutters.

○ Damage through and leading to rear buildings

- St. Stores.
- D. Domestic.
- F. Families.
- P. Persons.

Figures in distinct present the rate of Cubic Space to each occupant

- ✱✱ Houses where Typhus, or Typhoid Fever has occurred during the past Year
- ✱✱✱ Houses where Small Pox has occurred during the past Year
- † Houses where Scarlet Fever has occurred during the past Year
- B.H. Boarding House
- L.S. Sailors Boarding House
- L.S. Liquor Stores, or Drinking Places
- ___ Street Sewers.
- ___ Figures on Street Crossings indicate Elevation above High Water Mark.

Sanitary and Social Chart
OF THE
FOURTH WARD
OF THE
CITY OF NEW-YORK
To accompany a Report of the
4th SANITARY INSPECTION DISTRICT,
Made to the Council of Hygiene of the
CITIZENS' ASSOCIATION
BY
E. R. PULLING, M. D.
Assisted by
F. J. RANDALL.

Scale of Feet.

Contents

Introduction

SINCE THE EIGHTEENTH CENTURY, intellectuals have confidently predicted the end of religion and now we live in an age where science claims to rule. Yet when asked, about ninety percent of Americans said they believe in God. Gallup polls consistently show a third of Americans also believe in the divinity of Jesus Christ, have made a commitment to Him, feel their prayers have been answered, and believe God has a plan for them.

In America, ninety percent of the institutions that house and feed the homeless are private voluntary institutions. Of these, forty percent are religious—notably rescue missions dedicated to serving the poorest and most broken. For these islands of love and hope, religion is not some vague concept of goodness, nor is it mere psychology. Religion is the acceptance of the living presence of a God who can change lives. A rescue mission serves the essential purpose of Christian evangelicalism: to bring men and women to the Lord.

So it was with Jerry McAuley. Alone in a prison cell he was bathed in the presence of God and was given a mission to heal, teach, and bring to Christ drunkards, former criminals, the mentally unstable, the unskilled, and the poorly educated—all those rejected as the "undeserving" poor.

And so it continues. Charles Ross, anticipating his retirement at the age of seventy-three after serving the McAuley Water Street Mission for eighteen years, thought back to when he was first called to mission work. Ross, born in Kansas City, Missouri to a Plymouth Brethren family, was in business for twenty-one years until he "realized there was more to life than just buying nuts and bolts to make something to sell." In 1964 he became business manager for the Emmaus Bible School in Illinois (now the Emmaus Bible College in Iowa). In 1970 the Pacific Garden Mission in Chicago asked him to be its business manager.

"It took me three months to decide, asking God for guidance," he recalled. "One December morning just before Christmas, I called up the director and said I would take the job and he asked me to come for a look around. We went to the dining room just as the men were lining up for their lunch. It was a wet day and dirty wool overcoats stink when they get wet. I looked at the men and said to myself, 'Is this the way I'm going to spend the rest of my life?' It was as though I got a slap on the right side of my face and a voice seemed to say, 'Charlie Ross, but for the grace of God you'd be in that line.' As I was blinking inwardly, the other side of my face felt as if there were a smack against it and the voice seemed to say, 'Remember, Christ died for each one of those fellows just as He died for you.'

"I didn't hear audible voices but I felt it was the voice of God telling me, 'This is where I want you.' And I can say honestly from that day forward I never had any doubts about what I should do. I took the post of business manager in January 1970. After about a year I became assistant superintendent. I was there three-and-a-half years and then was asked to come to New York."

There are about 450 rescue missions in the United States today. Critics have accused their organizers of equating poverty with sin and of making the poor "sing for their supper." Conversions are called "nosedives" and those who enter their doors are dismissed as "cold-weather Christians" and "mission stiffs." If religious salvation is their reason for existence, they are said to be colossal failures.

"Rescue missions have always been the butt of jokes," Ross said. "Basically, it's because some people don't like the Christian message we preach. As it says in 2 Corinthians 4:3–4: 'But if our gospel be hid, it is hid to them that are lost: In whom the god of this world hath blinded the minds of them which believe not, lest the light of the glorious gospel of Christ, who is the image of God, should shine unto them.'

"We're not here to force anything down people's throats. We know a lot of men will be polite while they're inwardly sneering at the message. We never turn them away. We only say, 'Come and listen.' We let the Lord do the rest. I had a pastor who called up and wanted a bed for the night for some needy person. When we give a telephone referral we're careful to say a man will attend an evening gospel service, have supper, take a shower, and then go to bed. You would be surprised at the number of men who don't want to take a shower. We told the pastor all that. He objected and said the man was an atheist. I said, 'Listen sir. We're not saying we're going to make a believer out of him.

He can be an atheist if he wants; that's his free choice. But if he wants to take what we have to give he has to sit through the evening service. It goes with the turf.'

"Settled people with a comfortable life may object to asking someone to sit through a service, but not the men who come here. The very night when that pastor made his objections three men stood up and said what a tremendous lift it gave them to sit in the chapel and listen to the message. They didn't say how good it was to come and get something to eat; it was the service that eased their minds. It encourages them in what otherwise is a dreary life."

The men who come to the mission have a wide range of disabilities, intelligence, and talents, from men with schizophrenia, sociopathic personalities, and various degrees of alcoholism to former school teachers and other professionals. Magazine cartoons perpetuate a myth of homeless men on a park bench pleasantly drinking their lives away or innocently trying to subsist without work. Only about one-third have serious problems with alcohol or drugs. The other two-thirds come to the mission because they are severely destitute. They are where they are because they have few alternatives.

There is another myth that the men who seek refuge in city missions are mainly the broken and elderly. Although as many as ten percent who come to the McAuley mission on any night may be too old to work or physically handicapped, most are surprisingly young. Samples taken on two winter nights in 1989 showed about twenty-five percent were in their twenties, forty-five percent in the thirties, fifteen percent in their forties and the remainder fifty years and older, with one or two in their teens. The racial composition has also changed in the past twenty years, reflecting white flight from the inner city as well as the difficulty faced by poorly educated blacks in finding work in offices and factories that demand greater skills. Pictures of the chapel service a generation ago showed only white faces. Now the faces are seventy-five to ninety percent black, including men from the Caribbean.

A small percentage of men are belligerent and even dangerous. Political promises and slick advertisements of a wealthy society have also made some demanding. "They can drive you nuts," Charles Ross said. "They say, 'I want this and I want that.' But when Jesus Christ was on earth people turned away from Him; He never turned away from them. It says in Matthew 9:35–36: 'And Jesus went about all the cities and villages, teaching in their synagogues, and preaching the gospel of the kingdom, and healing every sickness and every disease among the people. But when he saw the multitudes, he was moved with compassion on them, because they fainted, and were scattered abroad, as sheep having no shepherd.'

"He told the disciples to help these people, so we don't say, 'Get out of here if you don't come around to our way of Christianity.' Our mission is compassion. We say, 'We'll give you what we've got. Just listen to what we have to say and make up your mind.'"

Every man who comes to missions needs patience and understanding. This is particularly true of the alcoholic. Living for years addicted to a chemical, fearing the pain of deprivation, frustrated by his inability to control this dependency, a man becomes convinced he is worthless. He is alienated from everyone, including God.

In 1956, the American Medical Association accepted alcoholism as an illness. To some this was progress but to others it was an escape. Does the disease concept absolve the alcoholic of all moral responsibility? A diabetic must still take insulin and follow a diet, and a cancer patient may still have to choose to undergo surgery. Can an alcoholic be excused from the obligation to get help for overcoming his illness?

It is here the message of a forgiving God who has a plan for each and every person has its force. Intellectuals may forecast the end of religion and skeptics may dismiss the ardent faith of evangelical Christians yet more than a century after the death of Jerry McAuley, the mission he started flourishes as the largest non-governmental institution in New York providing emergency shelter and food for men rejected or ignored by American society. For Christians, the mission is evidence of God's plan for a better world.

Does the disease concept of alcoholism excuse moral responsibility?

THE MEMORY OF
ERRY McAULE
I WILL GIVE
TO HIM
THAT IS
A THIRST
OF THE
FOUNTAIN
OF THE
WATER OF
LIFE FREELY

Existing McAuley Fountain in Greeley Square

1 The Funeral

IN THE FALL OF 1884 the Reverend S. Irenaeus Prime returned to New York City from his summer holidays. He had not been in the house for five minutes when someone came to ask him to conduct the funeral ceremonies for Jerry McAuley.

Irenaeus Prime was senior editor and part owner of the New York *Observer*, one of the many religious newspapers which circulated at the end of the last century. Prime, seventy-two years old and descended from an old conservative New England family, knew everyone who was considered worth knowing and was respected by all in turn. He was the last person who might be expected to call an ex-convict a friend, yet he did.

Recalling how he felt when he first heard of Jerry's death, Prime wrote: "It made me very sad. I did not know that this strange man had such a place in my heart that now he was dead I should feel as if the city and the world had lost a friend. He came often to see me and said little when he was there but seemed to love to sit near me and look up with a tearful eye and a pensive face and a heart, I doubt not, full of sweet hope and holy love. We never talked of the old, old times when he was a thief and a robber, when he was a drunkard and a blasphemer, when he was a convict in prison and afterwards an outcast and an outlaw. It is not in my memory that a word ever passed between us about those terrible days and nights of sin and shame, when he won distinction among the criminal classes as one of the worst of men, a dangerous character, unfit to be at large—as unfit to live as he was unprepared to die."

Jerry McAuley was all of that. Although in private he talked little of his past, he told his story thousands of times in public. Some heard his story by accident when they stumbled into his mission blind drunk or slunk in to escape the cold or beg a handout. Others came to hear his story out of curiosity, for Jerry was a wonder of his time. Second or third hand, he seemed an oddity: The Drunken Bum Turned Preacher. But no one heard Jerry or met Jerry and went away untouched. He was not an oddity. He was real.

He died in the afternoon of September 18, 1884. He took his wife to Central Park on Wednesday for a walk. Just as he returned at 5:30 in the evening he suffered an attack of what was then called "hemorrhage of the lungs." Nowadays we would say he was in the terminal stages of tuberculosis. He lived until 4:05 Thursday afternoon. His wife and others at his bedside said he turned his eyes toward Heaven, raised his hand, and with a brief smile said: "It's all right." Then his arm fell by his side, his eyes closed, and a moment later he was dead.

Few newspapers mentioned his death. However, the New York *Herald* on Friday carried a substantial report: "The voice of prayer and exhortation was heard last night in the Cremorne Mission on West 32nd Street but Brother Jerry McAuley, whose place had always been on the platform, did not appear. His work was finished and in an upper room the evangelist of the slums was lying dead. . . . The congregation which assembled was ignorant of what had occurred. But word of Brother Jerry's death had circulated and there strolled into the mission some figures familiar to the quarter but seldom encountered in a religious edifice. They were women who had been reclaimed from the resorts to the suppression of which the dead man's missionary efforts were chiefly devoted. There was not one of them but seemed deeply affected by the news. Mingled with the throng too were some hard faces of men who had evidently known the evangelist long before he had begun his mission and who had come in half bewildered by their surroundings and clearly at a loss how to regard the services."

The reporter told of a "typical mourner" who stood at the door, doubtfully handling his hat and peering in at the lighted interior. When he had confirmed the fact of McAuley's death, he said: "My, my, so that's the last of him. I ain't much on the relige myself and I don't hitch with these singing and praying folks. But Jerry McAuley was a brick. He was for sure. I've knocked around these parts some and I was down in the swamp when he tried to give religion a show in the Fourth Ward. Well, he never weakened there but started about the worst dives going and gathered in a good many poor fellows that were all the better for it. I can understand a man like that. He means business all the time."

The news of his death seemed to cause little stir.

Jerry had that rare, electric quality, known only to greathearted men, of seeming to make direct contact with everyone he met. Yet he never sought publicity and each of his friends thought he was part of a small band who, alone, knew and appreciated Jerry McAuley. So it was with Irenaeus Prime.

The funeral was scheduled for Sunday, September 21st. "As the hour approached," Prime recalled, "indeed all that day, my thoughts had been dwelling on the fact that New York has no consciousness of the loss it has met. The city knows not that one of the most useful men in it, one of the the most remarkable, wonderful men is to be buried today. Very few know or care about Jerry McAuley. We are going to the Broadway Tabernacle to talk of what he was and what he has done to a little congregation that will gather there. If it were Dr. Taylor, the beloved and honored pastor, the house would be crowded and the mourners would go about the streets. But poor Jerry—he is dead and who will be there to weep with us over his remains?"

Since Prime was to conduct the services he went to the church early. As he turned off Fifth Avenue and walked up 34th Street he saw a huge crowd standing in the sunshine, filling the streets and the square at 34th Street and Sixth Avenue. He walked on, wondering why they did not go into the church and take seats. When he reached the Tabernacle he found it was already packed. The police had to shout and push to clear the way so that he could get inside.

The services were scheduled for 2:30 but long before that a squad of six policemen had barred the doors. The crowds still came. They tried every door and pushed their way into the private entrances. A young lady arrived just at the opening of the services to find her way completely blocked. She pleaded with the crowd to let her in, saying she was in the choir. But the mass of people was too thick to be forced aside and she went away with tears in her eyes. The crowd outside grew greater and greater and more police had to be called to keep the Sixth Avenue car tracks from being blocked.

The church, one of the largest in the nation, was crowded from the front to the rear. Every seat was taken, all the aisles were packed, men and women sat on the pulpit stairs, crowded in the lobbies and corridors, and looked over each other's heads at the doors.

Reporters were struck by the variety of people: "old women, wrinkled and seamed" . . . "here and there sprinkled through the crowd the painted face of the scarlet woman showed itself" . . . "the tall silk hats of half a score of downtown bankers overtopped the straw hats of a few homeless tramps" . . . "a great many Negroes of both sexes" . . . "a great many gentlemen and ladies" . . . "the young shop girl who has been saved from temptation" . . . "gamblers and confidence men who seemed very ill at ease."

It was one of the largest funerals for a private individual ever held in New York up to that time. Yet the body in the black casket had been a drunkard so low that the meanest dives had once thrown him out. The open casket showed a thin, white face, high receding forehead, eyes a bit too close together, pointed nose, and strong chin. He could not have won hearts by his looks.

As his body lay in a coffin, on which was placed a simple cross of green smilax, it seemed that all that remained was to pay homage. That was why the crowd was so large. They came to say good-by and mark an end. This was a last offering of love and affection. A half dozen eminent businessmen and ministers came to the pulpit to eulogize him. One of the ministers recalled: "I remember the last time he left my study. I looked after him and felt a tender feeling for him such as I seldom feel for a man. I often used to drop in after a sermon to see him at his mission simply because I wanted to see how Jerry was getting along."

A *Herald* reporter was standing outside near one of the entrances talking to an usher when a shabby old man approached.

"Beg pardon, gents," he said, "but seeing as how you were connected here and seeing as how I ain't posted on ways and things, I thought I'd ask you a favor. I've heard it's the right thing to send flowers and such to put on the coffin of anyone who's been good to you. Well, I don't know, gents, whether I've got the rights of it or not. But there's something here for Jerry."

He took off his hat and felt inside with trembling fingers. He took out a little bunch of flowers.

"It ain't any great shakes," he said, looking at the reporter and usher to see if they disapproved. When they did not, he continued: "They're no great shakes, I allow, and I expect they mayn't set off the roses and things rich people send. I'm a poor man you know, but when I heard Jerry was gone I gets up and says to myself, 'Go on and do what's fashionable; that's the way folks do when they want to show a dead man's done a heap for them.' So there they are."

The usher took the flowers.

"When you drop them with the rest," the old man said, "though they ain't no great shakes, Jerry, who was my friend, will know; he'll know they come from old Joe Chappy."

"What did he do for you?" asked the reporter.

"A great deal. But it's long ago now. My girl had gone to the bad and was dying without ever a bite for her to eat. I got around drunk but it sobered me and I hustled about to hunt up some good man. N.G. They asked if she went to Sunday school and all that. Of course she didn't. How could the poor girl? Well they called her names, said she was a child of wrath and I went away brokenhearted, when I come across Jerry and he went home with me and comforted me and he said that Almighty God wouldn't be rough on the poor girl what didn't know no better. She died then but I ain't forgot Jerry."

Jerry McAuley was unique. He imitated no one but was imitated by many. He was the first person in the world to open the doors of a religious institution every night of the year specifically for the outcasts of society. He was the first to start what we now know as a rescue mission. He raised a beacon where men and women burdened with misery, broken down and shattered by debauchery and vice, homeless and hopeless, hungry, ragged, defiled and drunk, from the prison or from the gutter, were welcomed and made to feel that somebody cared for them. He showed them they could be saved in the spirit and made decent and respectable here and now in this life.

Nowadays the most active and tireless organization in the field of rescue work is the Salvation Army. It is so successful that it is often assumed that the effort to use religion and the Bible as a means of regenerating drunkards, derelicts, and prostitutes began with the Salvation Army. Actually, the Army came late to the field. General William Booth, the founder of the Salvation Army, began his preaching to the poor in England in the 1860's. He found many of his strongest workers from among drunkards and ex-criminals. Yet when his son, Bramwell Booth, began rescue work among prostitutes in 1884 he had to overcome his father's objections. It was not until 1888 that General Booth ordered Bramwell to do something for the homeless of London. Bramwell Booth's first reaction was to raise the traditional objections that charity should not be indiscriminately distributed and that it was hard to tell the difference between the deserving and undeserving poor. Although the first Salvation Army team arrived in New York in 1880,

a rescue home for women was not opened until October 1886, and a food and shelter program for derelicts and drunkards was not begun until about 1891.

It was in October 1872 that Jerry McAuley opened his first mission at 316 Water Street in New York. While he was alive those who came to scoff or be amused stayed to wonder and praise. George Kennan, the explorer of Siberia, spent many evenings at the Water Street mission in 1876 and later called it, "one of the most remarkable things to be seen at that time in the city of New York or any other city."

The crowds who came to his funeral probably expected that McAuley's work, and perhaps even his memory, would not last long beyond his death. But both lived on. In 1909 Ray Stannard Baker, the muckraker and exposer of evils, wrote a series of articles on religion in New York. He called the McAuley Water Street Mission "one of the most extraordinary institutions in this country."

John Henry Jowett, an Englishman who was a well-known preacher in Britain and the United States during the first quarter of this century, was pastor of the influential Fifth Avenue Presbyterian Church in New York from 1911 to 1918. After his own services on Sunday he used to visit the McAuley mission and sit quietly in the rear of the hall during the meeting. Later he returned to England. "The biggest thing in the city of New York," he once told a congregation, "is the McAuley Water Street Mission."

There are now rescue missions in every city of the United States where there is a skid row. Many of them are flowers from the seeds McAuley planted. There are also missions abroad which can be traced, directly or indirectly, to McAuley's efforts. Nearly a century has passed since he began his labors and the number of men and women who have been helped probably runs into the millions.

Thanksgiving Day Lunch, 1941

The Meaning of Conversion

THERE IS A LITTLE TRIANGULAR PARK formed by Broadway as it slants across midtown Manhattan, destroying the usual pattern of neat oblong blocks. Sixth Avenue and 32nd Street form the right angle and Broadway cuts across to form the hypotenuse. It is a tiny clearing in a jungle of skyscrapers with torrents of traffic roaring by on three sides like the streams at the bottom of a deep canyon. Pennsylvania Station, with its rivers of trains, is a block away. A block away in another direction looms the peak of the Empire State Building. There are Macy's and other large department stores, and beneath the streets a labyrinth of subway lines.

The park is called Greeley Square and there is a bronze, seated statue of Horace Greeley on a high pedestal. But no one pays any attention. All is hurry and rush. Thousands of feet go by every day, millions every year; twenty-four hours a day, seven days a week, always someone moving, busy, preoccupied, dodging traffic.

On a hot summer day a few people may stop to drink from an inconspicuous water fountain at the south end of Greeley Square. It is not like the utilitarian concrete fountains that the city usually installs. It is carved from a block of reddish marble. But no one notices: a sip of water and hurry on. Certainly almost none of these passing millions takes time to bend down awkwardly to read the inscription on the shaft of the fountain: "To the memory of Jerry McAuley. 'I will give to him that is athirst of the fountain of the water of life freely.'"

The memory of Jerry McAuley is now remote. McAuley himself never learned to write with any degree of assurance and almost none of the people around him were the kind who put their thoughts or stories down on paper. Either they were too busy with the struggle against impoverishment of body and spirit or they were men of commerce and banking who were more at home with a ledger than a diary.

Most of his early history has to be gleaned from *Transformed: or The History of a River Thief*, a pamphlet published in 1876, four years after he opened his mission on Water Street. For his later life there are transcripts of some of the things he said during his prayer meetings and occasional interviews on reminiscences. But the record leaves much to be desired.

Transformed was dictated and then transcribed into a formal prose which gives a meager indication of his actual style. It appears that he had the brogue of an Irishman and the accents and slang of the slums. One interviewer transcribed a few of his sentences like this: "There's some of us that's clane and dacent. There's more outside that's nayther." He probably dropped the "g" in words ending in "ing" and said "tief" instead of thief.

However, it is useless, if not misleading, to attempt to reproduce an unfamiliar accent without the use of an elaborate and technical phonetic alphabet. Even where the original source attempts to imitate his accent, we will, in this account, restore the customary spellings in the interests of clarity.

Some of the rough spots of McAuley's speech were probably rounded off later in life as he associated more frequently with people of higher education, but until he died strangers were aware of his antecedents with the first sentence he spoke. Yet he made a powerful, almost instantaneous, impression on bankers, businessmen, world travelers, uptown ministers, and society ladies.

Then, as now, a person's character was often judged by the outward signs of culture and education. McAuley overcame this handicap. He had been transformed. He was a new man with an inner strength and an aura of gentleness which overshadowed the indications of his earlier self.

In describing how this came about we will be dealing with visions, other voices, trancelike states, the fragrance of spiritual flowers, and copious tears. All this is something which ordinary experience leads us to view with suspicion, if not distaste. We immediately think of hysteria and hallucination.

We will also talk of revivals and prayer meetings. For several generations these have been easy subjects for debunking. Images from fiction and exposé literature come readily to mind: extravagant gestures, crude emotionalism, flamboyant preachers, lusty sinners.

Many people feel they can get along very well without leaning on what seems to be a religious crutch. They feel uneasy when they meet someone for whom religion is a deeply moving, compelling experience. Why go around preaching all the time? Why concern yourself with someone else's problems? Mind your own business, pay your taxes, take care of your family, have fun, and let the world wobble along as it always has. This is the routine of life: work, social and family obligations, and a certain amount of relaxation and pleasure.

Every now and then someone is dislodged from this routine. After search and trial and error he discovers there is a reality beyond the ordinary one. He finds a certainty and happiness he never knew before. He is transformed and often wants to talk about his experience and prod others into action or inward search. He might be called a troublemaker or thought of as an unnecessary irritant but he will not allow himself to be ignored. He has a sense of mission, a desire to do great things.

In religious terminology, a man who has been so transformed is said to be converted. But *conversion* is a word with a double usage and must be carefully explained. It can describe both an outer change and an inner change.

The outer change deals with the form or style of religious practice. This is the common usage of the word. A person is said to be a convert from one belief or sect to another. This outer change may take place without an inner change. A person might change his religion because he is physically persecuted or because of a more subtle social pressure which makes him want to conform to the practices of the majority. He might also change simply because he wants to marry a girl of another faith or because he enjoys the music of another church. Such a person might be called a convert but he is not transformed. He has not experienced the inner change of conversion.

At times the outer change of form coincides with an inner transformation. This happened with Jerry McAuley. He was born a nominal Roman Catholic and became a Protestant evangelist. However the change in the style of religion is not the crucial experience. It is the inward change that is important. A person might have been born and raised in a religious home. He might consider himself and be considered by others as a practicing Roman Catholic or a practicing Methodist or Presbyterian or any other sect. But these practices are peripheral to his life. Then, for some reason or other, he experiences conversion. He is transformed. Religious beliefs become real and alive. He knows in his heart and soul what the words and phrases mean. Religion becomes a living thing, a way of life.

In the pages that follow, when the words *conversion* or *convert* are used, they are meant in this sense of an inner change. Many of the men and women who will be described were, in fact, persons who returned to the beliefs of their parents. This does not make their conversion any less meaningful; it is the same inward transformation no matter what the form of the outward practice.

If conversion is something deeper than a change in form it is also something more than a mere change in philosophy. It is so real it can be felt, tasted, and seen. It is a deep emotional process with marked stages of development. One of the earliest descriptions of conversion can be found in the words of the Prophet Isaiah (6:5-8):

Then said I, Woe is me! for I am undone; because I am a man of unclean lips, and I dwell in the midst of a people of unclean lips: for mine eyes have seen the King, the LORD *of hosts.*

Then flew one of the seraphim unto me, having a live coal in his hand, which he had taken with the tongs from off the altar: And he laid it upon my mouth, and said, Lo, this hath touched thy lips; and thine iniquity is taken away, and thy sin purged.

Also I heard the voice of the LORD, *saying, Whom shall I send, and who will go for us? Then said I, Here am I; send me.*

These, poetically expressed, are the stages and result of conversion. First the conviction that something is wrong with the life one is leading. This can be a traumatic dislocation or a quiet although persistent feeling of unease. Whatever the symptoms, the sufferer eventually realizes he does not have the ability to solve the difficulty by his own efforts. Then comes surrender and a sense of the direct presence of the Lord. Finally, a feeling of release. There is a new meaning in life and often a sense of mission: "Here am I; send me."

Christianity, its later movements, and its major turning points are marked by the crisis of a converted man: St. Paul and St. Augustine, Luther and Wesley. Their biographies and writings are full of tears, tumults, and tensions. Said Paul to the Romans: "For what I would, that do I not; but what I hate, that do I."

One of the first men to study conversion as a psychological phenomenon was William James, the father of philosophy in the United States. In 1902 he published *The Varieties of Religious Experience*, a work which is still a major textbook on the subject.

Most people, if they are religious at all, are religious by habit. They follow tradition and routine. However, for those who have experienced conversion, religion means a direct, compelling contact with God. Their spiritual experience has given them a new life. They are twice-born. They are people for whom, as James wrote, "religion exists not as a dull habit but as an acute fever."

The experience of conversion is often marked by talk of weakness and sin. An average person, content with his day-to-day existence and not given to self-analysis and inward searching, often finds this morbid. Yet a person who is in real spiritual torment or mental anguish knows he is not well. He knows he is not complete. He knows that he has no will power and that he cannot simply will things to be better. He wants help, strong and immediate.

But first he must surrender his will. This element of surrender is the key to conversion. Every spiritual leader who has emphasized the conversion experience has pointed to the need for surrender. For instance, Martin Luther:

"God is the God of the humble, the miserable, the oppressed, and the desperate and those that are brought even to nothing. His nature is to give sight to the blind, to comfort the brokenhearted, to justify sinners, to save the very desperate and damned. . . . But here lieth the difficulty, that when a man is terrified and cast down, he is so little able to raise himself up again and say, 'Now I am bruised and afflicted enough; now is the time of grace; now is the time to hear Christ.'

"The foolishness of man's heart is so great that then he rather seeketh to himself more laws to satisfy his conscience. 'If I live,' saith he, 'I will amend my life: I will do this, I will do that.' But here, except thou do the quite contrary, except thou send Moses away with his law, and in these terrors and anguish lay hold upon Christ who died for thy sins, look for no salvation. . . . For He died not to justify the righteous, but the unrighteous and to make them the children of God."

In some instances this moment of surrender is accompanied by visions, the fragrance of flowers unseen, brilliant shafts of light, voices, and trances. This moment of surrender—and the later memory of this moment—is often bathed in tears.

"The stone wall inside of him has fallen," William James wrote. "The hardness of his heart has broken down. . . . Especially if we weep. For it is then as if our tears broke through the inveterate inner dam and let all sorts of ancient peccancies and moral stagnancies drain away, leaving us new washed and

soft of heart and open to every nobler leading. . . . Many saints, even as energetic ones as Teresa and Loyola have possessed what the church traditionally reveres as a special grace, the so-called gift of tears."

The person who has surrendered to God walks the earth with a sense of positive assurance. He no longer need worry. He can remain where he is and still be willing to live on. He may feel that he knows great truths which he cannot put into words. Above all, he has a sense of joy, of happiness every moment.

We will see this in the life of Jerry McAuley and the people around him. Yet the average person, religiously inclined or not, is well to be on his guard. No one nowadays accepts visions and trances and mysterious voices as positive evidence of the presence of something divine. Ecstatic states can be induced by alcohol, drugs, hypnotism, and, at times, mere suggestion and imitation. When the skeptic says, "Never mind your mumbo jumbo, show me your proof," he deserves a serious reply.

"Every religious phenomenon has its history and its derivation from natural antecedents," wrote William James. He was a pragmatist. He believed that all human thought and experience, including the various phenomena of religion, could be examined in the cold light of reason and be understood and given value.

Jerry McAuley was a man of his times and of his class. We will see that his vision and his work grew out of his experiences and the circumstances in which he lived. His conversion took place in Sing Sing prison under conditions that fostered discontent and self-analysis.

And now the religiously inclined person may object. To look for natural antecedents seems to play down and perhaps deny the saving grace of God. Not necessarily. The proof, said James, must lie in the result. If it is a true religious experience, something truly ethical must result.

We must expect to find the attributes which have been regarded in all religions as more divine than human; an abundance of charity and brotherly love, fortitude in the face of adversity, courage in the face of challenge, an ability to be heroic and yet humble.

In short, the man must become a living example of a wider life beyond the selfish interests of other men. Of course, it would be too much to expect that all persons who have the experience of conversion possess these qualities in the same degree. History demonstrates that saints are a rare breed. Yet all who claim to be converted should be raised above the level of what would be considered their normal abilities. When this happens we will know we are not dealing with hysteria or hallucination or artificial excitements.

The skeptic may still not be satisfied. "So what?" he may ask. "What difference does it make if a few people become holier than others, more humble, more heroic, or what have you?" In other words, what happens to a man after he surrenders himself to God and experiences conversion. Does this have a social value as well as a religious value?

One of the great paradoxes of Christianity is that although its followers speak mystically they act practically. We might not be able to understand them when they talk of a Heaven that we cannot locate with scientific instruments. We may be bored when they talk of eternity and salvation. But we can understand them—and assign a value—if they work here and now for the shortcomings and sufferings of the present.

Great saints have busied themselves establishing schools, hospitals, orphanages, and asylums. Although few would bestow that title on Jerry McAuley, we will see the works he established or inspired. The skeptic asks, "He had a vision. He thought he saw God. So what?" He can be answered with other questions. Is it worth while if someone helps to feed thousands of hungry men? Is it worth while if homes are established where ex-convicts can be rehabilitated and ex-prostitutes given refuge?

McAuley was a rare man. Few, of the thousands he influenced, achieved his degree of courage and compassion. But we can ask questions about the others too. Is it worth while if a rich man devotes part of his wealth and energies to feeding the homeless and helping ex-convicts and drunkards? Is it worth while if a gambler renounces his vice and becomes a quiet, respectable businessman, paying his taxes and supporting his wife and children? Is it worth while if a longshoreman ceases to be a drunk and puts in a good day's work?

All of this flowed from the experience of men and women who surrendered themselves to God after human agencies failed. The spiritual results of their surrender will be determined by God. The material results we can see and judge for ourselves.

3 Transformed

JERRY MCAULEY WAS BORN in 1839 in County Kerry, Ireland. His father was a counterfeiter who fled home to escape the law and may eventually have disappeared into the pit of a penal colony. Jerry never knew him. His mother may also have been in prison. At an early age he was put in the care of his grandmother. His earliest memory of her was of her saying her rosary and kissing the floor for penance. He would throw things at her while she was on her knees and she would rise to curse and swear at him. McAuley could remember thinking, although too young to shape the thoughts into words, that there was something wrong with a religion "that requires such foolish worship and allows such sinful ways." Of course, any boy who throws things at his grandmother as she is praying is hardly the one to talk about another's sins.

He probably had the rudiments of religious training, since he later knew the Lord's Prayer, but he was never taught or went to school. He roamed the countryside doing what mischief came to hand and suffering accordingly. "I got blows for me meat and drink till I wished myself dead many a time."

At thirteen he was sent to New York to the care of a married sister. For a while he helped his brother-in-law in some form of business. But he soon left home and boarded with a family on Water Street. He took up with two other boys and they supported themselves by working when they could and stealing when they could. Like most of the toughs of the neighborhood he learned to be a prize fighter. His main occupation was river thief. He and his friends kept a boat under the nearby wharves. They went out stealing at night, sold their loot in the day, and squandered the proceeds on clothes and drinks.

"I had no fear for any man living. I was a born thief. Stealing came natural and easy. A bigger nuisance and loafer never stepped above ground. I made good hauls. It was fair and easy to board a vessel and take what you pleased. The Fourth Ward belonged to my kind."

What little survived of the old Fourth Ward of New York City was obliterated in one gigantic sweep shortly after World War II and replaced by the dull brick towers of a low income housing project. No tears were shed. The Fourth Ward had been a slum for more than a century.

Before the American Revolution and for a generation thereafter it had been one of the finest sections of the city. George Washington and John Hancock lived there for a while. When the Brooklyn Bridge was started after the Civil War, a massive brick pier was stamped down on the prominence where Washington strolled. By the 1840's shipping and commerce had seized the waterfront, which formed one boundary of the Fourth Ward, and sailors and immigrants, along with the saloon and brothel keepers who preyed on them, pushed the old families farther uptown.

The worst conditions were near the river. At one time Water Street fronted on the river. Then the docks silted up or were filled with refuse and another block reclaimed to form South Street. This was repeated and Front Street came into existence. Houses were constructed on the reclaimed land as soon as the upper few feet were free of seeping water. Later basements were dug. People lived in them like rats.

Thousands of homeless children roamed the streets. Their parents were habitually drunk or had died or disappeared, perhaps on the journey over, crammed into filthy wooden ships, or carried off by the cholera, smallpox, and tuberculosis that were endemic the year around in the Fourth Ward. The children grew up to join gangs flaunting such names as the Daybreak Boys, Buckoos, Hookers, Swamp Angels, Slaughter Housers, Short Tails, Patsy Conroys, and the Border Gang.

That was Jerry McAuley's crowd; robbing, fighting, and drinking—and then spells in the city prison, called the Tombs because it was built to resemble an Egyptian monument. Sometimes he moved back

with his sister and mother, who apparently had immigrated later. Like most of the Irish newcomers, the McAuleys wanted to start afresh and leave behind the evils and sufferings of the old country. Jerry was a shame to them.

"None of my people would look at me. I disgraced them all. My sister begged me to clear out and not bring no more shame on them, and my mother the same. I'd a patch on my nose the year round and a black eye too, sometimes a pair of them. Get into a fight and smash things. Get taken up and off to the station house. Next morning up to the Tombs. 'Ten days, young man.' 'Six months, young man.'"

Many years later at his mission he would often describe what he was like in his wild youth. "Me and three men slept on some foul straw in the corner of a cellar on Front Street. Often the tide came in and we'd wake and the water well over us and rising. We kept a log there and we'd get up on the log and float round till it went down. One night some fellows stole the log and locked the door for fun. The tide was high and we were pretty drunk and couldn't find the log nor the door neither and before we kicked the door down the water was up to our necks and we sober enough and scared to death for fear we'd drown. Then I had another home. That was the same kind only I changed my base and tried a Brooklyn cellar instead of a New York one. There ain't much choice. Oh, wasn't I a dirty rag shop of a man."

The story played itself out. Jerry was such a nuisance and terror that even the rum sellers wanted to get rid of him. He was accused of highway robbery. He was guilty of many crimes but not that particular one. It did not matter. He had no one to contradict the evidence trumped up against him and was tried and convicted in short order. In January 1857 he was sentenced to fifteen years and six months in Sing Sing. He was then nineteen years old. His trip to prison is told in *Transformed*:

"I burned with vengeance but what could I do? I was handcuffed and sent in the cars to Sing Sing. That ride was the saddest hour of my life. I looked back on my whole past course, on all my hardships, my misery, my sins, and gladly would I have thrown myself before the advancing train and ended my life. It was not sorrow for sin that possessed me but a heavy weight seemed to press me down

THE TOMBS (*circa 1878*)
It housed the police courts and jail and was officially known as the Halls of Justice. Designed to resemble an Egyptian mausoleum, New Yorkers called it The Tombs and civic boosters bragged that it was the finest example of Egyptian architecture outside of Egypt.

when I thought of the punishment. I had got to suffer for my wrong doings, but I had an indignant, revengeful feeling for the injustice of my sentence. Fifteen years of hard labor in a prison to look forward to and all for a crime I was as innocent of as the babe unborn. I knew I had done enough to condemn me if it were known. But others, as bad as I, were at liberty and I was suffering the penalty for one who was at that hour roaming at will, glorying in his lucky escape from punishment, and caring nothing for the unhappy dog who was bearing it in his stead. How my heart swelled with rage and then sank like lead as I thought of my helplessness in the hands of the law, without a friend in the world.

"I concluded, however, before I reached the end of that short journey that my best way was to be obedient to prison rules, do the best I could under the circumstances and trust that somebody would be raised up to help me. When I arrived at the prison, I shall never forget it, the first thing that attracted my attention was the sentence over the door: 'The Way of the Transgressor is Hard.' Though I could not read well, I managed to spell it out. It was a familiar sentence, which I had heard many times. All thieves and wicked people know it well and they know too that it is out of the Bible. It is a well-worn proverb in all the haunts of vice and one confirmed by daily experience. And how strange it is that knowing so well that the way is hard the transgressors will still go on it."

What William James might call the "natural antecedents" of McAuley's conversion were those thoughts on the train to Sing Sing; the sorrow gained from a review of his past, the indignant feeling at being wrongfully punished, the combination of rage and helplessness. He was penitent and willing to obey the prison rules.

That feeling is exactly what a penitentiary was originally designed to nurture. When the Quakers became interested in prison reform in Philadelphia at the end of the eighteenth century, they drew on their own experience of deep, quiet meditation leading to an inward change of spirit. They designed a prison where the inmates were totally isolated from one another. Each man with his own cell and small yard surrounded by a high wall in which he could walk, work, and think.

Although the name *penitentiary* was retained to describe a maximum security prison, the idea of silent meditation became a hideous form of punishment. In later prisons the convicts were no longer totally isolated. They were brought together six days a week in communal workshops. But they were still forced to maintain silence.

The builder and first warden of Sing Sing was Captain Elam Lynds, who wrote: "It is the duty of the convicts to preserve an unbroken silence. They are not to exchange a word with each other under any pretense whatever; not to communicate any intelligence to each other in writing. They are not to exchange looks, wink, laugh, or motion to each other. They must not sigh, whistle, dance, run, jump, or do anything which has a tendency in the least degree to disturb the harmony or contravene to disturb the rules and regulations of the prison."

The main building of Sing Sing, on the edge of the Hudson River about thirty miles north of New York City, was a block of cells five tiers high with two hundred cells to each tier. The cells were back to back so that one hundred faced out on each tier, along which ran a narrow walkway. An outer wall was built around this cell block. The wall was eight feet from the face of the cells. It was pierced by windows only ten inches wide and twenty-four inches high, mere slits to admit the slender rays of the sun.

Each cell was like a coffin; three feet three inches wide, six feet seven inches high, and seven feet deep. There were, of course, no windows. Each cell was separated by a foot of stone from the cell on either side and by another thickness of stone from the cell in back of it. The door was iron-grated.

Week after week, year after year, the sun never reached in through those slits on the opposite wall to penetrate the gloom and damp of some of the cells. Other cells received the sun only a few brief passing moments during a day.

There was no plumbing. Just a bucket. A thousand buckets that filled and stank. The prison was built directly on the ground a few inches above the water's edge. The flagstones were always damp. The moisture penetrated up the walls and into the cells. It was cold and damp in summer and icy in winter. Each cell had a ventilator three inches in diameter which led to a small duct between the walls. This spread the odors and the dampness. It was a haven for vermin. Even if the cells could be cleaned and disinfected—which they were not, each prisoner simply swept the dust out so that it filtered down on the man below him—no one could get the fleas and lice and bedbugs from the ventilators.

The men were dressed in the horizontal stripes of a prisoner. They were mustered out of their cells

and marched to work. They stood in a line a few inches apart. Each man put his hands on the shoulders of the man in front of him. Then they marched in lock step; a shuffle rather than a step; a human centipede. A warder stood watching with a club. No smiles, no winks, no glances. If a man at work wanted to talk to his mate he twisted his mouth to the side and whispered. They used to say you could tell a man who had spent time at Sing Sing by his shifty eye, the shuffle of his walk, and the grimace of his lips when he talked.

The harsh discipline and total isolation imposed by Captain Lynds began to be eased a few years before McAuley passed beneath those ominously marked doors. A small library was opened with religious and otherwise edifying literature. Men who desired could be taught to read and write. An instructor would stand outside their cells and call the lessons into a group of grated doors. Gas lights were installed in the corridors.

McAuley was put in the carpet weaving shop and for two years not a word was said against him. He minded his work, was quiet and orderly, and all the keepers and guards spoke well of him. He said the Lord's Prayer every day from a feeling that it was right and that some way or other it would do

him good. He applied for teaching and learned to read and write. He improved steadily, especially in reading. He managed to get cheap novels, probably through the connivance of another inmate or one of the guards. He read them constantly to divert his mind from the dreary surroundings. From some of them he gained the hope that he might escape and he dreamed of murdering the man he believed responsible for putting him in prison.

Eventually, as with most prisoners, his health began to fail. For two or three years he suffered a great deal. He became restless and sullen and this brought severe punishment. Among other things, he was forced to wear the iron collar and was given "the showers"—a blast of ice-cold water on his head. The water was caught in a basin at mouth level so that a man choked. If he fainted he was revived and given another blast. "Punishment never did me a particle of good. It only made me feel harder and harder."

One Sunday morning when he had been in prison about five years, he went with the other inmates to services in the chapel. He was moody and miserable and hardly paid attention to what was going on. Almost accidentally he glanced at the platform and saw someone he thought he recognized. It seemed to be "Awful" Gardner, the boxer. At a second glance, he was not sure. He was used to seeing Gardner in rough clothes and with a rough face. Then the man spoke. McAuley was now sure it was Gardner.

In the 1850's "Awful" Gardner was well known in sporting circles in New York although he never achieved fame. He earned a brief mention in a few detailed histories of prize fighting as one of the seconds on the side of John Morrissey in the heavyweight title bout fought between Morrissey and Yankee Sullivan at Boston Four Corners, New York, in 1853. In the thirty-seventh round, Morrissey lifted Sullivan up and pinned him against the ropes. The seconds jumped into the ring and there was a general mix-up. After a while, when Sullivan was fighting "Awful" Gardner, the referee awarded the fight to Morrissey.

His real name was Orville Gardner. Like McAuley he was a Fourth Ward boy and a criminal. He attracted a good deal of attention in 1857 but for different reasons.

Gardner had been raised by a pious mother but grew up to be a fighter, thief, and hard drinker. He married and had a son. His mother, now a widow, lived with him and prayed three times a day that he would reform. When his son died Gardner tried to drown his sorrow in drink. One night he sat in a saloon with several other fighters. The room was hot and close and filled with smoke. He went out for air, happened to look up at the bright sky and saw two stars.

"I wonder where my boy is," he thought. With one of those sudden resolutions which often mark the career of converted men, he returned home and knelt to pray with his mother. Then he took a two-quart jug of whisky and rowed across the river to some woods in Brooklyn where he fought a weird match with the bottle. He told himself he would either drink himself to death then and there or never drink again. He set the jug in a clearing and talked to it. "Now it is give you up forever or never leave this place alive."

He struggled for nine hours. Once he thought he would smash the jug but then thought the smell of the whisky would be too tempting. He knelt and prayed for help. Finally he knew he had won. He dug a hole in the ground, picked up the jug, holding it at arm's length, and dropped it in the hole. He covered it up and stamped down the ground. He never drank again.

This was Gardner's conversion. He broke off from his boxing companions and took up with ministers

TORTURES IN SING SING
In the shower bath, the prisoner was doused with cold water, which collected in the trough at the level of his mouth and nose. He gulped in the water until he fainted. He was revived and given the treatment again and again. The iron collar, which the prisoner was forced to wear day and night, was simply uncomfortable and made him the butt of ridicule. The cat-o'-nine-tails was applied for trifling misdemeanors, such as talking in line.

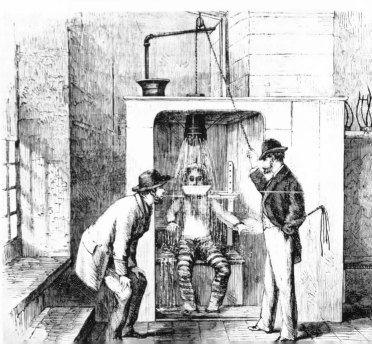

CHAPEL SERVICE IN SING SING
The platform where "Awful" Gardner refused to stand and the little table to which he went instead are in the distance, behind the guard in the center aisle.

and missionaries. Under their sponsorship he told his story to others in the hope of reforming them too. That was why he was at Sing Sing.

Gardner said he did not feel he belonged on the platform with the ministers. He came down and stood by a desk on the floor. He began by saying he had once worn prison stripes and then told the story of his conversion. As he talked he began to cry. He knelt down and prayed and continued to sob. McAuley felt tears filling his own eyes. He raised his hand slowly to wipe them off, ashamed that his companions or the guards would see him weep. He wished that he were alone or that it was dark so that he might cry openly unobserved.

"I knew this man was no hypocrite. We had been associated in many a dark deed and sinful pleasure. I had heard oaths and curses, vile and angry words from his mouth, and I knew he could not talk as he did then unless some great wonderful change had come to him. I devoured every word that fell from

his lips though I could not understand half I heard."

One sentence impressed him deeply. Gardner said it was a verse from the Bible.

Sunday was the most dreary day of the week in prison. After the morning chapel service the prisoners were marched to the dining hall to take their plates of dinner and then marched, with their food, to their cells where they were locked in until the next morning. These were the long dismal hours when the whispers, sighs, and groans of a thousand men echoed against the blank walls and the smell of a thousand bodies and a thousand buckets filled the damp and gloomy air. McAuley had generally provided himself with a novel to help pass these hours. But on this Sunday he had none.

That sentence he heard from Gardner kept recurring in his mind but he could not remember exactly what it was. It occurred to him to look it up in the Bible. Every prisoner was given a King James version of the Bible as part of the few possessions allowed

20

him in his cell. McAuley had put his Bible away in the ventilator on the day he entered prison and had not touched it since. He reached in, took it down, beat the dust from it, and opened it. He soon realized that he did not know where to turn to look for the verse but the day loomed long ahead and he thought he might as well start at the beginning. He began reading page after page. The book captured his mind and heart from then on.

"On and on I read. How interested I grew. It seemed better than any novel I had ever read and I could scarcely leave it to go to sleep. I was glad when released from work that I might get hold of my Bible and, night after night, when daylight was gone, I stood up by my grated door to read by the dim light which came from the corridor." Whenever he could sneak the chance he tried to tell his mates in the workshop what he had discovered. He told them it was a "splendid thing."

He never found the verse which started him on the search. He forgot about it in his interest in the book itself. One night he found some verses in 1 Timothy, chapter 4:

Now the Spirit speaketh expressly, that in the latter times some shall depart from the faith, giving heed to seducing spirits, and doctrines of devils; speaking lies in hypocrisy; having their conscience seared with a hot iron; forbidding to marry, and commanding to abstain from meats, which God hath created to be received with thanksgiving of them which believe and know the truth.

He threw the book down and kicked it around the cell. It seemed to be a trick to condemn Catholics.

"There's their lies," he told himself. "I always heard the old book was a pack of lies. That's the way they hold us Catholics up." Something seemed to whisper to him, "Go get a Catholic Bible, then you can prove this to be false."

He went to the library and asked for a Catholic Bible. They looked at him sharply, wondering why a convict would deliberately come to ask for a Bible. But they gave it to him and he returned to his cell. He turned to the same chapter and there were the same or similar words: "Forbidding to marry . . . commanding to abstain from foods." There were notes in the margin to explain the text. But this made him suspicious and increased his confusion.

"It surely is the Word of God and they are trying to get out of it," he told himself. He compared various chapters of the two versions and found that although there might be slight differences in the words the meaning was always the same. He was in despair and could not decide what was right or wrong.

He read the entire Bible through a second time and enjoyed it even more. "The Book of Revelation particularly astonished me." He wanted to believe what he was reading but felt it was beyond his understanding. The tension was building within him. He felt he wanted to change in some way but he also felt he would be a traitor if he broke with Catholicism. One night he was resting from reading, walking up and down those meager seven feet that were his world.

"I was thinking what a change religion had made in Gardner. I began to have a burning desire to have the same. I could not get rid of it but what could I do? Something within me said 'pray' but I couldn't frame a prayer. The voice said: "Don't you remember the prayer of the publican: God be merciful to me a sinner?'

"I thought of my own religion in which I had been brought up and I asked, 'Why can't I be good in that?' Then I thought, 'But that will not save me as Gardner's does him. It does not keep me free from my sins.'

"There was a struggle in my mind. 'If I send for the priest,' I told myself, 'he will tell me I must do penance, say so many prayers and do something for mortification and such as that. If I ask the chaplain he will tell me to be sorry for my sins and cry to God for forgiveness. Both can't be right.' The voice within me said, 'Go to God. He will tell you what is right.'

"What a struggle I went through. I knew I ought to pray but if there had been ten thousand people there I couldn't have been more ashamed to do it than I was there all alone. I felt myself blushing. Every sin stared me in the face. I remembered the 'Whosoever' in the Bible. 'That means you,' said the inward voice. 'But I'm so wicked,' I replied, 'Everything but a murderer and that many a time in my will.'

"The struggle did not seem my own. It was as if God was fighting the devil for me. To every thought that came up there came a verse of Scripture. I fell on my knees and was so ashamed I jumped up again. I fell on my knees again and cried out for help and then, as ashamed as before, I rose again. I put it off for that time and went to bed."

The tension built and built for three or four

weeks. Then suddenly it eased and he found some release. "At last the Lord sent a softness and a tenderness into my soul and I shed many tears. Then I cried unto the Lord and began to read the Bible on my knees." McAuley moved beyond the stage of ordinary religion. "The Sunday services seemed to do me no good. They were dry and dead to me." He was struggling toward a direct experience of the divine, with no need for church or minister or priest.

A woman missionary, whom McAuley identified only as Miss D., began to visit the prison. She was told that McAuley had suddenly become religious and was talking about it. He was sent for one day and met Miss D. in the library. They talked and then knelt down to pray. McAuley was embarrassed but knelt beside her. To hide his shame he covered his face with his hands. Then he peeked through his fingers and saw that she was crying.

"An awe I cannot describe fell on me. It seemed dreadful to me, that prayer of that holy woman."

The crisis returned greater than ever. The breaking point was near. "That night I fell on my knees on the hard stone floor of my cell. I resolved to stay there whatever might happen till I found forgiveness. I prayed and then I stopped. I prayed again and stopped. But still I continued kneeling. My knees were rooted to those cold stones. My eyes were closed and my hands tightly clasped and I was determined I would stay so till morning."

He told himself that if he got no relief from the unbearable tensions by the time he was called he would never pray again; he would die rather than pray.

"All at once it seemed as if something supernatural was in my room. I was afraid to open my eyes. I was in an agony and the tears rolled off my face in great drops. How I longed for God's mercy! Just then, in the very height of my distress, it seemed as if a hand was laid upon my head and these words

came to me: 'My son, thy sins, which are many, are forgiven.'

"I do not know if I heard a voice yet the words were distinctly spoken in my soul. I jumped from my knees. I paced up and down my cell. A heavenly light seemed to fill it, a softness and a perfume like the fragrance of flowers. I did not know if I was living or not. I clapped my hands and shouted, 'Praise God! Praise God!'"

Looking back years later, McAuley dated his conversion from that night. His struggles were not over. He would again take to drink and become a worse drunkard and criminal than ever. But in that night he first found the way. He told the story many times at the mission he later established.

"I was ignorant. I knew nothing of the Christian life or its peculiar duties or perils so I had to learn by bitter experience. Some persons have asked me, 'Do you really believe you were converted before you fell?' Yes, I was. I know I was converted while in a prison cell. Why, I was so happy I fell like a dead man on my cell floor and didn't know anything for a long while. When I got up I couldn't contain myself. I knocked things around and shouted and I suppose made a terrible to-do. The keeper heard it; a tall old Jew we called Shadpole because he was so long and slim. Slipping along with his slippered feet to my door he peeked in between the bars and hollered, half-scared like, 'What's the matter in there?'

"I didn't answer him but kept right on. I couldn't help it. He yelled again, 'Say, what's the matter?'

"'Oh, I got religion,' I shouted. 'I got RELIGION!'

"'I'll give you *religion*,' he growled. He took down my number for a cold shower bath."

McAuley was too carried away by his experience to care for anything. The next morning he was called to work and nothing happened. He felt the Lord had made Shadpole forget it or wipe the number from his slate.

Reclaimed

AFTER HIS CONVERSION McAuley experienced the customary sense of joy and contentment: "From that time life was all new to me. Work was nothing; scowls and harsh words nothing." Like many converts he felt he had to be more perfect even in slight things and gave up smoking. And like Isaiah, who heard the Lord asking, "Whom shall I send?" and replied, "Here am I; send me," McAuley had a sense of mission. He began to try to convert the other prisoners.

Although the silence and harsh discipline were designed to break the spirit of the convicts, Sing Sing was regularly shaken by fierce, suicidal revolts. One, which took place before McAuley's conversion, was led by a convict named Jack Dare. McAuley and Dare were close friends; they were in the same workshop and if they had any little luxuries they shared them.

"Jack Dare was the first man I began to pray for. I approached him on several occasions with the subject but he repulsed me with sneers. He seemed to think I was playing a bold game to get out of prison but he learned at last that I was in earnest. He found me several times weeping and poring over my Bible. Once he lifted his hand to strike me and even spit at me. But when I told him that I had no resentment and could stand it for Jesus' sake, that astonished him. I said nothing more for a week and he seemed to be getting worse all the time but I felt sure the Spirit of God was striving for him and I kept on praying. One day he told me he had been praying but it seemed dreadful to him to pray. I knew all about that from my own experience.

"Not long after this as he came out of his cell one morning to go to work I caught sight of his face all lit up. He was at the head of the column and I near the foot. He just glanced at me with a smile and an upward turn of his eye to Heaven and then I knew it was all right with him. I could scarcely keep from shouting. The first one he told the good news to was the keeper. 'Jack,' he said, 'I'm glad you've got religion.' It was not that the keeper cared for religion but he was afraid of Jack. He was such a desperate character and now he knew he would have no more trouble with him."

McAuley had a half hour a day during the evening meal when he could whisper his preachings to the men on either hand. Later the regular keeper was relieved and the rules of silence were considerably eased. He had his men picked out and went from one to the other saying a few earnest words. He believed that several of the inmates experienced conversion. This went on for about two years. "My cell seemed all that time like Heaven and I cared very little whether I ever came out of it or not. No one could insult me. If my comrades abused me I felt that I could pray for and forgive them."

Through the efforts of the women missionaries who visited the prison he exchanged, by dictation, letters with a few pious ladies on the outside. The two which have survived are made up of simple religious sentiments. In one he mentioned that he had memorized twelve Bible verses and had learned the hymns, "Jesus, Lover of My Soul" and "Prayer is the Soul's Sincere Desire." These activities helped to persuade the authorities that he had been reformed.

On March 8, 1864 he received a pardon and was set free. He had been in prison for seven years and two months and now was about twenty-six years old.

"My faith was so simple I felt the Lord would give me anything reasonable I might ask. And I never had a doubt until after I came out of prison and mingled with Christians. Their wavering, unstable, half-and-half faith staggered me." He now began to learn the hard lessons that would go into the shaping of his mission on Water Street. He called this mission, "The Helping Hand." He needed a helping hand when he came out of prison, determined to lead a new life, but none was offered.

"When I got out of prison I was more lonely than I had been in my cell. I could not go back to my old haunts and companions and I knew no others. If I had found a single Christian friend at that time it would have saved me years of misery. I must say that it does not seem to be right to turn men out of prison and make no provision for their future well-being. Many a poor fellow has been driven to crime and back again to his prison cell for want of kindly counsel and direction when he first came out again into the world. I wanted to do right, to please God. The first thing I did was to inquire for a prayer meeting. I was told of one but when I got to the door I was afraid to go in. I had never been to a Protestant meeting and nobody invited me in."

He kept away from the Fourth Ward but still had to find some place to stay. The only friend he met told him of a place where he could board. It was over a "lager bier" saloon. This was a new drink for the slums, imported by the wave of German immigrants; so new that it was still spelled as a German phrase. McAuley had never heard of it. He was told it was a harmless drink, wholesome and good like root beer.

"I drank it and then began my downfall. My head got confused. The old appetite was awakened. From that time I drank it every day and it was not long before I went from that to stronger liquors. The night I stopped praying I shall never forget. I felt as wretched as I did the day I went to prison."

For a while he had a job in a factory which

made hats. The workers called a strike and he was one of the leaders. They were all fired. Unemployed, he drifted back to the Fourth Ward and to crime.

There was a story that Cherry Hill and the Fourth Ward had been cursed for their sins and deserted by God. The story was often told by Jerry Sullivan, a County Cork man who kept a shoe repair shop on Water Street:

"'Twas of a Saturday night years ago when the Hill had had a drop and the devil was in them and what with the singing and the dancing and everyone rushing up and down the Hill yelling, you wouldn't believe the row. Then they began a-cussing and a-fighting and the blood began to flow till someone afraid of murder run for the priest. And sure the priest he come and he talks to them and threatens them but they wouldn't heed. So then he walks the length of the street, calling on them to remember the judgments of the Almighty. But the devils only laughed and swore the harder. So the priest—God help us—when he got to the top of the Hill, he turns around and looks down it and hears the men and women, aye, and the children, all blaspheming and cussing. Sure, 'twas like listening at the gates of hell. Then the man of God he stretches out his hand and, says he, 'May the curse of the Almighty be upon this Hill, for 'tis the wickedest place on earth.' And bedad, the curse stuck to Cherry Hill till the Irish all cleared out."

McAuley found a partner named Tom Wilson and they lived in a tenement at 17 Cherry Street. Maria Fahy, an Irish girl who sometimes worked at one of the variety houses on the Bowery as a waitress or entertainer, lived with them as Jerry's girl. Another girl, Nellie, lived with them as Tom's girl. They were all heavy spenders and heavy drinkers. The Civil War was still on. Jerry and Tom went into the "bounty business," which appears to have been a routine dodge of the confidence men of the times. Men who enlisted were paid a bounty and others, who could recruit volunteers, were given a reward equal to half the bounty received by the man who signed up.

"Rascally business that. I would pick up men wherever I could find them, get them half drunk, and coax them to enlist. I became a sportsman and went often to the races. We went boating on the river. We would buy stolen goods of the sailors, compel them to enlist on fear of being arrested, and we took the bounty. We went on for some time in this thieving, racing, speculating, and bounty

business. We kept a recruiting office in New York and another in Brooklyn and found plenty to do and might have grown rich if I saved what I made."

Sometimes he would remember with joy the days back in Sing Sing. He felt he was rushing downward at a furious speed and tried to drown his conscience in whisky. When the war ended they took their boat out on the river to buy and sell stolen and smuggled goods. They paid off in counterfeit money to increase the profit but soon had to give the whole game up. "No one would steal for me when they found I gave them nothing for it." He sank back to his earliest occupation as a river thief, boarding vessels at night and stealing what he could. Incidents began to occur which made him realize he was heading for a quick death. Having once had a vision of Heaven, hell was real and it loomed large.

On December 11, 1866, soon after nightfall, Tom and he took the boat and rowed across the river to Brooklyn looking for chances. They nosed around Greenpoint but were disappointed. They pulled down to the Williamsburg Ferry and hitched the boat to the ferry Idaho to be towed across to New York. Steam boilers were new then and easily exploded. The boiler of the Idaho blew up soon after the ferry pulled into the stream and the flames quickly spread. They began to untie their boat to get away when two men jumped from the ferry and grabbed on. They rowed these men to shore and came back, not to save lives but to see what booty they could pick up. By this time another ferry had come up and taken most of the passengers off. But a few more jumped into the river.

"We saved one Christian woman. We held on to her as she clenched the sides of the boat with her hands. The whole scene was terrific. The fire raging, the screams of the perishing, the struggles of the poor creatures in the water, impressed on my mind deeply the thought of the last day and fiery hell to which I knew the sinner must go. And yet God used us wicked people in the midst of all this terror and confusion to save His children. My partner wanted me to let the people go and pick up the cloaks, hats, and various things that were floating in the river. But I said, 'No, I haven't got so low as that yet.'"

As it happened no one was killed or seriously injured, due mainly to the arrival of the other ferry. The newspapers the next day mentioned that some people were rescued by a small boat but gave no details.

EXPLOSION ON THE FERRY IDAHO
The artist called upon his imagination to show many small boats in the river. Newspaper accounts the day after mention only one boat. McAuley himself later wrote that his small boat was the only one at the scene.

"Another night in Brooklyn we stole a rope fender off a ship, the whole cost of which was not more than a dollar and a half. And yet for that we could run such fearful risks. The captain of the vessel saw us and seizing his revolver fired at us once, twice, four times. The balls came so close that I could feel them as they whizzed past my head but they did not hit. After I got around the wharf and out of danger I felt frightened more than before. Something whispered, 'If that bullet had hit you, where would you have been?' The response of my conscience was, 'In hell.' "

More than a year passed until the next brush with death. McAuley sank lower and lower. Whenever he thought of reforming he remembered the text, or thought he heard it whispered to him by Satan: "For it is impossible for those who were once enlightened and have tasted of the heavenly gift and were made partakers of the Holy Ghost. . . . If they shall fall away, to renew them again unto repentance." He stayed drunk to drown his misery. He was sodden one night as they were set to plunder a ship tied up in Brooklyn and could not

do his share. He remained in the boat while Tom boarded the ship. He was so drunk he fell overboard. The little boat went in one direction and the tide carried him in another direction out from the wharf. He sank to the bottom of the river and then rose to the surface. He sank again and rose. Then he sank for the third time.

"This is the last and now you are lost," a voice seemed to say inside him. He thought he could see hell opening and heard the shrieks of the condemned. Then another voice said, "Call on God." He felt he could not; that he was too mean. But then he did call, inwardly, for help. He felt he was being lifted up to the surface. The boat drifted back so that he could grab it. The experience sobered him and he managed to climb back in. He felt he had been given his last chance and that if he ever went stealing again he would be killed and sent to hell. But this only made him angry and he drank more than ever to make himself insensible to the nagging voice.

He was determined to go out on the river again come what may. But Tom had an accident and they

25

had to stay ashore for a while. They were running low on money and Maria and Nellie told them to find some way to get food and drink.

Jerry was lying in the room when he heard voices in the hall. One was his landlady who had stopped someone. The other was the voice of a cultured man.

"Do you love Jesus?" asked the man, apparently in an effort to get her to stand aside.

"No indeed," replied the landlady. "Do I love Jesus? And who is He?"

"My good woman, and don't you know who Jesus is?" the man responded. The landlady stood aside and he continued on upstairs to visit someone. The landlady came into McAuley's room.

"Who is that?" he asked.

"It's one of those tract peddlers," she replied.

"Why don't you treat the man with respect?" McAuley scolded her. He picked himself up from the floor and went out into the hall. He thought that the man, whoever he was, could find him an honest job. He stood there with his small eyes, bleary with drink, an old hat like a tarpot, a tattered red shirt, and ragged pants with the legs stuck in the tops of his boots. The tract distributor came down the stairs, saw Jerry and was obviously frightened. He had been chased or kicked downstairs by men like this. Jerry began to speak but the stranger, out of caution, suggested they talk on the street, thus giving him room to run if he had to.

They went down and talked as they walked up the street to the New Bowery. This was an extension of the Bowery, cut through to open a straight road to Pearl Street and the main commercial district of New York. The stranger's name was Henry Little. He took Jerry to the Howard Mission at 37 New Bowery. There they met another man who said if McAuley signed a pledge to give up drinking they would see what they could do about finding him an honest job.

"The idea struck me as it never had done before that a drunkard like me couldn't get work and there was no hope of decent employment unless I did reform. So I signed it. But I told them I should not be likely to keep it and that I had taken it many times before and broken it. 'Try again,' they both said, 'and ask God to help you.'

" 'Well, to please you, I will,' I said. I went right home from there and told my partner what I had done. How he laughed. 'You take the pledge,' he said. He had a bottle of gin in his hand at that moment and turning out a glass offered it to me. 'Tom,' said I, 'I have just taken the pledge.' But I drank it and as I put down the glass I added, 'Now this is the last drink I shall ever take.' 'Yes, till you get the next one,' said he."

Little had followed McAuley back to the house. He came in just as Jerry put down the empty glass. McAuley kept as far away as he could so that Little could not smell his breath. The missionary invited him to go out for a walk. They strolled down toward the river. McAuley told him he was going out that night to steal. He said they were broke and needed the money.

"Jerry," Little said, "before you do that I'll take this coat off my back and pawn it and give you the money." McAuley looked at the coat. It was worn and old. Little was obviously not a rich man. Little went away and soon came back with fifty cents. He gave this to McAuley and asked him to take a verse from the Bible with it: "Seek ye first the kingdom of God, and His righteousness; and all these things shall be added unto you."

McAuley did not go out boating that night or any other night. He had at last found a helping hand.

It was the time of what came to be called the John Allen excitement. It was a curious page in New York's history, when many religious people thrilled to the thought that religion had penetrated into the heart of iniquity in the Fourth Ward.

 # The John Allen Excitement

Soon after the civil war a reporter named Oliver Dyer tried to make a living in New York as a free-lance writer, an uncertain existence even now and an impossible one in Dyer's day. The few magazines which existed had specialized interests or were content to cover only the great and seemingly world-shaking events: wars and earthquakes and the doings of kings, presidents, and politicians. There was little chance for a reporter to develop his own stories.

It was Dyer who touched off the John Allen excitement in the fall of 1868. Later, when the affair had nearly petered out and Dyer was ridiculed as a "bohemian writer," he delivered a lecture at Cooper Union which illustrated his style and motivations. Dyer said he had wandered for years through the slums and decaying neighborhoods and had found many strange things. For instance, he had met an old Negro, a former slave, who sang songs which were moving. Dyer had thirty school girls from the Howard Mission sing one of these songs. The first line went: "Nobody knows the troubles I sees. . . ." He thus anticipated, among whites, the discovery of traditional American spirituals.

The Brooklyn Bridge was still in the planning stage and would not be completed for another fifteen years. Dyer predicted New York would grow to an unbelievable size and that bridges would be needed across all rivers, including the wide expanse of the Hudson River. The George Washington Bridge across the Hudson would not be built until 1931.

That was Dyer. He larded his message with snippets of songs and visions to come. What he really wanted to tell them about was the fantastic growth of crime and vice in New York. He marshaled his dull, dry facts. There were 5,500 liquor shops, 647 houses of prostitution, and 1,648 billiard saloons with bars and gambling halls attached. He gave the number of robberies in a single year, the number of murders, and the number of homeless men. He said $1,481,368 was stolen every year in money and property. But he knew the audience could not appreciate this heavy dose of statistics so he drew them a picture.

He said if you put all the grog shops, all the houses of ill-fame, and all the billiard saloons into one continuous street it would reach from City Hall to White Plains, then a town about thirty miles north in the bucolic wilderness of Westchester County. Every night along this street, said Dyer, there would be a murder every half mile, a robbery every one hundred and sixty-five yards, six outcasts at every door, at frequent intervals men dividing the loot, eight preachers trying to convert the criminals, and thirty newspapermen to report on it all.

A person listening to the lecture could be excused if he lost the point—the growth of crime and vice —while savoring the image of that fantastic street.

Early in 1868 Dyer began searching for someone to publish his report on crime and vice, and found S. S. Packard, who put out a monthly called the *Phrenological Journal*, which extolled the new science of bumps on a person's head as keys to character. Packard had already sensed there was a market for a magazine catering to the growing curiosity of Americans. He also understood the value of enticing readers with publicity and catchy titles. He had decided to bring out a new magazine to be called *Packard's Monthly* when Dyer came to him. They were well matched. Dyer contracted to write a series of articles under the general title, *The Shady Side of Metropolitan Life*. The first article would appear in the second issue of the magazine, due to be published in July. Packard then got busy and early in July 1868 posters appeared in large letters on the side of walls and wagons:

THE WICKEDEST MAN
IN
NEW YORK
see Packard's Monthly

The wickedest man turned out to be John Allen, a strange character even among the many strange and awful saloon and brothel keepers of the Fourth Ward. His real name was Evert E. Van Allen. He came from a respectable farming family in upstate New York. Two of his brothers were Presbyterian ministers and another was a Baptist minister. A fourth brother was a fairly wealthy merchant in the city. Allen himself had been a teacher. For seventeen years he had kept a saloon and dance hall at 304 Water Street, with rooms above the bar where the girls could take their customers. The door from the street led directly into the bar. The dance hall was in a separate room in the rear.

Allen appears to have been psychopathic or otherwise deranged. He kept religious books and newspapers on the tables of the bar and in the dance hall. In the midst of a fight or a fit of swearing he

*John Allen
and His Son Chester*

Allen's Dance Hall

sometimes would break off, run into the dance hall, fall on his knees, and pray long and loud for himself and those around him.

A reporter later recalled visiting Allen in his saloon just as the Civil War was ending. Allen insisted on showing off his son, Chester, who was about two years old. He had the child awakened and brought to the bar. Allen said the boy was a genius and could already read. He stood the sleepy-eyed child on a table and asked him a series of questions, which were promptly answered in a bright, if mechanical, fashion:

"What state do you live in?"

"New York State."

"What country?"

"United States."

"Who's the President of the United States?"

"Lincoln."

"What's Lincoln?"

"Son of a gun."

"What's McClellan?"

"Nice man."

"What'll you do when you get to be a man?"

"Marry."

"What'll you do to your wife when you marry her?"

"Mash her head."

Dyer began his article by telling of Allen's background and his predilection for religious literature. He described the bar and its inmates, saying a sailor home from a long voyage might regard the girls as beautiful but decent men could only regard them with "sorrow unspeakable."

He said he visited John Allen's one night in the company of Albert Arnold of the Howard Mission, three clergymen, and a policeman to keep them from harm. The place was going full blast. Thirteen girls were waiting in the bar while, in the dance hall, there were three musicians, seven customers, and an equal number of girls.

Allen gave the visitors a hearty welcome and promptly called for Chester, now about five years old. The boy demonstrated that he could read and answered a series of questions on ancient history, "both sacred and profane," geography, and politics. He danced a breakdown on the table and said his prayers, to the accompaniment of his father's jokes.

Allen led them into the dance hall: "I've three brothers who adorn the sacred calling and grit and grace run through our family like the Tigris and the Jordan through the Holy Land. I'll watch over you like a hen over her chicks and you shall leave my premises as virtuous"—he paused—"as you came in." Then a big laugh. The clergymen, to change the subject, suggested they sing a hymn. Allen said the girls would choose one. The girls explained they knew hymns not only because Allen kept hymnbooks around the saloon but also because they had been to Sunday school, which did not make the ministers very happy. They sang a hymn with the chorus:

> *There is rest for the weary,*
> *There is rest for you,*
> *On the other side of Jordan,*
> *In the sweet fields of Eden,*
> *Where the Tree of Life is blooming,*
> *There is rest for you.*

Dyer wrote that he returned several times after that, bringing scores of visitors, many of them clergymen. They always received a cordial welcome and Allen let the women sing a hymn.

Arnold, of the Howard Mission, decided to make a strong effort to reclaim Allen. On the night of May 25th, Dyer wrote, he went with Arnold and six clergymen from different parts of the country. It was a little after midnight when they arrived at the saloon. The yellow shutters of the green house were closed and they thought it was too late. But a light shone through the window over the door. They shouted. Allen stuck his head out of an upstairs window. He explained he was shampooing his hair, something he did every night to sober himself before going to bed. The visitors went into the saloon and found the women in the dance hall smoking their pipes after an exhausting night. Allen came down and invited the visitors to have a dance with the girls. When they refused he said, "Well then, let's have a song."

There were eleven girls. They sang "Rest for the Weary" and "There's a Light in the Window for Thee, Brother." At the end of the hymns Arnold tapped Allen on the shoulder.

"John, old boy, give us your hand," he said. "I feel just like praying here for you."

Allen shook hands but said, with an oath, "Pray? Do you mean pray? No sir, never."

"Well John," said Arnold, "I am going to pray here anyhow. If I don't pray loud I'll pray soft. You shan't lose the prayer at any rate."

Allen ran out into the bar shouting, "I won't hear you," and closed the door behind him. Arnold invited the girls to pray. The visitors knelt on the floor as did some of the girls. Others bowed their heads. It was a moving prayer and some of the girls began to cry. A few of them, with tears in their eyes, rose to their feet, crowded around Arnold and begged him to take them away. They said they would work their heads off if honest work could be found for them; they would submit to any hardships if only they could be restored to a Christian life.

Here Arnold had to hem and haw and give evasive answers. He was not prepared for success. He had finally managed to bring sincere prayers into John Allen's dance hall. Moreover, these prayers had borne fruit; the prostitutes were repentant and wanted to lead a new and better life. Yet Arnold had to admit defeat. He knew there was no Christian home in the city which would take in a woman who admitted to having been a prostitute; at least he had never heard of any such Christian home.

This was the point Dyer had been leading to all along. He was not really interested in John Allen. He wanted to draw attention to the prostitutes, to make his readers see them as human beings and not as stereotypes of sin. He wanted something to be done to help them.

He concluded his article with his usual burst of statistics. He said that on the average a prostitute lived only five years after entering the profession. He said there were forty dance halls within a half mile of John Allen's and many more scattered throughout the city. He estimated that 10,970 girls worked in these places. Thus, he wrote, it took 2,194 girls a year to keep them in business. He further computed this at "a trifle over six girls a day, Sundays included. Six fresh girls a day from the Sabbath schools and virtuous homes of the land to feed the licentious

Prayer Meeting at John Allen's

maw of this metropolis of the Western world."

But Dyer had overreached himself. Instead of evoking sympathy for the girls, which might lead to help for those who wanted to reform, the article focused attention on John Allen. He became famous. In turn, Allen was carried away by the publicity and allowed the ministers to hold daily prayer meetings in his saloon. People flocked to 304 Water Street to see the wickedest man in New York.

Dyer had never said Allen was converted—to the contrary, the impression was that he was unredeemable—but those daily prayer meetings seemed to prove that he had got religion. He became a new wonder. The newspapers spread stories of the growing crowds and there was talk of a great new revival. At one meeting, at five o'clock in the afternoon, fifteen hundred people filled all of Water Street from Dover Street to the south to Roosevelt Street to the north. Strangers wanted John Allen pointed out to them. A newspaper reported: "Little Chester was the center of great interest."

This upset the routine of the street. A "bucket shop" which sold whisky at ten or fifteen cents a bucket according to the quality, uncertain in any case, reported business was off by a third. The owner of a crude distillery said dance-hall keepers were buying whisky by the gallon where they used to buy by the barrel. He complained: "John Allen and the whole herd of Methodists are taking the honest bread right out of a man's mouth." Slocum, the owner of a dance hall at 318 Water Street, complained, "Something has got to be done or we shall all go up the spout."

At midnight August 30th John Allen announced that he was closing his dance hall. On Sunday, September 1st, officials of the Howard Mission revealed that John Allen's saloon would now be used exclusively as a house of prayer and a Home for Fallen Women. A sign was posted asking anyone who wanted to hire "magdalenes" to apply inside.

At noon, the time appointed for the service, the crowd was packed inside "like sardines in a box, emitting an ancient and fish-like smell that pervaded all the air and made it anything but pleasant to breathe." Eight clergymen took part. There were prayers, admonitions, speeches, and a few testimonies from those who had been converted—all punctuated with shouts of "Glory to God." John Allen said that since he had become so famous he intended to join a church, but not immediately. When the services ended he stood at the door shaking hands with those who went out, telling them to come again the next day at noon when another prayer meeting would be held.

The meeting of September 4th was attended by someone who wrote an account published the next day in the *New York Times* under the pseudonym, "Philanthropist." He described the services briefly, mentioning "the testimony of Samuel Irving, the converted gambler, swearer, and Sabbath breaker—as he was pleased to designate himself—who gave a very thrilling account of his own conversion, which seemed little less marvelous than that of Saul when on his way to Damascus."

A reporter from the *Herald* attended the same meeting. In contrast, he spoke of "dealers in piety" and "sensationalists." He called it a "love feast" with praying "mostly of the snuffle order, with shakes in the voice." On succeeding days other reporters noted that the crowds which jammed the former saloon were not the prostitutes, thieves, and bullies who were the normal inhabitants of Water Street but refined gentlemen and elegantly attired women who called each other sinners while "poor forlorn creatures in the homes of infamy immediately opposite sat in the doors and invited the passers-by to lechery." Policemen were kept busy trying to sort the pickpockets from the respectable.

The *Herald* reporter on September 7th commented: "The solution of the original conundrum 'Who is the wickedest man' loses the greater part of its attraction in the novelty of the other interrogatory: Is Allen humbugging the parsons or is there a compact between them to fool New York?"

On September 11th, the Howard Mission announced the movement had taken a step forward: religious services would also be held at the groggery and sailors' boarding house at 374 Water Street, kept by Thomas Hadden. In reply to the newspaper innuendos, the statement added: "From our knowledge of the movement, gained by our personal presence and participation in the meetings, we see no reason to doubt that the work is truly of the Lord. If in any case there have been manifestations of indiscretion or untempered zeal, they have evidently resulted from the spontaneous nature of the awakening and the absence of definite control, inevitable in such a case."

The crowds, with the reporters in pursuit, headed for Tommy Hadden's place. He was known as "Shanghai" Hadden from his habit of robbing the sailors who were unfortunate enough to seek lodgings from him. The two filthy and smoke-begrimed rooms were so packed for the announced services by the ministers and their respectable following that "very few of the ungodly ones could get near enough to hear the prayers offered for their salvation."

With interest beginning to go elsewhere John Allen set out on September 18th for what was announced as a lecture tour of New England. He took along Slocum, who ran the dance hall a few doors away. But they got no farther than a bar in Hartford, Connecticut, where they were thrown out as a disgrace to their profession and returned to the city sodden drunk.

An article in the *New York Times* on the following day tried to put an end to the fiasco. It recalled "the ever-memorable reformation of 'Awful' (Orville) Gardner, the notorious pugilist and gambler who, nearly eleven years ago, suddenly forsook the prize ring and the card table with their vile associations and began to live like an honest man and a respectable member of society." It said the same popular interest that was aroused by the reformation of Gardner in 1857 had been awakened by the news that the "king of Water Street dance house keepers had abandoned his wicked business." There the similarity ended. Gardner was still firm in his new life but Allen had never changed.

The *Times* said Allen had merely rented his dance hall to the clergymen for $350 a month; that Hadden was also receiving rent for the use of his place; and that he was playing along with the ministers because he was scheduled to be tried in a Brooklyn court on a charge of having robbed a sailor and hoped to escape sentence by pretending to be reformed. The *Times* also disclosed that the clergymen had rented Kit Burns' rat pit for an hour a day at the rate of $150 a month and that services would begin there in a few days.

The article continued: "The daily prayer meetings are nothing more than assemblages of religious people from among the higher grades of society in what were once low dance halls. There is an unusual amount of interest displayed at these meetings and much good has doubtless been accomplished thereby but it is also a fact that there are few and sometimes none of the wretched women or ruffianly, vicious men of that neighborhood present. Those classes are not reached at all and it is false to say that a revival is going on among them."

Officials of the Howard Mission confirmed that rent was being paid for the use of John Allen's place but denied any money was going to Hadden. They also denied there had been any attempt to deceive. They said an agreement to pay Allen had

been reached only after his place had been closed; they felt it was wrong to make him bear all the costs. The money paid him represented only two-thirds of the actual value. But this explanation was overshadowed by the news that prayers would soon be heard at Kit Burns'—one of the most infamous places in the city. Even those who had never been near the Fourth Ward had heard of the rat pit at 273 Water Street.

There was a bar at the entrance from the street. The walls were decorated with pictures of prize-fighters and dogs and two stuffed dogs stood on the counter. Burns was a leader of "the fancy." He often assumed the obligation of setting up the stakes and ropes for a prize fight. He raised his dogs as rat killers and constantly bragged of his "purps."

Kit Burns

The Rat Pit
273 Water Street

The rat pit was in the rear: an amphitheater with a pit in the center and the seats rising steeply at the sides. Fifty to one hundred rats would be turned loose in the pit, allowed to cower for a while and then a dog set on them. Bets were placed on how long it would take to kill all the rats or how many would be killed within a certain time. Sometimes a sport from another part of the city or from out of town would bring his own dogs and there would be a match to see which dogs could kill an allotted number the fastest. When this paled then the dogs

COOLING OFF THE DOGS
A fight between dogs
was an alternate amusement to
having a dog kill rats.

*Prayer Meeting
at Kit Burns'*

might be set to fight one another. And when even this grew boring, there was always Kit's son-in-law who, for a fee, would jump into the pit and kill the rats with his teeth.

A reporter hurried over to ask Kit Burns what he thought of the revival.

"Well, I'll be honest with you," Burns said. "I suppose most of us remember when we were little children and weren't up to what we see around us now, for it's my opinion the world is a mighty sight worse than when I was a boy and I'd just like to see it bettered. But I don't believe in dead beats. I've known Johnny Allen fourteen years and he couldn't be a pious man if he tried ever so hard. You might just as well ask a rat to sing like a canary bird as to make a Christian out of that chap. He's a fraud. So's Tommy Hadden; so's Slocum. I don't want to say a word against them preachers for they've paid me a pretty fair rent for the pit, but if they ever want to reform the girls in Water Street and shut up its rum mills they've got to do it in some other way than by howling for it. You can stun a man by shouting into his ears but you may yell until you're black in the face and you'll never succeed in making sour milk sweet. That's my opinion."

Burns was determined to "do the square thing" for his patrons. He cleaned the blood from the floor of the arena, swabbed and swept the stalls. He put a table in the center of the pit with a pitcher of ice water on it. He even considerately placed a spittoon nearby. The appointed hour came and the clergymen and a few ladies took their places. "The remaining space was occupied by the supernumeraries, choristers and friends of the mission, the representatives of the press, and as many of the curious public as had managed to elbow their way through the miscellaneous crowd which choked up the passages leading to the pit, thronged the barroom, bulged over the sidewalks, and greatly obstructed the business of the thoroughfare."

"This is sheer humbug," said a businessman who wandered over a few days later to inspect the gathering at Kit Burns'. "If they pray ever so earnestly here among themselves what good does that do to the poor unfortunate women in the neighboring bagnios or the depraved men out on the street there."

Kit Burns soon soured on his new tenants; "reverend lessees," one newspaper called them. When they overstayed their hour he hurried them out. Then he turned to the reporters, tilted his top hat forward on his head, and said: "Them fellows has been making a pul-pit out of my rat pit and I'm going to purify it after them. Jim! Bring out them varmint." A dozen rats were hoisted out of cages by their tails and tossed into the arena. A bull terrier was turned loose on them and the sports amused themselves with shouts and imitations of the missionary choir. It was such a hit that Burns did it every day. He said it "ratified" the religious meeting. His fertile imagination was his downfall. He gained so much publicity that he could no longer be conveniently overlooked by the police, especially after someone was beaten up in a nearby alley soon after leaving the prayer meeting. The Society for the Prevention of Cruelty to Animals forced city officials to have the rat pit closed and the "ratification" meetings ended with the prayers.

John Allen's place again began to be noticed. It was newly painted with a sign which said: "Water Street Mission and Home for Fallen Women." A little boy had thought of a good thing. He had admission cards printed and stood outside shouting: "Here you are. Carte de visite of the wickedest man in New York, only five cents."

The Home for Fallen Women was out of business, despite the sign. Allen reported his girls had been insulted and had left: "I have not lived among them for seventeen years without learning something about them. I know their vices and their virtues. Yes, you may sneer, sir, I said virtues. Some of them have many virtues. They have feelings also, feelings which those missionaries should have respected but did not. They should have been treated more considerately on Blackwell's Island [a prison] than they were at those meetings. One preacher cried, 'Oh, God, we thank Thee that these scarlet whores of Babylon have come to seek salvation.' Another pointed them out and exclaimed: 'Behold the harlots whom we are going to take to Jesus,' and so the poor girls were hooted at, stared at, and finally shamed from repentance."

The excitement soon petered out. When the month expired, John Allen retook possession of his place

A SENSATION FOR THE SAINTS.

Cartoon from Leslie's Weekly

and resumed his old occupation. The publicity, however, had made him a man too notorious to ignore. On October 17th he was arrested by Captain Thorne of the Fourth Ward station house on a charge of keeping a disorderly house and of stealing fifteen dollars from a sailor from Baltimore. His wife, another man, and four girls were arrested with him. He then gave up the business for good and, for a while, ran a grocery store on Roosevelt Street. He failed in this too and dropped out of sight. A brief notice in a newspaper reported his death in October

"RATIFICATION" MEETING
By chance, the artist attended on a day when a weasel was put in the ring to kill the rats. Newspaper accounts invariably speak of dogs being used.

1870 at his father's home in West Perth, New York.

Hadden too quickly relapsed, if he had ever been reformed in the first place. He ended up with a ten-year sentence in the New Jersey Penitentiary on a charge of grand larceny.

Toward the end of the excitement, late in September, the *New York Times* had commented: "The moral that points Aesop's familiar fable of the mountain that labored and brought forth only a mouse has never perhaps found a more complete exemplification than in the great expectations and insignificant results of the Water Street project for the recovery of the degraded creatures of that locality. That is to say, the great moral revolution among the wretched keepers and inmates of the low dens of infamy existing in the Fourth Ward that was expected would follow the sensational efforts of certain philanthropists and reformers has not made its appearance nor is there the slightest indication of its approach."

This criticism was too facile and too hurried; neither the *New York Times* nor any other newspaper stayed on the scene long enough to observe the results. A beachhead had been established in the perpetual war against the forces which degrade mankind. John Allen took his saloon back but another saloon was rented a few doors down the street. This was to become the first home of the McAuley Water Street Mission.

 Beginning a New Life

THE NEWSPAPERS CRITICIZED the Water Street revival but maintained their faith in revivals as a method of reclaiming men. They were opposed to the form, not the substance. The *Herald* on September 5th, even as it began to expose the failures of the movement, suggested what might be the correct way to convert the sinners of Water Street:

"We regret to say that the work of 'changing the hearts' of the fallen creatures in Water Street promises to be a failure. The instruments engaged in it, even if sincere, are not calculated for the caliber of mind they address. What is wanted is a man of enthusiasm, one of their own class, master of rough language and homely bits of philosophy, and who intuitively knows exactly the emotions which govern his hearers and how best to direct them for their special benefit."

Without knowing it, the *Herald* was describing Jerry McAuley. When John Allen reclaimed his saloon, the building at 316 Water Street was rented and the meetings continued there. The missionaries remained in the neighborhood to follow up on those who might have a change of heart. It was probably while on such an errand that Henry Little first met McAuley.

Later, the day after pawning his coat and giving the fifty cents to McAuley, Little returned to the house on Cherry Street with two women missionaries. They stayed and talked and prayed.

"I wished they wouldn't but I had not the courage to say so," McAuley recalled. "Day after day my new friends followed me up so closely I could get no chance to drink. 'Tom,' I would say, 'I'm going to turn over a new leaf.' But Tom would answer, 'Will the Lord come down from Heaven to give you beefsteak?'"

Little was living with Mr. and Mrs. Franklin Smith in a house nearby on Monroe Street. The Smiths invited Jerry and Maria to come for tea. Little lent McAuley a coat for the occasion. They ate, sang a hymn, read a chapter from the Bible, and knelt down to pray. Mrs. Smith, who was herself employed as a missionary, led the prayers, pleading for all of the souls around her.

Jerry later said: "I thought my knees would bust and I looked through my fingers to see if she wasn't almost ready to quit. Her pleading face was turned to Heaven, tears streaming from her eyes as she was talking to Jesus about me, and I thought, 'Oh, that woman loves my soul.'"

Jerry began to cry too and they asked him to pray for himself. He said he did not know how. He did know, of course, but felt he could not pray because he was so wicked. They asked him to pray the

Franklin Smith

*The Howard Mission and
Home For Little Wanderers
37 New Bowery*

prayer of the publican: "God be merciful to me a sinner." He did so, repeating the words over and over. "Put in, 'for Jesus' sake,'" they urged him. He did this too and felt "a sudden calm joy." He remembered shouting, "I am saved."

McAuley probably fell into a trance since he had a partial memory of what happened. The events of that moment were so powerfully moving that they left a permanent impression on all who were in the room. Franklin Smith was moved so deeply that he would devote the last twelve years of his life to the Water Street mission.

Many years later, in talking to others, Smith remembered the scene: "There was a shock which came into the room, something similar to a flash of lightning which every one present saw and felt. Jerry fell down on his side prone on the floor with tears streaming from his eyes. 'Oh, Jesus, you did come back, you did come back,' he cried. 'Bless your name.'" Little and the Smiths were frightened. They jumped from their knees and ran out of the house and into the street.

After that McAuley broke with Tom Wilson, who continued in his old life and was sent to prison. Wilson later died during an attack of delirium tremens.

With the help of the missionaries, McAuley found small jobs around the waterfront. It was difficult. He was an ex-convict and a known drunk.

He attended the revivals at 316 Water Street and tried to tell of his conversion but felt choked by a great lump in his throat. "I would jump up and hang on to the seat in front and say, 'I love Jesus' and flop down as if I was shot. But I always felt better for it." Little stayed close to him and they walked the neighborhood arm in arm. McAuley welcomed this support. His old companions thought he was shamming to get something out of the parsons and jeered as he passed.

On Sundays he went to the regular services at the Howard Mission on New Bowery. The main purpose of the Howard Mission and Home for Little Wanderers, to give its full title, was to save the slum children. It boarded about twenty children at the mission; some were orphans, others were from homes that were temporarily dislocated. There was also a day center where other children were fed, clothed, and given some schooling, with a strong emphasis on religion. The children were taught to sing in chorus and were taken around the city for concerts as a means of raising funds. A collection of their songs became a popular hymnbook under the title, *The Little Wanderers' Friend.*

It was at the Howard Mission that McAuley met Alfrederic Smith Hatch who, more than any other person, was destined to be his helping hand. Hatch was born near Burlington, Vermont, in 1829. When he was twenty years old he was slender and delicate and suffered from asthma. His father, who was a doctor, sent him to New York to get a job as a sailor in order to build his health, carefully instructing him to find a "temperance captain." Young Hatch had never even smelled salt water up to that time. Nevertheless he found a ship and made two voyages across the Atlantic in 1849–1850. He learned to climb the masts and stand on the icy, careening deck in the midst of a winter storm. But more than that, he learned to live with and even admire some of the roughest, dirtiest, swearingest, drinkingest men alive.

The voyages apparently cured whatever ailed him since he lived to reach his seventy-fifth year, the

*Bathing Children
at the Howard Mission*

ALFREDERIC HATCH AND FAMILY, 1871
This oil, by Eastman Johnson, is often reproduced as an example of a fashionable post-Civil War American home. Hatch, seated at the desk to the right, is shown with his parents, wife, and many children. Johnson charged one thousand dollars a head for the painting. It was completed just as the baby was born. Hatch asked how much it would be to add the latest addition to the family. Johnson replied: "One thousand dollars." Hatch paid.

father of eleven children and swarms of grandchildren. There is a picture of the Hatch family in the Metropolitan Museum of Art in New York. Alfrederic Hatch, balding, with stately sideburns, sits in the living room of his fashionable home at 49 Park Avenue, surrounded by his large family. The scene is the epitome of Victorian respectability. Hatch never smoked or drank and practiced his religion every day but the sea had washed away whatever trace there was of stiff-backed Vermont puritanism. No matter how dirty or degraded a man might seem, Alfrederic Hatch was willing to give him a chance as long as the man was willing to try.

About ten years after his career at sea Hatch got a job as cashier in the Bank of Jersey City in New Jersey, where he met Harvey Fisk, who was master teller of the Bank of the Commonwealth in Jersey City. Fisk had connections with bankers in New York. In 1862 they formed a partnership under the name of Fisk and Hatch. They were dealers in government bonds and immediately began to make their fortunes. Fisk and Hatch was one of the three firms which raised almost all the money needed by the Union to carry on the Civil War. Alfrederic Hatch became one of the pioneer members of the newly consolidated Stock Exchange in 1865.

Hatch was a supporter of the Howard Mission and was among those who preached from the door of John Allen's dance hall when the crowd extended from Roosevelt Street to Dover Street. He was also one of those who seemed to be doing so little good at the meetings in Kit Burns'. Henry Little introduced McAuley to Hatch at a meeting at the Howard Mission. Hatch recalled: "His criminal and prison life had left an unmistakable impress upon him and his appearance told plainly enough what he had been. To the ordinary observer he was perhaps as hard and hopeless a looking case as one would be likely to encounter in tramping the worst streets of New York day and night for a month and in his dull eye, rough aspect, and illiterate speech there was little promise of the future evangelist."

McAuley continually turned to Hatch for advice. As he began to grope for a new path he had to care for Maria as well as himself. Maria pronounced her name Mariah. Even as a drunk and thief Jerry had watched after her tenderly. Her father had disappeared and her mother had died when she was young. She was raised and educated in New England and, although her family had been Catholic, she had attended Protestant Sunday schools. Unfortunately she ran away to New York and for a while sank so low she lived with a few girls in one of the terrible cellars of the Fourth Ward.

When McAuley left Tom Wilson he arranged for Maria to live in the house at 316 Water Street. She attended the prayer meetings but only to accompany Jerry, not out of personal conviction. One day Jerry and Maria came to the Howard Mission and met Hatch. McAuley explained they were not married and asked what they should do. Hatch gave the easiest answer—get married. But Maria was unsure of herself and Hatch then said they must remain apart. As difficult as this was, McAuley agreed. He was determined to face his problems squarely. It was arranged for Maria to live with a family in New Jersey.

Maria is a somewhat shadowy figure in the accounts of McAuley's life. She is often mentioned but generally only as someone at McAuley's side. However there are sufficient hints to show that she was his greatest source of strength, aside from God. In many ways her role was more difficult. It was hard enough for McAuley to seek a new life among respectable and perhaps straight-laced churchgoers. But how much more difficult was it for Maria? Religious society in the last century did not easily forgive a fallen woman. If she followed McAuley she would be an easy target for scorn and condescension. It was no wonder she hesitated. And then, because she hesitated, she had to part from the only man who had treated her with love and respect. It was a cruel situation yet she passed through this time of trial and emerged stronger than ever. Through cour-

age she found faith and through faith she found strength and triumph.

McAuley found a job with a ferry company that was building a new slip at the foot of Catherine Street. He had left his old friends and old haunts. Maria was out of the city. Henry Little had gone away too. McAuley was depressed and lonely and felt he had to see Maria. He took the stagecoach on a cold, snowy Sunday. They reached the halfway house and all the passengers went into a bar for a drink to warm themselves. McAuley stood to one side. He felt the passengers looking at him as if in pity because he could not afford a drink.

He was still a man of touchy pride. Once he had been king of a place like this. He went up to the bar and asked for a sarsaparilla. The bartender looked at him and handed him a bottle of gin and a glass. He took a drink, got back into the stage, and continued his trip to see Maria.

He stayed too long and missed the return stage. He had to put up at a hotel. Again alone, far away even from Water Street, he went into the hotel bar and drank heavily. He became drunk and hardly knew what he was doing. He went out of the hotel and found a church that was open. He sat in a pew and cursed God and cursed himself. He thought he could never go back to Water Street and disgrace his new friends. He decided to commit suicide.

He left the church and found his way to a railroad station and stood on the platform. He thought he would lie down on the tracks and let the train run over him. But he was still on the platform when the train arrived and the conductor, probably thinking he was a confused drunk, pushed him inside.

The next night he went to a prayer meeting, con-

Maria McAuley
(circa 1872)

fessed his relapse, and asked the congregation to pray for him. Yet he fell to drinking once more after that.

The Sunday after this relapse he went to the Howard Mission and saw Alfrederic Hatch on the platform. Hatch smiled and nodded to him. McAuley thought he could not face such a man and tried to slip out the door after the meeting. But Hatch caught up with him outside the door and held out his hand.

"Jerry, what is the matter?" he asked.

McAuley put up his hand, as if to ward Hatch off.

"I'm not fit for you to speak to me," he said.

Hatch insisted that McAuley tell what had happened. McAuley did so, saying he had been in hell for days. Hatch shook his hand hard, then put both his hands on McAuley's shoulders and looked him straight into the eyes.

"Don't give it up, Jerry," he said. "Try again and keep trying."

Hatch gave him his business address, 5 Nassau Street, and said whenever McAuley was in need he should come there for help. He meant it. His staff was used to many an odd character showing up at the banking house, with its mahogany paneled walls and carved desks, and being promptly allowed into Hatch's office, there to beg a job or a handout. The offer gave McAuley new courage. He told himself he would never visit Hatch just to ask for money. He went to 5 Nassau Street often for encouragement and advice and was always received, even if the banker had to break away from a business meeting.

Once again McAuley's religious enthusiasm was awakened. He was still employed by the ferry company and was told to report for work on Sunday. He went to his employer and said he was not only reformed but was also trying to live a Christian life which meant strict observance of the Sabbath.

"Jerry," said his employer, an old sea captain, "You are no better than I. I am a Christian man but I have to work on Sunday and you must too. I want you to come tomorrow to work." McAuley stayed home and when he arrived at the ferry slip on Monday he was told he had been fired. He was learning that not all Christians were the same. He went to the captain and tapped him on the shoulder.

"Captain," he said, "have you discharged me for wanting to keep the Sabbath?" The captain remained leaning over the side of the ferry and did not reply. Jerry spoke again: "Captain, have you discharged me for trying to do right?"

The captain turned and replied: "Jerry, you haven't

accommodated me and I can't accommodate you." McAuley said good morning and walked away.

He found other jobs but would keep tripping over his principles. He was still finding his way. Apparently he fell back to drinking several times. He got fighting drunk and barged into a prayer meeting to pick a quarrel. But he was always forgiven and his new friends remained faithful.

After about a year McAuley found the way. He gave up smoking as well as drinking, joined a church, and found room and board with a devout Christian family. Few people understood him. He was a stranger to his new friends and an oddity to his old ones. Late in 1870 McAuley was ferreted out by Julius Chambers, then an eager young *Tribune* reporter. Chambers later became a flamboyant Hearst editor. He recalled his adventures in *The Book of New York: Forty Years' Recollection of the American Metropolis*. Writing in 1912, his memories of 1870 were somewhat hazy. He apparently did not take time to check his facts. For instance, by 1870 McAuley had been out of Sing Sing for six years and his paleness could hardly be ascribed to "prison pallor." Nevertheless Chambers' is one of the few accounts of the new life McAuley was learning to live.

Chambers was told to write an article on river thieves. He bought a suit of rough clothes and began to frequent waterfront haunts.

"After a few nights," he recalled, "I was taken to the 'Catamarket Club,' a dingy second-story room on South Street, north of Catherine. On my second visit I saw a tall, cadaverous man, with strangely white cheeks, due, I afterwards knew, to 'prison pallor.' His face appealed to me. His fine gray eyes had in them a look of hopelessness and lament I could not resist. I talked to him but he was shy. He read me right. He told me I was not a sailor or a tough, like the men and youngsters about me. He refused to drink—said he never again would touch 'the damnable stuff.' I invited him to Dorlon's at Fulton Market to have supper. He accepted with anxious reluctance. A novice could see he was hungry but he still distrusted me. We went and I gave to him all he could eat. He admitted it was his first food in twenty-four hours.

"I then made a confidant of him. I told him I was a *Tribune* reporter but didn't mention the character of my assignment. He admitted to me he had been a river thief; was recently out of prison, after a long term. He was tired of a career of crime; he thought he could be of use to wretches like himself haunted by officers of the law and repudiated by respectable people. . . . After we had met several times I told him what I sought; he proved to be a mine of information. He had a thief's honor, however; he wouldn't 'peach' on former pals."

McAuley could easily have gained fame by retailing details of his previous escapades. But to the end of his life he kept to his resolve not to talk about his life of crime. Except for the generalities included in *Transformed* his past is a blank. It was not, as Chambers imagined, a thief's honor. He was determined to present himself by what he hoped for in the future rather than seeking cheap glory or publicity by dwelling on what he had been in the past.

McAuley went from job to job, preaching his new religion, trying to live it and being mocked and called a hypocrite. Once, with the help of Alfrederic Hatch, he found a job at the Custom House at four dollars a day, an excellent wage.

"But there I preached Jesus too much and was soon turned away. Then I got steady employment in another place where also I testified for Jesus. I had been there only a little when a companion began to swear. I reproved him. 'We can get along without swearing,' said I. 'What,' said he, 'are you a churchman?' 'No, I am a Christian or trying to be one,' I replied." The others jeered at him but he kept on and through his example a German workman experienced conversion. Ultimately McAuley lost that job too.

Once, while out of work, he went to see Hatch in his office. Hatch could not think of anything offhand but had an idea.

"Jerry," he said, "I have got a job for you if you will take it."

"I'll take anything that's honest," McAuley replied.

"Well Jerry," Hatch continued, "I have a little yacht down in Gowanus Bay that wants watching until I can sell it. Now I want you to go and live on it and take good care of it, keep everything clean and in good order, and see that nobody runs off with anything and I'll pay you and give you your grub."

"Will you trust me to do that?" McAuley asked. The feeling of being trusted was new to him. Hatch did not consider the furnishings of the little vessel valuable, some silver plate and a few other things. But McAuley thought it was all solid silver and worth a mint of money. As an old river thief he knew Gowanus Bay was infested with robbers. The responsibility was heavy. He lay awake at night with a revolver cocked and ready, starting up and creeping to the deck at the slightest sound resembling the dipping of muffled oars into the water.

Many years later, with his Irish way of self-mimicry, he would give a funny performance of himself on the yacht. He wanted to illustrate the great change in his life. He would picture himself sitting under the awning of the yacht sipping lemonade out of a silver cup and contrast this with the life he had led before.

In reality it was an experience with deep meaning; it marked another point in his rehabilitation. "When I found I was trusted like that by a man who knew all about my past life I began to respect myself and think, 'Jerry McAuley, there is a chance for you after all; you will be somebody yet before you know it,' and it gave me a big boost." In his later effort to rehabilitate others trust became an act of deep symbolic significance. Honesty, complete and unswerving at whatever cost, also took on deep meaning.

McAuley's last job before opening his mission was as a porter for a firm on Broadway which sold sewing machines. Hatch had some connections with the company and heard of the opening. He used the job to test how well Jerry's reformation was going. He asked Jerry how he should recommend him. Should he tell the company that McAuley had been a thief and drunkard and had spent time in Sing Sing? Or should he hide the facts and take a chance that the past would not be discovered? If he told the truth McAuley might not get the job.

McAuley did not hesitate: "I don't want any hiding or dodging. I won't be a fraud in any way, whatever else I am. I want to be just Jerry McAuley and nothing else." Hatch sent him down to apply for the job while privately telling the company that he would guarantee the loss if McAuley stole anything. After some hesitation about how the other workmen would feel next to an ex-convict, McAuley was hired.

Afterward, when Jerry dropped into the banking office for a chat, Hatch told him of his subterfuge and made a joke of it: "If you should get away with half a dozen truck loads of sewing machines some night it might break me."

Jerry laughed and then became serious. He said: "You'll never be ashamed of me or sorry you said that. If the cellar where I work was a gold mine or had diamonds lying all around loose, your promise will never cost you a cent."

About three years passed this way after the John Allen excitement. The house at 316 Water Street had become a temporary lodging for homeless men with a reading room for sailors waiting in port; a place where they could pass the hours without throwing their money away in the rum mills and dance halls. Officers would come in from the ships looking for men to fill out a crew.

One day McAuley was sitting in the room when a captain came in and saw him.

"Is that the kind of people you keep here?" he shouted. "He's a dirty thief and a scoundrel. He robbed my ship and stole a hundred dollars' worth of sugar and he ought to be in the pen." The captain kept shouting and swearing. McAuley knew the charge was true; he had stolen the sugar but that was many years ago.

McAuley had been working steadily and for the first time in his life he had saved some money which he kept in a bureau in a house on Pearl Street, where he was then living.

"Captain," he said, "I have a hundred dollars and if you'll come home with me I'll pay for your sugar."

"You pay a hundred dollars, you dirty thief? You haven't one hundred cents. You'd like to get me in your house and murder me."

"No one shall touch you. Come with me and I'll pay." The captain continued to swear and shout. McAuley's always quick temper showed itself. He got up, grabbed the captain by the collar, and dragged him out. "You'll come and I'll give you the money."

McAuley was tall and strong and the captain went along muttering, "You have a hundred dollars. You thief." They reached the house and went up the stairs, the captain beginning to sweat with fear. Jerry unlocked the door and the captain then realized he would not be harmed.

"Jerry," he said, "I believe you are just fool enough to pay that money."

"Yes sir," McAuley replied, "here it is." He went to the bureau and produced the hundred dollars.

The captain turned it aside, saying, "Jerry, I stole the sugar before you stole it from me so keep your hundred dollars." The incident showed McAuley that he could face up to his past and make amends to anyone he had harmed. His purpose in life was now ready to unfold.

At about this time Maria returned to New York. After staying in New Jersey she had gone to New England to live with her sister. She thought of how Jerry had changed and sought her own inspiration in the Bible. Then, as she was sitting one day in a small church in Massachusetts, she experienced conversion and began to live anew. She returned to New

York and found employment as a Bible reader, going into the saloons and dance halls to seek converts, and visiting tenements to read to immigrant families and help them with their problems. Some of the earliest supporters of McAuley's mission were people Maria had comforted in her missionary rounds.

Early in 1872 she and Jerry were married at the Howard Mission. Alfrederic Hatch and a few of their friends were at the wedding. Hatch had prospered with the passing years. He was a director and vice-president of the Chesapeake and Ohio Railroad, vice-president of the Old Dominion Land Company, and a director of the St. Louis and San Francisco Railroad. But he still visited the McAuleys in their new apartment on Division Street.

"I had taken tea with them one night," he recalled, "and we sat talking. They told me a great deal of their past lives. Their thoughts were all of the wonderful things that God had done for them and their talk of the past seemed to bring home to them with renewed force that night the blessedness they were enjoying. Maria looked around the cheerful room and then at Jerry and drew a long breath and said, 'Can this possibly be us?'"

Hatch was undoubtedly the only Wall Street banker who visited a porter working in a basement: "Jerry worked in the packing room in the basement which had an entrance down a flight of steps on the side street. When I wanted to see him I used to run in that way. One day I called and did not see him in his usual place. I waited a while and presently he came out from behind a pile of packing cases in one corner with a radiant face. He said, 'When I get lonesome and discouraged and feel the blues coming on I go down on my knees behind that great pile of boxes and pray and then I am all right again.'"

40

Jerry McAuley
Photographed on His Wedding Day
1872

7 The Vision

JERRY MCAULEY HAD A VISION. He saw what he believed God wanted him to do.

"One day I had a sort of trance or vision. I was singing at my work and my mind became absorbed and it seemed as if I was working for the Lord down in the Fourth Ward. I had a house and people were coming in. There was a bath and they came in and I washed and cleansed them outside and the Lord cleansed them inside. They came at first by small numbers, then by hundreds, and afterwards by thousands. Before I came out of this vision I was in tears. Something said to me, 'Would you do that for the Lord if He should call you?' I answered, 'Yes, Lord, open the way and I will go.' I felt that I could go down there where I had always lived. I was used to the filth and felt sure I should be called to work for Jesus there."

His vision had its natural antecedents. It was part of a greater vision which had energized the English-speaking world for two centuries. Christianity, as we know it, was shaped during the Industrial Revolution in Great Britain. The conversion experience of the Puritans set the movement going. At first this new personalized religion was kept with a select group of "saints"—as opposed to "strangers."

Then came John Wesley and revivalism. Wesley taught that conversion could come not just to a select few after long and deep thought but to anyone, anywhere, "in the twinkling of an eye." He emotionalized religion. He took his preachings to the open fields and thereby reached the unchurched multitudes. He did not want to reach their minds. He wanted to stir their hearts, to make them look inward. Wesley's revivalism became, for all practical purposes, American Christianity. It suited the needs of a society which emphasized the role of the individual. It answered the need of a nation in perpetual turmoil. It reached out to the pioneer and later to the millions of unchurched immigrants in the city slums.

When wave after wave of immigrants poured into New York, the earlier settlers, who had become the new rich and middle class, abandoned their neighborhoods and small churches and moved uptown. Their decaying homes became slums or were re-placed by tenements; rookeries with scores of families crowded into what were designed to be single family dwellings. Revivalism sought to reclaim the lost ground. Missions were set up—perhaps just a room above the street—and missionaries and visitors were sent out to distribute tracts.

On the surface, this may seem to be bland pietism. But much of the philanthropy and many of the great social welfare institutions of the United States developed because missionaries were willing to seek out people where they worked and lived. The mission stations were like the Special Service camps in Viet Nam. They were outposts and beachheads in the jungle of slums from which the troops could fan out to engage misery in hand-to-hand combat.

The rich and middle classes moved elsewhere but some still had their personalized religion which compelled them to practice compassion and charity. They maintained an active interest in what was happening out in the jungles. They contributed enormous sums of money to schools, universities, orphanages, hospitals, and mission work. Some also gave their time and talents by serving on boards or committees or going down into the slums to preach sermons or teach a Sunday school class.

For several years the missionaries had become more and more aware of the need to do something for the homeless men of New York. The crumbling yellow pages of the annual report for 1870 of the New York City Mission and Tract Society contain one of the earliest accounts of what the newspapers were later to call the "tramp menace."

"One of the veteran city missionaries, located near the Five Points, had his heart stirred within him as he saw crowds of unfortunate and friendless men drifting past him daily and he drew them into his mission room and when they were hungry he fed them from his own table and at night, instead of sending them to the police station for lodgings, gave them a blanket and a place on the benches of the mission room.

"This practical philanthropy becoming known, two of our downtown merchants craved the privilege of furnishing the means needful for carrying it on and have ever since footed the bills. This good mis-

Underground
Lodging Cellar
Spots were rented
at three cents a night

sionary, with his limited accommodations, last year . . . gave to worthy and deserving men 1,468 lodgings and 1,820 meals.

". . . About the same time one of the leading Nassau Street bankers, having on his hands on Water Street a house he had purchased to redeem it from the rum trade and the business of prostitution, offered it to the City Mission for their purposes and they, having cleaned and improved it, opened it for a free reading room for workingmen where they will also give lodgings and meals to the unfortunate and deserving."

This, of course, was the building rented as a place to continue the meetings begun in John Allen's dance hall. When the owner objected to having it used as a prayer hall, Alfrederic Hatch bought it outright. Later the meetings ended and the building stood vacant.

Meantime Hatch's philanthropic activities expanded. He became a member of the executive committee of the City Mission, then the leading religious and charitable organization for the section of New York below 14th Street. The quick response to the need for lodgings is a good example of how reports from the missionaries out on the front lines were fed back to a command post and got action.

In May 1872 the City Mission established Carmel Chapel at 134 Bowery. Carmel Chapel would later be moved elsewhere and develop into a flourishing church. It began as a simple mission station and

reading room. Soon more signals were flashing back to headquarters: "It is simply heart-rending to be obliged to turn away really needy men on a cold, blustering night when we know they have no alternative left them but the street and the station house."

Someone from Carmel Chapel described what a police station lodging room was like: "Imagine then a room about twenty by ten feet. Along the wall is placed a slightly raised and inclined platform, extending the whole length of the room. On this the men lay themselves down, side by side, without mattress, covering, or pillow. Drunk or sober, ragged or not, covered with vermin or cleanly, it makes no difference, side by side they lie, the air reeking with offensive odors and vibrating to lewd jests and horrid oaths. One man was discovered at our chapel stealing some old newspapers. On being asked what he did that for, he replied that he expected to spend the night at the station and he wanted a small roll of papers for a pillow as the bare boards were awfully hard."

Police Station Lodging

42

Carmel Chapel was organized by the Reverend John Dooley, then just beginning a career that would make him a legend among the religious and social workers of lower Manhattan. At first Dooley tried to meet the needs of some of these men by buying tickets, at reduced rates, valid for a night's lodging at a rooming house. The tickets, at fifteen cents each, proved too expensive. He then persuaded the City Mission to rent a large loft at 185 Spring Street, which he fitted out with seventeen beds, a number of benches, two baths, and a lavatory. It was opened in March 1873 and provided a place to sleep at an average cost of eight and a half cents a night per man.

At that time the various types of religiously-inspired social work were not as clearly defined as they are now. Most Protestant activity in the lower part of Manhattan was coordinated through the City Mission Society. When Dooley began his home, the YMCA assumed responsibility for feeding the men. Within a few years the YMCA assumed full responsibility. The Spring Street house developed into the Bowery branch of the YMCA.

Dooley's dormitory was the prototype of skid row lodging houses. Commercial operators copied the idea of crowding a number of beds and bunks into a single large room and soon flop houses lined the Bowery and similar streets in every large city. In the single year 1888 four and a half million such lodgings were provided in New York alone.

However, the problem of extending charity to homeless men ran headlong into Protestant ethics. Everyone would admit the need to help children, widows, and the aged and infirm. But Protestantism stressed the value of individual struggle and salvation. Work had a kind of religious value. Then what to do with those who wandered the streets asking for charity? The obvious answer was to supply workhouses and if they did not choose to enter these places, then there must be something evil about them. Their sufferings were the just punishment for this evil.

The old ethics were considerably softened as society became more industrialized and more complicated. Wesley and his followers introduced a greater measure of compassion. It was conceded that man

Bowery Branch of the YMCA 1879

was not entirely the master of his fate. But an attempt was made to distinguish between one man's fate and another's. Whenever a bed or meal was provided as an act of charity the search was for the "deserving" poor. The Spring Street lodging house was opened to "worthy" men. Other missionary reports speak of "bummers" and "revolvers" in contrast to "persons of good name and respectability who have suddenly overtaken misfortune or been turned out of doors for want of means."

"The shameless beggar, the incorrigible vagrant, and the barefaced imposter" were sent to the police lodging house.

It was these men whom McAuley wanted to help. This was the originality of his inspiration. He did not go to the Bowery, which was then, although garish and loud, still a respectable working class street where someone from uptown could seek relatively safe entertainment in a variety hall or beer saloon. He returned to the depths of Water Street.

There had been some improvement following the John Allen excitement. The mission station and sailors' reading room was open at 316 Water Street and—most surprising of all—Kit Burns' rat pit down the street had been transformed into a home for reformed prostitutes. Burns retired early in 1870 near the end of his sordid life; he was to die in 1873. The house was opened in February 1870. The former rat pit became a kitchen, the bar was turned into a chapel and the rooms upstairs were furnished as lodgings. Henry Little served as missionary and was in charge of the Sunday services; a matron lived upstairs with the girls. The home was to remain open for many years but without much success.

Water Street was still untamed. With John Allen's and Kit Burns' closed, the honors for the most sordid dive probably went to the Hole-in-the-Wall at the corner of Dover Street. It was run by Charley Monell and presided over by a giant Englishwoman, over six feet tall, known as Gallus Mag because she kept her skirt up with suspenders, or galluses. She had a pistol in her belt, a club strapped to her wrist, and would bite an ear off an opponent in a knockdown, drag-out fight. She preserved the ears in a jar of alcohol as trophies. There was also the Fourth Ward Hotel at the corner of Catherine Street, with a tunnel leading under the streets to the East River, where bodies of murdered sailors could be dumped.

When McAuley went to some of his friends and told them of his vision and asked their help, they tried to discourage him.

"I went to a certain minister and he said, 'Why, you're wild, Jerry, to try to start a mission down there. Why, they'll kill you the first thing and fire you and the benches outdoors together.' 'Well,' I replied, 'Let them. I've taken and given a good many hard knocks for the devil and I think I can stand and take a few for the dear Lord Jesus, so I shall start right there where I am most needed and where no one else wants to go.' 'Well, go on then if you must,' he said, 'and here is five dollars for you anyway and God bless you.'"

One reason for McAuley's later success as an evangelist was his facility for rephrasing and reworking the Bible to illustrate a point. He once told a meeting at his mission how his work had been divinely ordained:

"Did you ever read in the Bible about that fellow in the tombs? He tore all his clothes off and broke his chains and nobody could help him. But Jesus came along and saved him and put a new suit of clothes on him, shoes and all—no second-handed things; but what did the fellow do? Why, I expect he straightened up his coat collar and put on a white choker and said, 'Well, I guess, Lord, I'll go along with you and have a good easy time and folks will think I'm respectable.' But Jesus said to him, 'Go back among the people that knew what a miserable old tramp you were and tell them what wonderful things God has done for you.' And I can imagine I see him go back and get up on an old barrel and tell the people what a miserable wretch he was until Christ found him."

During the summer of 1872 McAuley went with Maria on a tour of the camp meetings around New York; to Sea Cliff on Long Island; Sing Sing on the Hudson not far from the prison with its awful, yet wonderful, memories; and finally to Ocean Grove in New Jersey. Camp meetings were mammoth gatherings where religious families had their spiritual springs replenished. Each day's meeting ended with the singing of the hymn, "God Be With You Till We Meet Again," and the audience walked out into the moonlight in a mood of deep emotion.

The McAuleys were welcomed as notable converts. Jerry told some of the story of his life and described his vision. He was still not sure how his inspiration would work out in practice. In one explanation at about this time he said he wanted to rent a building and fit it out for men who had just come out of prison; he would have cots for them to sleep on, and bread and coffee to give them in the morning, and a prayer meeting in the evening.

His testimony at the meetings ended with a re-

CAMP MEETING AT SING SING,
*The once-rustic area has now become a place of vacation h
and is called Ossining, after the nearby*

quest for contributions and he raised four hundred and fifty dollars during the summer. It was only then that he went to Alfrederic Hatch. They talked one Sunday after the service at the Howard Mission. McAuley described his vision and told of the money he had raised.

"He seemed to discourage me a little at first," McAuley recalled. "He said, 'Jerry, if you start a mission you will have to give your time to it. You have got a good situation and good wages where you are respected and trusted, which you will have to give up. Don't you think you can serve God and do good and earn your bread and butter at the same time right where you are?' I thought then and knew afterwards he was trying to see how much I was in earnest."

After this show of reluctance, Hatch agreed. He asked the City Mission to return the building at 316 Water Street. Since Carmel Chapel had just opened on the Bowery and showed signs of flourishing, while the work at Water Street had never developed into much, the City Mission agreed.

In October 1872 McAuley and a few helpers took possession of the Water Street house. They used the four hundred and fifty dollars for cleaning and repairing, and put up a sign: "Helping Hand for Men."

8 The Mission Started

THE MISSION GREW BY INSPIRATION and trial and error. A few days after hanging out the sign Jerry, Maria, and a few others stood in a corner of the large downstairs room singing the only hymns they knew well, "Rock of Ages" and "There is a Fountain Filled with Blood." No one came. Jerry discovered that the old man he had appointed door-keeper would not let any one in. "He had the door locked and kept them all out. He wasn't going to let any of those bad characters in to disturb our meeting—not he."

There were rows of wooden benches with an aisle down the center leading to a small platform, with a reading desk, a small organ, a wooden arm chair

for Jerry, and a few benches for important visitors. Maria could play the organ, a skill she probably acquired during her youth in New England. The reading desk was for the visiting minister or lay preacher who would conduct the services. Finally, since this was an evangelistic mission, there was an empty bench at the foot of the platform where penitents could come to pray. Its value was more symbolic than real. If there were too many for the length of the bench those remaining would simply kneel in a line extending out on either side.

The only model McAuley had to follow was that of a small mission church in the slums, with Sunday worship services, a Sunday school for children, a Bible class for adults, occasional prayer meetings, and perhaps casual facilities for reading religious literature. After about a month he was given donations for a Thanksgiving dinner. Everyone was invited and asked to bring friends. With this the real life of the mission began.

"We gave a good dinner to one hundred and fifty poor people and, afterwards, Brother Rue proposing to give thanks for the grand day we had experienced, we had a kind of family prayer meeting. We got together for prayer and singing and while this was going on, the outside people flocked in and crowded the house. Such a night I never saw; sinners crying, 'God have mercy on us,' 'Lord help me,' and while I was on my knees the Lord said, 'You had better open the door every evening.' And so I did." From that night on the mission was open seven nights a week. Later an eighth meeting was added on Sunday afternoon.

Many of the seats were filled by drunks and tramps looking for a place to rest or to escape the chill of the night. They discovered here was a place that was not looking for the "worthy" and the "deserving." No matter how dirty a man looked, how foul he smelled, or how uncertainly he stood on his feet, he was given food and a place to sleep and offered a helping hand.

"I suppose I was the first one to open a place for tramps and we would have as many as fifty or sixty at once to provide lodgings for. They would be stretched out on the benches and then on the floor until there was not room to put your foot down without stepping on them. They were a terribly degraded set, hungry and alive with vermin, but we looked beyond all that and saw only souls for whom Christ died and whom He desired to save, and every now and then God found a real jewel among them."

McAuley realized that if he were to compete with

The First Mission

the noise and shouts of Water Street he had to show signs of life himself. A regular item in the mission's budget was new hymnbooks; they were quickly thumbed to tatters by dirty, calloused hands. If the chapel did not fill up fast enough at the start of the meeting he would call out the number of a hymn with a chance for scope and volume: "Pull for the Shore" or "Let the Lower Lights be Burning." Then he would shout, "Open both the doors there wide. Now sing so they can hear you clear down to Dover Street and up to James Slip."

If the singing was too weak to suit him during a meeting he would start over: "Try that again; sing as if you meant it and don't go to sleep over it. It will do you good. Why, if people should judge by the way you sung that verse they'd think your religion was an awfully dull and uphill business. Now let's raise the roof." And they did.

He was a natural preacher and made up little parables, using words and phrases they all understood. He never troubled himself or his listeners with philosophy or theology. He had a parable about flies which he used to turn aside those who asked for explanations or assurances:

"I'm no hairsplitter and what God says to me I believe because He says it. You heard about the fellow who was describing a little fly to another friend and talked about the various parts of the fly and so on and wondered how they could have been produced. 'Look,' says he, 'at this tiny foot. How could it ever have been made?' 'Oh don't bother me,' says the other, 'God said, "Let there be flies," and there was flies and I know there is plenty of them and that's enough for me.' Some people are hairsplitters. They ask: 'If I get religion, how will so and so come out.' Well, let God take care of that and do you do your duty."

He believed that Jesus would take a personal interest in each man's life. It was more than belief; it was knowledge. For proof he pointed to himself. Once a bedraggled character from Water Street came to him and insisted that conversion was the work of his imagination.

"Well," Jerry replied, "Good for imagination."

"Well, that's all it is," the man repeated.

"All right," Jerry said. "I used to be just like you are now; wretched, ragged, friendless, homeless, and unhappy. Now see me. I am contented, have a good conscience, and everything I need. Say. Why don't you imagine yourself into it too? It's so e-a-s-y [dragging the word out] and it's certainly better. Just imagine it, why don't you."

Sometimes the platform would become a stage and he would act out a comical little play. He would tell a bit of his criminal career and of how drunk and miserable he used to be and then illustrate the change:

"Just look at me now [holding up his coat with a funny gesture and twist of his head as if looking himself over]. I have everything a man could want. I have plenty to eat, a good home and good clothes, and I am respected and trusted. Think of it: Jerry McAuley, the biggest bum that used to hang around

this ward turned into a respectable citizen. Why a few years ago, if a man with five dollars in his pocket met me coming down the street he'd cross over on the other side and lucky for him too. But now I go downtown, walk into a big banking-house, take an armchair, put up one leg over the other, and talk with the boss as big as life. And they don't set any detectives to watch me either or send for a policeman to run me out. This is what Jesus has done for me—made a man of me—and He will do it for you too if you let Him."

His message was as blunt as that; it pays—in this life—to serve Jesus. To many this seemed crass materialism; a degrading of the spiritual qualities of religion. But McAuley realized that the customary revivalist emphasis on hell and damnation had no meaning to an audience largely composed of outcasts. They were experiencing hell on earth. They did not need to be taught the penalties of sin. But they did have to be shown the rewards of righteousness. They first had to discover that "Godliness is profitable unto all things, having promise of the life that now is," and only then would they be able to concern themselves with their place in eternity: "of that which is to come."

The fiasco of the John Allen excitement was not repeated. McAuley derided "kid glove sinners" who might be drawn to Water Street out of curiosity or to strengthen their own righteousness under the pretext of reclaiming others. His temper would flare up and he would want to "fire them out."

At the end of a meeting anyone who wished was given a chance to get up and pray. One night a man stood and began praying in the stereotyped way of many revivals; he prayed for all the poor sinners in the room, for the heathen, and for everything else except himself. Jerry kept still for as long as he could and then interrupted in a harsh, flat voice: "Look here, my friend, you had better ask God to have mercy on your soul."

He paraphrased the Bible as he saw fit: "I read that Scripture about the prodigal son a long time ago and I thought I was like one of those characters and I thought the other didn't have much religion either. Why he got mad when the poor wanderer came home and then went off grumbling and growling. He was one of those nice, goodish boys who brag about always staying at home and taking care of everything—very nice, precise folks—kid-glove sinners; but they are usually like this fellow—not half as good as they think themselves to be. For here is your never-did-wrong chap growling and

Interior of the First Mission

getting mad at his poor old father, and it don't say the prodigal ever did that. What did he growl about? Why, because the father loved his own child and was glad to see him coming home after staying away so long; was glad to see him even though he was in rags, barefooted, and heartsick. There are some of those steady brothers around yet. Well, I praise the dear Lord I am his child tonight."

The mission was not for the nice, precise folks but for the prodigals. He talked to them straight in language that was their own: "The trouble with some men is they have no backbone and if everything don't go to suit them they let go, fall down, and stay there. If a man knocked one of you down, would you stay there and let him kick the life out of you? No? Of course you wouldn't. You'd get up and try to save yourself, wouldn't you? Well, that's the way to do with Satan; if he gets you down by some foul blow, don't you lie there and let him kick you to death but jump up and strike out for yourself."

He never called any man a bum or any woman a "whore of Babylon." They were all men and women living as he and Maria had once lived. He took as his guide the story of Zacchaeus in Luke 19. As Jesus was passing through Jericho He saw Zacchaeus, a tax collector and wealthy man, who had climbed a tree to get a better view over the heads of the crowd. Jesus said: "Zacchaeus, come down at once for I must stay at your house today." The people grumbled, saying Jesus would be the guest of a sinner but it turned out that Zacchaeus was moved to give half of his wealth to the poor. McAuley told the story in his own fashion:

"Jesus saw Zacchaeus up in a tree and knew him, knew all about him. But I notice He didn't call him an extortionist or a robber or any hard name but merely said, 'Come down Zacchaeus, I am going to take dinner at your house today.' Didn't accuse him of anything. He never does. Never calls those who come to Him hard names. He never called one of those poor unfortunate women a magdalene once— not once in His whole history. No sir. The bigger the sinner the more tender Jesus was. He never was harsh, only with one class of people—those hypocritical Pharisees; those dead church members who professed religion but hated Christ and were only hypocrites. He went for them and so He ought and so do I go for them and I intend to keep it hot for them."

Some conventional churchgoers came to the meetings and were shocked at the way McAuley made free and loose with the text of the Bible. They did not like the way he continually referred to the sordid details of his past life. Nice people did not act or talk that way at religious gatherings.

But he made many new friends too. He soon gained the help of two of the most active philanthropists in New York: Morris Jessup, a banker who, among many other activities, would become founder of the American Museum of Natural History in New York; and William E. Dodge, of Phelps, Dodge and Company, who was a member of Congress, a founder of the YMCA, and head of the New York City Mission and Tract Society.

The new help came at a critical moment. McAuley's earliest supporter, Alfrederic Hatch was driven to the verge of bankruptcy by the great financial collapse of 1873. With this twist of fate, Hatch found comfort in the man he had originally comforted. He wrote: "When clouds and darkness gathered about my own pathway I was uplifted and comforted by the simple and childlike yet robust faith of Jerry and his wife and by their sublime trust in the living providence of God."

When the mission had been open for awhile Sidney Whittemore, a well-to-do businessman, decided that since he was such a "big gun" in the church he should go down to Water Street, shake Jerry by the hand, and encourage him to keep up the good work. When he proposed the visit to his wife, Emma, she objected; it was not a place for decent people to go. But she went along with the understanding that they would go only once.

The room was crowded and a place had to be squeezed out for them near the platform. McAuley opened the meeting and the testimonies followed. The Whittemores felt themselves deeply moved and when the invitation for prayers was given they both stood and, with emotion, asked the congregation to pray that they might return to God.

At the end of the meeting those who felt drawn toward conversion were asked to "come to the bench." This was always the crucial moment, the time of trial, the moment often evaded. When Jerry

48

Emma Whittemore

saw someone whom he felt was ready to surrender himself, he would go and encourage him to step forward. The Whittemores were surprised to hear themselves singled out. They went forward and knelt at the bench with drunkards, tramps, thieves, and prostitutes. McAuley stood over them and said, "Now pray, every one of you, pray."

He moved down the benches to listen to the prayers one by one. When Sidney Whittemore's turn came he said, "God be merciful to me a sinner." Emma Whittemore did the same. McAuley stood over them a while and then placed his hand lightly on Mrs. Whittemore's shoulder. She looked up and so did her husband. They saw tears running down McAuley's cheeks. He said, with great tenderness, "Ah, put in 'for Jesus' sake.'" They did and before they rose from their knees they knew their lives had been changed.

Sidney Whittemore became one of the firmest and most abiding of all the supporters of the mission. His wife too. Many years later Emma Whittemore established scores of successful rescue homes for prostitutes. Shortly after the turn of the century she joined the Salvation Army and her house for women in New York became part of an even greater effort for the rescue of women.

9 The Dirty Turncoat

WHEN JERRY MCAULEY BECAME A CONVERT to Protestant evangelism and opened his mission in the Fourth Ward, he violated every principle of his class and kind.

The epithets "turncoat" and "traitor" have a special sting for an Irishman. If British rule over Ireland had any purpose, aside from sheer economic exploitation, it was to get the Irish to accept Protestant practices and English values. The only easy road to status was for an Irishman to turn his back on his religion and his culture.

The Catholic Church and Irish culture went together. Priests, being themselves despised, were not the protectors of an established order or of vested privileges. They were protectors of the people. A man who turned against his church was a traitor of the deepest dye.

Instead of loyalty to country there was loyalty to family and neighborhood. The family was the heart of society. A man was nothing outside of his family; his family was his personality. He was as strong or as weak as his family and they prospered or fell together. A collection of family loyalties made up the loyalty of a neighborhood which, for most people, hardly extended farther.

Irish immigrants brought these values virtually unchanged to the United States. Large extended families lived in one or two tenements. Old Irish neighborhoods clustered in a single block. The Irish built their little churches and stood off the rich New York Protestants who seemed to resemble so closely the rulers they had left behind.

Jerry McAuley had sufficiently disgraced his family as a thief and drunkard but these were familiar failings to the Irish in New York and could be borne. But to become a Protestant and set up a mission and start preaching in your own neighborhood was the ultimate in disgrace.

One of his sisters tried to persuade him to give up what seemed to be a mad career. He explained the reasons for his new life, with citations from the Bible. His sister was illiterate and realized she was out of her depth. She was sure the parish priest would convince him of his errors. McAuley had no desire to engage in argument but went with her to the priest to please her.

Strangely, the priest had been born into a Protestant family but was later converted to Catholicism. The debate was doomed from the start. Both were men who had reached their convictions not by habit or imitation but through trial and insight. Each had opted for a different road. McAuley reasoned on the basis of the Bible as an inspired work. The priest readily accepted this but said the traditions of the church could not be ignored or waved aside. They parted with no opinions changed.

McAuley's sister was content with persuasion, the priest with friendly debate, but the neighborhood would settle for nothing less than threats and violence. The toughs and hoodlums smashed the windows with bricks and threw garbage in the door. Wire screens were put in front of all windows, except one in the rear, which seemed safe. Then one night a brick came through this window, narrowly missing the head of a visitor who was playing the organ.

"What was that?" he asked.

"Oh, that's nothing," McAuley replied. "They send whole paving stones sometimes; that's only a piece of brick."

One Fourth of July night the opposition combined patriotism with interference. They put a barrel in the middle of the street and set someone to watch at the door of the mission. Whenever anyone got up to testify a pack of firecrackers was exploded in the barrel and the man's voice was drowned out by the din. This happened several times till McAuley had an idea.

"Now I want you to watch me," he said. "I'll select a hymn ahead of time and the moment I say, 'Sing,' just sing with all your might, and when I say, 'Testify,' be ready to spring right up."

A man got up to speak and the explosions began.

"Sing!" McAuley shouted and they sang so loud they drowned out the fireworks. When the pack finished McAuley shouted, "Testify," and the man jumped up again to tell his story before the next pack could be lighted. When the explosions resumed they were again drowned out by a hymn. Eventually the harassers ran out of firecrackers and had to be content with shooting roman candles at the windows.

The meetings were generally in the charge of visiting ministers or laymen. One night McAuley came down from his quarters above the mission a bit late. The meeting had started and the chairman was reading a text from the Bible. As McAuley came down the stairs he heard a yell like an Indian war-whoop: "Silence." The chairman almost dropped the Bible as McAuley entered. Maria pointed to a giant of a man sitting in the congregation. McAuley did not want to interrupt the reading so he sat down. There was another yell. He walked down the aisle to where the man sat. They later learned his name was Jackson.

McAuley looked at him: huge, with broad, strong shoulders, and his red shirt open at the neck to show a hairy chest. McAuley spoke to him gently, still not wanting to upset the meeting; telling him that order had to be kept. Jackson just pointed over his shoulder as if to say that someone else had made the noise. McAuley went back to his place on the platform.

The Bible reading resumed. McAuley looked directly at Jackson. He saw him drop his head below the level of the man in front of him and then came the yell for the third time. McAuley knew he was in for it. If Jackson got away with this the meetings would never go on undisturbed. McAuley called for "Rock of Ages" and walked down the aisle. He looked at the great brute. He felt the work of the Lord was at stake and there was no turning back. He told Jackson he had to leave.

"Ah, go on," Jackson growled. "What's the matter wid you?"

"Come," said McAuley, "you must go out or I'll put you out."

Jackson did not move. McAuley reached out and caught him by the collar. Jackson reached his arms back and locked his hands around the back of the bench. "Go ahead, old fella," he grinned.

McAuley got a tighter grip on Jackson's shirt collar and surged backward. By this time everyone else had jumped off the bench. Jackson was dragged to his feet and the bench with him. The congregation continued to sing "Rock of Ages," all eyes on the fight. McAuley dragged Jackson and the bench into the aisle. The bench hit the ceiling and Jackson's grip was broken. McAuley grabbed him by the throat. Jackson struck out with a right jab from the shoulder. McAuley had not forgotten what he knew of the manly art; he fended off this and other blows and kept shoving Jackson nearer the door. When Jackson was not striking he was clutching at whatever he could grab: benches, even the heads of those foolish enough not to stand aside.

There was a final lunge to the door, built of solid wood two inches thick. They both slammed into it and split the wood apart and tore the whole door off the hinges. McAuley's grip was still on Jackson's throat. His face was turning color and he begged for freedom, promising to behave. McAuley threw him on the sidewalk, returned to the meeting, and joined in for a final chorus of "Rock of Ages."

A few weeks later someone else began a disturbance. McAuley saw that he had been drinking and, with customary tolerance, said, "Don't mind that poor fellow, friends. He has been taking a little too much gin."

"Not a drop of gin, Jerry. Nothing but good old bourbon whisky," the man replied. McAuley then realized he was deliberately causing trouble and had to be bounced. He called for a hymn and started down the aisle when the man suddenly lay down on the floor.

"All right, young man. If you prefer going out that way I've no objections," McAuley said and took him by the collar and dragged him down the aisle

A Fourth Ward Groggery

and out the door.

McAuley did not make things easier for himself. He had come to the Fourth Ward to do more than preach. He wanted to end the vice and crime that was destroying so many lives, as his own had almost been destroyed. The cellar dives seemed to be the worst. They had names like "The Well" and "The Man Trap." About a dozen men and women inhabited these holes, where the tide seeped in twice a day. Sometimes a girl would dart out and grab a sailor's hat and run back into the den. He was wise if he let it go for, if he followed it in, he would probably be beaten and robbed, if not murdered. The denizens of these holes died off as quickly as the rats they resembled but there were always others to replace them.

McAuley discovered that a rich man, considered one of the respectable men of New York, owned the houses where these cellar dives flourished. It seemed simple. He had only to go to this good Christian, explain to him how his property was being misused, and the matter would be cleared up. "He paid no more attention to me than he would to a barking dog," McAuley recalled. He later found out why. Each hole brought the rich man rent of from thirty to forty dollars a month. McAuley was still learning the ways of the kid glove sinners.

He went to someone with important friends and explained what was going on. He was assured he did not have to worry any longer; that it would all be attended to and Water Street would be as quiet as Fifth Avenue.

A few days later he looked out his window and saw several policemen outside looking up. He could

not understand what was wrong and thought the mission might be on fire. He ran out and asked them what was happening. "We've been sent down here to watch the mission," one replied.

"Why," McAuley exclaimed, trying to keep his temper in check, "I didn't want anyone to watch the mission but I want to break up these dens around here."

"Oh, we've got nothing to do but to obey orders," the policeman said. "All the orders we got was to come here and watch the mission."

At first McAuley charged into everything around him, thinking he could clean up Water Street by himself. Just as often the police would make him out to be the culprit, accusing him of causing a riot or interfering with an officer on duty. William Dodge had him appointed deputy sheriff but warned him not to interfere with the police as they did their duty.

One day Jerry was standing in the door of the mission when a fight broke out across the street where two new buildings were under construction. The fight began when a workman turned a hose on a well-dressed stranger passing in the street. The stranger objected. The workman picked up an ax. As he raised it to strike the stranger he glanced over and saw McAuley watching.

"What are you looking at, you dirty turncoat, you miserable hypocrite you?" he shouted. McAuley told him to be quiet.

"Come over here," the workman yelled and added a string of curses. McAuley walked over and grabbed him by the collar. His mate slipped behind McAuley and was about to hit him with a shovel. McAuley

Saloon in a Water Street Tenement

pushed the first into a pile of sand and threw the second on top of him. A policeman arrived and McAuley asked him to arrest the man who had started the row. Then a second policeman came up and whispered to the first. Instead of arresting the workman they dragged McAuley off to the station house while the people in the street laughed and shouted, "There he goes . . . the dirty turncoat . . . bad luck to the likes of ye."

At the station house, the second workman made a complaint that McAuley had struck the other in the nose and had knocked him down.

"Is that so?" said the sergeant. "He hit you? Show me the marks."

"Him lave any marks on me, I'd knock his brains out," the first workman replied.

"Faith he did," said the second and they were about to have a fight of their own when the foreman came in. He wanted to get the men back to work. He said they had been drinking and denied there had been a fight. Now the captain was angry.

He shook his fist at McAuley and shouted, "I'll lock you up anyway. I'll break up that old nuisance of a mission for you. It keeps the whole place in an uproar. I'll send you back to prison where you belong. That old mission is a nuisance.

Another policeman darted in. "He has a shield on, too, captain. And he has a great big club down there at his mission to knock men down with." The captain tore McAuley's coat open and was about to rip

the shield from his shirt. McAuley pushed him back, ready to fight if the badge was touched.

Just then Maria came in. She had been told Jerry had been taken to the station house.

"You go see Mr. Dodge or Mr. Hatch," Jerry shouted to her. Maria first went to Hatch, who could not leave his office. He put her in a carriage and sent her off to Dodge, who said he would get a special court convened if necessary so that McAuley would not spend one night in jail. But it was not necessary. The captain knew it would be difficult to make out a case and that McAuley had powerful friends. He let him go with a warning, "I'll make it hot for you."

Once a policeman aptly named Savage was put outside his door, ostensibly to protect McAuley, but he was in league with the saloon keepers. Savage would walk into the mission while a meeting was in progress, stamp with his heavy boots across the room to a shelf where Bibles and a few newspapers were kept, pick up a paper, throw it down and stamp, stamp, stamp back to the door. He was a brute who one night almost clubbed a woman to death beneath McAuley's window.

Still McAuley kept at it. He would lie in bed at night and hear the hideous sounds of the street: the music, the snatches of song, the laughter, the groans, and the occasional cry of "Murder! Murder!" He went from person to person seeking help but received only promises.

10 Early Faith

AT FIRST, McAuley wanted to test the truth of his vision and made it a rule never to ask for money or go into debt: "We found ourselves more than once with very little money in the treasury. Then again we would feel rich when we found we had ten dollars in cash. We borrowed no trouble about finances but trusted wholly in the Lord. Before the cold weather set in the workers prayed earnestly for the winter's supply of coal. Two businessmen were talking about it just then in their offices downtown. One of these men had been converted but a few months before at the mission and felt moved to send in a thank-offering to the Lord. The other had been for many months a devoted worker there. Said the first,

'Let us join and send them coal enough to last the winter months.' The thought was of God, before whom the earnest prayer had just gone up. It was done and all trouble on that score was settled.

"On another occasion a gas bill came in and there was not a cent in the treasury; but it was taken to the Father to whom belongs the silver and gold. In the course of the day a letter was received containing just the amount of the bill and the carfare of the messenger who should go to pay it."

During the first year 5,144 men were given lodgings, 26,261 meals were supplied, and a great deal of donated clothing was distributed. It was always touch and go, however.

"One night we found the mission without a cent and forty odd tramps to feed and nothing to offer them. It was a time to test my views, for I had declared I would let the Lord have His way and whenever He ceased to provide, I would accept it as evidence that He did not want us to go on, and, as He supplied our necessities, would consider He was pleased to have us continue. I felt for those poor hungry men. Some of them had probably not tasted a bite of food for two and three days. They had no money to help themselves and when they came on Saturday night we usually kept them over Sunday. But on this night we were broke.

"We proceeded to the mission room and commenced the services and some souls were saved. But even when nine o'clock had come, strange to say, no one had handed us a penny. As the meeting drew to a close and nothing come, oh how dark everything seemed! My faith trembled. I could hardly keep from crying as I looked into the hungry faces of the poor tramps and converts. I spoke to my wife about them and she replied, 'The Lord will provide. You see if He don't.'

"I closed with a heavy heart and dismissed the meeting and my wife took her position at the door as usual to shake hands with the folks as they went out. A lady passed out with her husband and, after going five or ten yards, suddenly stopped and coming back to my wife said, 'Mrs. McAuley, we keep a baker-shop on Cherry Street and I just happened to think you had better send up and get five dollars' worth of bread.' "

That was Maria's post at the door. Sometimes a drunk would come up and cry over her. Sometimes a tough from the neighborhood would come up and sneer at her or insult her. But she shook every man's hand, no matter what his race or condition; she smiled and looked at him and said, "Come again tomorrow night." Often it was this final act of humanity that melted the stone in a man's heart.

At another time they were out of money and closed the meeting with silent prayers for help. As the people were leaving someone came up and gave a small package to one of the worshipers, saying, "Here, hand that to Jerry." The package, unmarked, was brought to McAuley who opened it and found one hundred dollars inside.

McAuley had been around missions long enough to know it was the custom to print an annual report on the progress of the work and, in the process, thank those who had helped. He was too busy to arrange for one at the end of the first year but he did manage to issue a report in October 1874, summing up the work of two years. To him, of course, the mission was a tremendous undertaking and he thought the report should be on an equally large scale. He ordered ten thousand copies. When he mentioned what he had done to some of those who had contributed to the mission, they were indignant at the waste. They asked where the money would come from to pay the printing bill. Jerry had no answer.

He decided to make the best of what appeared to be a bad thing. One Saturday morning he asked a convert, "Happy Charlie" Anderson, to help him. They hoisted large packs of reports on their backs and started uptown, stopping at churches along the way to ask if they could leave the reports on the pews. They were refused, except at three churches.

The next morning a carriage drove up to the mission and two well-dressed women stepped out. McAuley thought they had seen his report. Then he thought it was too early, unless they had read the report while they should have been listening to the sermon. Apparently this was what happened. They came in, talking about the work, and each handed McAuley fifty dollars. They left, refusing to give their names.

"I was happy, 'What a miracle! One hundred dollars. Whew! Three cheers!' said I, hardly able to hold myself in, 'We're safe now.' "

That was not the end of it. A few days later another young lady found an escort and came down to the mission. She is identified only as Miss S. She said she had found the report on her pew, had carelessly turned the pages and became so interested she did not hear a word the pastor had said.

She returned a number of times and it became apparent she was in spiritual turmoil. One Sunday night she took a diamond-cluster ring from her finger and as she walked out she passed it to Maria while saying goodby.

"Here, Mrs. McAuley, take this and sell it for the good of the mission," she said. "Do pray for me, won't you? I'm an awful wicked sinner."

Miss S returned the next afternoon at tea time. She knelt and prayed with the McAuleys and was converted. The time for the meeting arrived. As they went down to the chapel, Miss S said, "You must not ask me to speak in the public congregation. If you should it seems to me I should faint."

"All right," McAuley replied, "If you faint, I'll have someone ready to pick you up." After the opening ceremonies, Miss S was the first to jump to her feet to testify, with glowing face and words. Her life was changed from then on and wherever she lived she volunteered her services as a missionary for a church or chapel.

At times there were only a hundred men and women at a meeting. At other times there were as many as four hundred, with people standing at the back and in the aisle. About thirty or forty were converts who attended regularly. But there were always new faces and new experiences. The meetings began every night at half-past seven and ended at nine. The Sunday afternoon meetings were from two-thirty till four o'clock; a total of 417 meetings a year.

There were two variations. A large dinner was held in the chapel on the afternoon of Thanksgiving day. On December 31st, after the evening service, a Christmas tree was uncovered and presents distributed to converts and their families.

Nearly two hundred hymnbooks had to be replaced every year. Sometimes a drunk in a neighboring saloon would take up and sing the chorus of a song remembered from his childhood.

There would be hymns while the room was filling, then a reading from the Bible, followed by a short statement by Jerry. The testimonies would follow immediately. This was the heart of the meeting.

This was not a conventional church with a preacher to instruct the worshipers with a sermon. Here the members of the congregation were their own preachers. Neither was it a conventional revival meeting, with fiery exhortations and loud declarations of faith. Sometimes a seaman, used to the competition of wind and wave, might declare loudly, "God spake peace to my soul one day at four o'clock in the afternoon on board the ship *George Peabody* at Pier Fourteen," and punctuate his testimony with an explosive "Amen." But usually the voices were small and matter of fact.

When the men and women of the Fourth Ward discovered they would not be hooted at for their lack of education or sneered at for their simplicity, they were eager to talk; so eager that McAuley imposed a one-minute rule:

"These long-winded fellows kill the meeting. Wind them up and set them a-going and they don't know when to stop. Now speak short. If you've come in here with a long yarn all fixed up nice, with a beginning and a middle and an ending, just cut off both ends and give us the middle. I was a poor drunkard, a miserable loafer and tramp without a decent coat to my back, full of wickedness and sin

and a terror around this terrible ward. Jesus picked me up and saved me and has kept me saved. Glory to His name. There's my testimony and it didn't take me a minute to tell it either."

He meant it too. He had a little bell he would ring when someone got long-winded. He also had signs posted on the walls, again shocking the primly pious by the seeming harshness of the injunction:

SPEAKERS ARE
STRICTLY LIMITED
TO ONE MINUTE

He underscored the rule with a story of stirabout:

"I want you all to testify and tell what God has done for you and be as short as you can. You have, probably, all heard about the three men with the pot of stirabout, haven't you? Three hungry men had a pot of stirabout set before them but only one spoon and the stirabout being too hot to use their hands, one man was to use the spoon and then pass it to the second and so on. Now what would you think if one fellow took the spoon and kept it all the time and let the others starve? Well, pass the spoon."

McAuley knew from his own experience the value of sincere testimony sincerely told. Sometimes Orville Gardner would come to a meeting and sit on the platform while McAuley pointed to him and told of his own conversion. He also knew how hard it was to take the first step.

Once a sailor asked him how he could trust Jesus. McAuley replied, "Can't you trust the Lord from here to the door?" The sailor said yes, he could do that. "Then can't you trust Him from the door to the corner?" The sailor exclaimed, "Yes, I see it!"

McAuley never stopped trying. He later recalled the case of a hard convert: "We did pray for him, it is true, and to be honest with you I got discouraged over him. I thought his one of the hardest cases that ever came into those doors. Think of it: two years praying steadily for one man before he yielded."

He knew his methods were right and he ignored the rebukes of visitors from uptown: "We did not know how to put on airs but went right in for solid work. We would go into the congregation and talk to the people and lead them to the altar. One night my wife got a young lady to come and we knelt down beside her to help her to the Lord. Several of the pillars were sitting quietly on the platform doing nothing and one of them—a 'big gun'—said sneeringly, 'Jerry and his wife will talk that girl to death.' Wife heard it and arose and took her seat but I didn't hear a word and 'twas well I didn't. Just as wife got up the Lord wonderfully saved the girl. Oh how happy she was! It was a good thing we did run the risk of talking her to death for she died shortly afterward and went to the triumphs of faith."

An old longshoreman named Padgett was brought in one night soon after the mission opened. He had been a gambler and thief and was now a drunk and so was his wife. They were reduced to a few rags of clothing and were literally taken in from the gutter. They were converted and became devoted supporters of the mission. Old Padgett, as he was invariably called, once told his story to a visitor:

"My clothes and my wife's and all we had in the world wouldn't a-brought a dollar at auction. I earned wages but I swallowed them and so did she. I bummed round here with Jerry before he ever got sent up and I wouldn't believe my eyes the night I come in here and seen him clean and respectable. I give my heart to God that very night and the next day I says, down on the docks, 'I've stuck boys. I'm not going to serve the devil no longer.'

" 'You,' they says, 'You. That's a great go. Here, old Padgett, we'll give you this one day for your holding out. No, we'll give you till you get the first dollar. We'll see about you then.' Well, they've seen. I ain't fallen, though I've been tempted many a time."

Most of those who came to the mission were simple people like Padgett. Society seldom bothered to condemn them for being drunk and dissolute because nothing better was expected of them. But McAuley did expect better of them. He showed them how to find religion and, at the same time, how to find contentment in a peaceful, orderly life.

In 1874 a blacksmith came in. He was a mean-tempered drunk, without a coat to his back or shoes on his feet and ready to fight any man. His wife was a drunkard too. They were both converted. He would testify: "God has given me and my wife clean hearts and clean ways and everything we need and has given me a humble spirit. If a man now strikes me on one cheek I think I am willing to turn to him the other also, if I can serve God. I swing my sledge every day at work with heavenly thoughts and sometimes I forget my mate on the other side of the anvil and keep striking as if it was one more blow for Jesus."

Sometimes a convert would be well known among his kind; a man like Rowdy Brown. He was a mate on the Liverpool packets and a savage. He hated religion. He once saw a man sitting in the f'c'sle of a ship reading the Bible. Without a word, Brown kicked the man in the mouth, knocking his teeth out, and permanently disfiguring his face. He was afraid of no one. He once stood boldly and cursed a man who had two pistols in his hands. The man fired both guns. Brown was hit but survived.

He was living at Rhode's New Sailors' Home on Pearl Street when he heard that a chum had been converted at Jerry's. He grabbed a bottle of whisky and started toward the mission. He swore that if his mate got up to testify he would tear his mouth open and pour the whisky down his throat.

The meeting began and Brown sat holding his black bottle, waiting for his shipmate to stand up. He listened intently to be ready to act. He felt himself tremble. They were telling stories and describing feelings that could have been his own. When his chum testified Brown just sat and listened. When prayers were invited at the end of the meeting Rowdy Brown stood up and called out, "Oh, pray for me."

Everyone knew him. McAuley and others gathered around and Brown moaned and seemed to be torn with anguish. He became calm and went home. He returned the following night and still did not feel converted. But he went home and prayed and as he got into his bed he suddenly felt the thrill of conversion. He jumped out of bed again and shouted praises of God so loudly he awakened his roommate, who thought he was drunk.

Rowdy Brown became as rough and ready in his new life as he had been in his old. He would sometimes grab a sailor on the street and drag him into the meeting. When the invitation was given for prayers he would go over to someone he believed should be saved and hoist him up to his feet. He would come back from a voyage and give a sizable part of his earnings to the mission.

He even started his own rescue mission at sea. There is a story told of him aboard the West India brig *Nellie,* in the harbor of Matanzas, Cuba. He stretched a big canvas on the deck as an awning and had a sign painted: JERRY McAULEY'S PRAYER MEETING HERE THIS AFTERNOON AT THREE O'CLOCK. He sent boats out to collect sailors from other ships and touched off a small revival in the port. He later retired to Canada, where he died. There was every indication that his conversion held firm to the end.

Another early convert was also named Brown—Jack Brown. Like McAuley, Jack was a graduate of the Fourth Ward, the East River, and Sing Sing.

Jack Brown's first memory of his mother was of her lying drunk on the floor. She smothered one of her children to death one night by rolling over on top of the baby while drunk. Jack's parents lived over a saloon and he grew up to hate the smell of whisky. His father died when he was six and he left home when he was eight to support himself as a newsboy. He was arrested for stealing and sent to the House of Refuge, the juvenile prison of New York. The officials taught him religion and thought him a bright scholar. The other inmates taught him how to be a professional criminal and they too thought he was bright.

He was about fourteen when he was released and made straight for Mickey Hagan's saloon. Hagan was a receiver of stolen goods and Fagin for young river thieves. He would sell boats, rent them, or let them out for a part of the loot.

Within a year Jack was the leader of his gang. He thought of a daring scheme and used it many times. The gang patrolled the waterfront by day until they found a pier where a ship was partly unloaded and the cargo stacked on the dock. Then, at night, they rowed with muffled oars, hardly drawing a deep breath, until they were under the dock. Slowly and steadily they bored a hole through the beams with a large auger. It went straight into the sacks and the coffee, spices, or other produce poured down into bags they held beneath. All the while a watchman would patrol the dock with pistol cocked and not know a thing.

Three years passed and Jack thought he would never be caught. He was cornered a dozen times but always slipped away. He was shot twice but recovered. He once was knocked overboard into the freezing river and had to swim under water to reach the dock and escape. Then he was caught. He fought like mad but the handcuffs were slipped on him and he was marched to jail.

His trial was short. He was sentenced to ten years in Sing Sing and that was considered a mild sentence given to him in view of his youth. He was about eighteen. He screamed he would kill anyone who tried to take him away and they had to chain him like a beast. The warden was warned to deal with Jack as the devil himself.

He continued to fight for the first six months in prison and hardly a week passed that he was not punished. He suffered the shower bath until he fainted, kicks and cuffs, floggings and half rations. He was reduced to skin and bones.

He realized he would soon be dead if he did not behave and he decided to calm down. It took him a year to learn to control himself. A new chaplain came and helped him to reform. He was transferred to another cell where things were easier and did the work of two men in the shops to prove his new way of life. He studied and learned to read. Eventually he was granted a pardon, five years and one day after he had been brought in. The chaplain brought it to him.

"Jack," he said, "You're very young yet and now is your chance. Try to be an honest man and pray for help. I wish I knew if you will pray."

"You'd make me if anyone could," Jack replied, "but I ain't sure of the use of it yet. I wish I was."

He tried to find work but no one would have a jailbird. He would have returned to the river but he knew he had lost his nerve. A friend took him to Mickey Hagan's saloon and he was hired as a bartender. After the experiences of his childhood he was still a confirmed teetotaler, probably the only nondrinking bartender in New York. The smell of whisky made him sick but he stayed on the job for three years. There were fights every night. Being sober he could keep order where no one else could.

He hated every minute of it. He saved his money and then, one Saturday night, he got his pay and left.

"Get another man," he said, "I'm done," and walked out with Mickey shouting after him. He looked for work for three months, answering advertisements in the papers and inserting his own. He went every place he could think of but he always admitted squarely that he was a jailbird and the answer was always no. He cut down on the amount of his food to make his money last. Finally he had spent everything and pawned his clothes so that he could not take a decent job if it were offered him. He tried to live in City Hall Park but the police slapped him on the feet with their clubs and drove him away.

One night, after going without food for two days, he got tired of it all. He started to walk slowly down Beekman Street toward the river. As he got nearer something seemed to pull him on and he began to run. "It's the end of all my troubles," he told himself and plunged over the side of the dock. Instead of sinking into the river he hit his head on a boat and was knocked unconscious.

He was taken to Bellevue Hospital and remained

there six weeks, slowly recovering. He was determined to kill himself once he got out. But one night he began to talk to a man in the next bed and told him his whole story.

The man said, "I don't know but one man in New York that'll know just what to do and that's McAuley of Water Street. You go there soon's you can stir and tell him your story."

Jack laughed. "I'm done telling," he said.

"Try him," the man insisted. They talked more and the man kept insisting and Jack finally agreed. He got out of the hospital sick and trembling, still without home or money. Bellevue was at the river's edge. Jack stood and looked at the water. He thought that in his weakened condition it would be easier to drown himself now. But he was proud that he had always kept his word. Since he told that man he would go to McAuley's he turned away from the river and began walking the mile and a half south to Water Street.

He was too weak to do more than go in and sit and listen. At the end he got up to leave and fell over in a dead faint. He was taken upstairs and put to bed in a room next to the McAuleys'. He recovered consciousness and saw Jerry standing over him. He looked around the small, clean room.

"You'd better not keep me," he said. "I'm a jailbird and a rascal and nobody alive wants to have anything to do with me."

"Be quiet," Jerry replied. "I'm a jailbird myself but the Lord Jesus has forgiven me and made me happy and He'll do the same by you." Jack was kept at the mission for a week and treated as a member of the family. They urged him to give himself to God.

He told them, "When I see a man that's always been respectable come to me and give me work and say he's not afraid or ashamed to, then maybe I'll believe in your Lord Jesus Christ you talk about." That same night a gentleman came to him at the mission and offered him a job. The only account of this meeting does not give the man's name but it apparently was Alfrederic Hatch. It would appear that McAuley spoke to him about Jack.

"You don't need to tell me a word," Hatch said. "I believe you are honest and you can begin tomorrow if you're strong enough. It's light work and it shall be made easier at first."

Brown's conversion took place at that moment. "I looked at him and it seemed as if something that had frozen me all up inside melted that minute. I broke out crying and couldn't stop."

Hatch knelt and began to pray: "Dear Lord, he is Thy child and he has always been Thy child. Make him know it tonight. Make him know that Thy love has followed him and will hold him up so that his feet will never slip again."

Jack was too deep in emotion to speak. Hatch, realizing what was happening, walked away without another word.

"Some of the men shake their heads," Jack said later. "They say it wasn't a regular conversion. All I know is the sense of God came into me then and it's never left me."

Conversions like this, however—the swift transformation of a man—were rare, considering the hundreds of men who filled the chapel almost every night of the week. Most men came, if they came at all, for the warmth of the room or to beg a handout.

 # How Character Can Be Changed

IN SEPTEMBER 1876 the old building was torn down and replaced by a three-story brick building. Only the chapel on the ground floor was fully finished, with seating for about two hundred persons. An airshaft led up through the first and second floors to a skylight on the roof. On the second floor, on three sides of this shaft, there were windows so that a person could look down into the meeting room. The

second floor was roughed out into rooms for the McAuleys, the janitor, and a few converts. They all lived together as a single family. The third floor was left unfinished.

The building cost about fifteen thousand dollars. The annual operating expenses were about two and a half thousand dollars. Jerry and Maria were paid four hundred dollars a year as salary. A full-time janitor and general assistant received one hundred and twenty-five dollars.

The building was ready by the end of the year. On December 9, 1876 the mission was legally incorporated. The first trustees were Alfrederic Hatch, Sidney Whittemore, John D. Phyfe, Frank Storrs, and Jerry McAuley.

Two other supporters appeared and soon became trustees. One was James Talcott, a wealthy merchant. He later would become president of the New York State Chamber of Commerce and one of the founders of Barnard College in New York City.

The other was Robert Fulton Cutting whose father had been president of the Stock Exchange in 1863. The Cuttings were, and still are, one of the old families of New York, active in business, banking, and philanthropy. Fulton Cutting was then in his early thirties. He would later become famous as a leader of the political reform movement in New York and president of the Citizens Union.

Many New Yorkers would long remember 1876 as the year that Dwight L. Moody and Ira D. Sankey, perhaps the most effective evangelists since Wesley and his immediate successors, held a tremendous series of revival meetings in New York. They packed Barnum's old Hippodrome.

Religion was a living thing for almost all Americans—but skepticism was growing. To some, religion seemed a pale thing, a mixture of superstition and crude emotions, compared with the new discoveries of science and technology. It also seemed an inadequate answer to the problems of the world. The rich were hard put to find lavish ways to spend their wealth. Robber barons ransacked the earth's resources. Politicians looted the public treasuries. Nations armed for greater wars. Meantime the millions of the poor lived in squalor and degradation. "What good did revivals and prayer meetings do?" the skeptics asked.

So it was with George Kennan. Kennan, who died in 1924, is best remembered as an authority on Russia. Shortly after the Civil War he was sent to Siberia to help plan for a telegraph line that would extend from Alaska to Europe. He returned three years later to write *Tent Life in Siberia*. In 1870 he went back to Russia for a horseback trip through the Caucasus, which resulted in another book. In 1876–1878 he worked in and near New York and came to know the McAuley mission.

Then he went to Washington as assistant manager of the Associated Press but, apparently tiring of the sedentary life, returned to Russia in 1885 for a care-

PLATFORM AT THE SECOND MISSION
It remained virtually unchanged as long as the building stood. The cane-backed armchair next to the reading desk was Jerry's place on the platform. The chair has been preserved through the years and is kept, unused, in an upstairs room at the present mission.

ful study of the Siberian penal colonies. The book which resulted from this trip, *Siberia and the Exile System,* made him nationally famous. At the turn of the century Kennan was a dashing foreign correspondent, lecturer, and writer. He knew the world and he knew what people were like.

He was reading the New York *Sun* one day late in 1900 when he saw a brief account of the twenty-eighth anniversary of the McAuley mission. It awakened memories and stirred feelings which he shaped into an article for the weekly newspaper, *The Outlook:*

"I could not help wondering whether, among the people who thus met to do honor to Jerry and his work, there were any of the men and women who helped him carry on that work in the early days and who bade me welcome when, attracted by curiosity, I strolled into that mission house for the first time one close, warm evening in the summer of 1876.

"Does 'Happy Charlie' still meet incomers at the door with face aglow with friendliness, helpfulness, and love as he once met me or has he given place to other and later converts? Is the work carried on now with the simpleness, the earnestness, and the absolute sincerity that characterized it then or have the methods of the workers become ceremonious, formal, and stiffly ecclesiastical, as such methods are apt to become when no longer inspired by an earnest, straightforward, and deeply sincere human soul?

"I have not had an opportunity to visit the Water Street mission since Jerry McAuley's death but I still vividly remember the impression it made upon me when he conducted it and I am still of the opinion that, regarded merely as a psychological and spiritual phenomenon, it was one of the most remarkable things to be seen at that time in the city of New York or in any other city."

From notes kept through all the years, Kennan reconstructed the events of a summer evening in 1876. An artist friend named Metcalf came to him and said, "George, I want you to go with me tonight to Jerry McAuley's prayer meeting."

"Prayer meeting," Kennan repeated. "I don't go to prayer meetings." He considered himself "a doubter, if not a confirmed skeptic."

"I know you don't," Metcalf answered. "Neither do I as a rule but this isn't a common prayer meeting, it's Jerry McAuley's." Metcalf explained that McAuley had been a thief and river pirate, had been to Sing Sing, and now was running this prayer meeting on Water Street. Kennan agreed to go. Metcalf advised him to put on an old suit of clothes and leave his watch and chain behind.

"I give you due notice," Kennan said, "that I don't take any stock in the cheap claptrap of your revival meetings. They work up a lot of excitement but it doesn't last and what's the use of it? Character isn't made or changed in that way."

"Isn't it?" Metcalf asked. "Perhaps Jerry'll give you some new points on character changing."

They walked down the Bowery as dusk was deepening. The concert halls were already going full blast; "Volks," "Atlantic," and other beer gardens were filling up, and here and there a peddler stood on a corner keening "H-o-ot co-o-rn," a sound which was to remain in the memory of New Yorkers and remind them of the smells and sights of the summer streets when they were young.

They turned left into the vast slum of the Lower East Side, with narrow sidewalks swarming with dirty, half-clad children, long rows of carts and wagons backed up against the curbs for the night, knots of men with inflamed faces standing at the entrances of the high, dirty tenement houses, and slatternly women with disheveled hair and dresses open at the breast leaning out of windows to scream at the noisy children below. A drunk would reel along the path or a woman dressed in tawdry finery would brush against them and leer significantly. Great sink holes in the middle of the street, filled with black, slimy mud, gave off a sickly odor, like decaying bodies. Boxes and barrels of garbage blocked the uneven sidewalks and from the green swinging doors of the saloons came the smell of sour beer, stale tobacco smoke, and sawdust saturated with spit.

As they turned into Water Street, with its rum shops, gambling hells, brothels, and cellar dives, the noise grew louder; cries, oaths, and laughter mingled with the notes of drums, horns, violins, and hurdy-gurdies turned at a crazy speed. As they passed Roosevelt Street and neared the mission it seemed a perfect pandemonium.

Metcalf shouted that all this was not accidental; the rum sellers and dance house keepers were trying to overwhelm the prayer meeting with noise. As Kennan and Metcalf approached the mission they could hear the familiar strains of the hymn, "What a Friend We Have in Jesus." The words, mixed with the banging of the musical instruments, the hurdy-gurdies gone mad, the curses of the children, the shrieks of their parents, and the shuffle of sailors' feet in the dance halls, were strangely appropriate:

Have we trials and temptations?
Is there trouble anywhere?
We should never be discouraged,
Take it to the Lord in prayer.

Handbill for
George Kennan Lecture

"Happy Charlie" met them at the door: young, blue-eyed, light-haired, with what Kennan described as a "peculiar expression of contentment and serenity on his face."

McAuley came up. It seemed to Kennan there was nothing prepossessing in his appearance to justify Metcalf's eagerness to come to the mission. "The only things about him that I liked were his kindly, steady eyes and his straightforward, simple manner."

They were shown to a bench at the side of the room and Kennan looked around as another hymn was sung. It was obviously an audience recruited from the slum: sailors, stevedores, coal heavers, poor mechanics, drunkards, loafers, tramps, streetwalkers, and plain bums. Among them were a few men and women with bright faces and simple clean clothes. Kennan assumed they were recent converts. Only four men had the appearance of gentlemen and two of these were obviously helping McAuley in his work.

One of these four stood up and read a chapter from the Gospel of John. Kennan thought he might be a Wall Street banker but did not record his name. Then Jerry began to speak, earnestly, but quietly, with enough animation to hold anyone's interest:

"Why do you come to this prayer meeting? Is it to thank God because you're happy? No. You come here because you're wretched and miserable. You know you're living in the gutter and you know it's your own fault. God didn't put you in the gutter. You went there of your own accord. You gave yourselves up to the service of the devil and you've got his wages. How do you like 'em? Is he a good paymaster? Are you satisfied? Of course you're not. I know because I've tried the devil's service myself. I've been a thief; I've been in jail; I've played checkers with my nose on a prison grating just as some of you have. I've been as low down as any man or woman in this room. I crawled up out of the gutter at last, with God's help, and now I want to get you out. You feel that you're sinners. You feel, deep down in your hearts, that you're low, miserable and degraded and I tell you that you'll never feel any better or be any better until you stop sinning and come to Christ. Now if there's any one of you who has manliness enough left to say to me, to this company, and to Almighty God that he's going to try to stop sinning and live a new life, let him get up and say so."

Almost before he said the last word two or three men were on their feet. Kennan became absorbed. In less than ten minutes he forgot who he was, how he came there, and what he had thought about religion and prayer meetings. He forgot his skepticism and surrendered to the drama of the proceedings. It was not the form of the meeting which carried him away. It was the spirit. Each man seemed to be stirred with emotion and spoke with fierce, impassioned sincerity.

"For the first time in my life," Kennan recalled, "I saw human souls naked. If there be anything more interesting on this round globe of ours than the self-revelation of a human being who has forgotten all conventionalities, abandoned all pretenses, and lost all self-consciousness in a fiery, passionate impulse to do and speak the truth, I have yet to discover it."

Thirty or forty men and women testified, capsuling their misery into the allotted minute. Among them was an elderly man, with iron gray hair and dissipated face. "I am a confirmed drunkard. I have lain out all night in the gutter. I have spent for drink all I had in the world. My wife died of a broken heart. I have sunk to the lowest depths of degradation. God help me." He choked with sobs and said he had stopped drinking for about a week. "Only God and myself know how I've suffered. Help me. Pray for me. I'm afraid I can't hold out." He broke down with great, impassioned weeping and stood in agonized entreaty. "Happy Charlie" went to him and put an arm around him.

"God will help and we will help," said McAuley, rising to the desk. "Let us first ask the pity and the help of God." He prayed a few simple words for the support of the weak and tortured man, who sank back to his seat. Another got up and another drama began.

A quarter of a century later Kennan wrote, "Before I went to Jerry McAuley's prayer meeting I might have asked, 'What can my soul possibly have in common with the soul of an East River thief, of a confirmed and degraded inebriate, or of an abandoned woman from the slums?' And yet the emotions that lived and died in that Water Street mission more mightily stir my heart, even now, than any royal tragedy ever represented on the stage or recorded in the history of humankind."

As they stepped into the street after the meeting he suddenly became conscious of the drums, horns, hurdy-gurdies, and shouts. He could only suppose the noise had continued through the meeting but he had not heard a thing except the testimonies.

Kennan went back again many nights. As a reporter he was interested in the human drama. He also went "for the moral uplifting that it always gave me."

In going back he discovered his own humanity. "To my great surprise I soon found that I was linked to those Water Street outcasts by a hundred unsuspected ties. Outwardly, and at a cursory glance, they seemed to be nothing more than average representatives of a debased and degraded social class with whose appearance I had long been perfectly familiar; but psychologically they were to me unturned leaves in a great book of human life and on some of those leaves I found recorded my own thoughts, my own experiences, and my own deepest emotions."

Kennan found this was not like any prayer meeting he had ever heard of. There was never any attempt to work up feelings by standard revival methods. Everything was sincere, without concealment, evasion, self-consciousness, or pretense. When Kennan and Metcalf arrived one evening they saw two decently dressed young men sitting together. During the testimonies the men stood, one after the other, and spoke the pious words that were conventional, even recommended, in the churches of the time. But the words did not ring true in the atmosphere of the mission.

"That's the first insincere note I've ever heard in this prayer meeting," Kennan whispered to Metcalf.

"Hold on a minute," Metcalf replied. "Wait till you hear what Jerry says to them." The second finished, declaring that he knew he was "washed white in the blood of the Lamb."

Jerry rose, walked to the desk, and said quietly, "If you want to get religion and follow Christ, feel honestly and speak the truth. God hates shams."

"What did I tell you," Metcalf whispered. "I knew Jerry'd spot them."

"Yes," Kennan replied, "he spotted them all right. But what a bombshell that admonition would be in some church prayer meetings that we know of. It would put a stop to the exercises."

Kennan came to feel that the Water Street mission was the only spot in New York where his feet stood "on the solid rock of absolute verity and fact."

That winter he was sitting in the mission watching the people assemble when a portly, fashionably-dressed man of about forty-five came in. He looked around somewhat bewildered and when no one came to show him to a seat he went and sat in the corner near the organ. He seemed to fit the pattern of a gentleman, church member, good husband and father, good contributor to foreign missions, and a worthy man who did his business honestly. The meeting began and Kennan promptly forgot about the visitor.

The hour of testimonies passed quickly. There was a lull. Kennan looked around and saw the visitor on his feet. His eyes were red and swollen and although he held a handkerchief the tears flowed unhindered down his cheeks. He seemed to want to speak but could not control his emotions. He stood there for fully half a minute with quivering lips and tear-wet face. Then he spoke.

He identified himself and said he was the deacon of a church on Ninth Street. "I came down to this meeting out of curiosity and because this afternoon I had nothing else in particular to do. Now I want to confess in the presence of Almighty God and this company that I am a liar and a hypocrite. I have pretended to be a Christian—perhaps sometimes I thought I was a Christian—but now I see that the truth was not in me. I have had my lesson and I am going back to my church. With God's help, I will say to them what I have just said to you. Pray for me, that I may have courage enough and strength enough to show to them there the honesty and sincerity that I have learned from you here. So help me God, I will henceforth live the real Christian life if I can."

Kennan went back often enough to see some of the fully-rounded life of the mission. "It was touching as well as inspiring to see the eagerness with which new converts would throw themselves into the practical work of the mission and the unwavering persistence with which they would follow it up, regardless of time, money, comfort, and personal convenience. One man for a whole year had been coming down to that prayer meeting from 129th Street. Another was coming there every night from Staten Island, and many more were devoting every hour they could steal from sleep and labor to the Water Street mission and its work."

He could have mentioned others. The wife of the blacksmith who swung his hammer "with heavenly thoughts" visited the sick and destitute of the Fourth Ward. A German and his wife who lived on a gravel scow and earned only six dollars a week once kept a reclaimed outcast for six weeks while he was learning to walk in his new life. The converts worked for anyone in need. When a man came and told of the troubles of his family a woman volunteered, "I have no money but I can sew. I'll cut up one of my sheets and make some clothes for the children." Another woman cheerfully volunteered to wash the filthy rags of a thief.

Converted drunks like "Happy Charlie" Anderson were a special band. They were always ready to steady a man when he gave his testimony and see that he did not have to live his new life alone. The older converts watched the progress of the newer ones, cheering and strengthening them in their hours of depression and temptation; seeing that they were fed and clothed; helping them to find work until the newly rescued might qualify as a rescuer himself.

Former convicts were another band. There were men like John O'Neill who had spent five years in Sing Sing. He came down to the mission and found a new life and, as a bonus, a girl whom he married. He was one of the most warmhearted of men, joyful and bubbling over with happiness.

There was also Jack Brown; his health destroyed, consumed by tuberculosis, but eager to save others. "I'm down on the docks o' nights," he told a visitor. "I know the signs and now and then I can help one that's far gone. I'm going myself you see. There ain't much left of me but a cough and some bones but I shall be up to the last. God is that good to me that I'll go quick when I do go, but quick or slow I bless Him every hour of the day for the old mission and my chance."

12 Bliss of the Purified

LIKE GEORGE KENNAN, Helen Stuart Campbell was a modern person. Her father was president of the Continental Bank Note Company and she was married to an Army doctor.

She was one of the new breed of emancipated women who struck out on their own. In 1864, at the age of twenty-five, she published her first book. By the time of her death in 1918 she had published about twenty books. She began with children's books and went on to books about housekeeping and cooking. Then her interests became wider.

She wondered where the world was heading and whether there were any new solutions in the theories of "German socialism" or the communism of Pierre Prodhoun. The more she talked and debated the more mixed up and confused everything seemed.

"For myself and others like me the venerable religious 'truths,' long established social 'laws,' and well-known historical and scientific 'facts' seemed years ago to dissolve before my eyes, leaving in their place only a question. One ism after another presented itself, seeming at first to meet the demand for truth then paling and fading away under the light of investigation. Church people were stupidly intolerant; radicals equally so. Where I belonged had long been a mystery to myself."

In 1878 someone took her down to the McAuley mission. It was only a few blocks from a place which, as a well-established writer, she knew well— Harper's publishing house on Franklin Square. But she had never gone down Dover Street, past the towering pier of the Brooklyn Bridge, past the rows of tenement houses intermixed, here and there, with a few gabled roofs which evoked memories of the old Dutch section. Many of the houses were wooden structures, leaning and bulging with cracked roofs and broken windows. It was not the place for fine ladies. It was the foulest of the city's red light districts, with women crowded on benches outside the "sailors' boarding houses" awaiting the call of customers.

"In men and women both, as we passed on, only the wild animal seemed left; brutal, lowering faces stamped with every sign of violence; oaths and horrible words the current speech."

They saw a large lamp outside the plain red building with "Jerry McAuley's Prayer Meeting" written on the glass on two sides. Unlike the rest of the street, here the sidewalk was swept and clean. A policeman stood nearby to drive off mischievous boys. They pushed open the door and a bell tinkled to warn the janitor that visitors had come. But it was not necessary; the crowd was gathering and the meeting was about to start.

They went to the platform and took a seat on one of the benches reserved for visitors. Mrs. Campbell looked around. She noted the reading desk, the small cabinet organ, the vacant armchair, the Scripture texts on the walls, and the framed cards in heavy black letters telling speakers to limit themselves to one minute.

The congregation came in; two of them hatless, another without shoes or coat and with matted hair and dirty face. Jerry and Maria came in from a rear door. Maria went to the organ. Jerry went to the vacant armchair and sat looking at each new arrival with eager interest.

Mrs. Campbell studied his profile and saw immediately what he was. She was not a modern, scientific woman for nothing. She had read the latest theories of Cesare Lombroso, the Italian criminologist, who had shown with graphs and statistics that there are born criminals and definite criminal types. You could tell them at a glance by such things as a slanting forehead or long ear lobes or a large jaw or excessive hairiness.

She whispered to her companion, "It is useless to say Jerry McAuley is an honest man. He cannot be. He was born to be bad. How can he help it with that type of head?" She looked at him again. The retreating forehead, the small and deep-set eyes, the heavy, projecting nose and wide mouth could indicate nothing but a bully and ruffian. The tall, well-knit frame, long arms, and great hands showed brutal strength. The keen, quiet way he observed the audience was like a powerful animal thinking of possible danger and ready to annihilate an enemy.

But the woman at the organ—she was different; sweet, motherly-looking; face and figure full of strength and helpfulness; deep gray eyes wide with feeling.

McAuley called out, "Number Four," and the familiar words of a Moody and Sankey hymn rang out with an intensity and heartiness she had not been prepared for. Punctually at half past seven McAuley got up and went to the desk. "Let us pray," he said quietly. The congregation knelt and again Mrs. Campbell was surprised. There was no ranting or shouting, just quiet appeal.

He rose from his knees and sat in the armchair while another hymn was sung. Then he returned to the desk and read the story of blind Bartimaeus from the Gospel of Mark. He spoke with deep reverence. Mrs. Campbell found she could forget his brogue and slum pronunciations.

"And so you see," he concluded, "that the Lord was willing to give His time and His mind to any that would be asking either. I tell you, my dear friends, there's nothing like it. Joshua commanded the sun and moon to stand still and sure 'twas for his own interest he did it. But Jesus Christ Himself stood still and spoke to the blind beggar. You'll never get ahead of that."

McAuley recited, briefly, the story of his conversion. Before anyone else could get up to testify, Mrs. Campbell heard a voice behind her. She turned. It was Maria, getting up from the organ and coming forward.

"And I tell you the same thing. I've been through it all and in my very worst drunken fits—and I drank all the time—there was a power that could save me even then. I was so lost and degraded I don't want to think of it. I couldn't speak of it if I didn't want you to know that this dear, tender Saviour goes seeking that which is lost. He found me and today all I want in the world is to make every one know His power and have the peace and comfort I have, every hour of my life."

If Mrs. Campbell had been surprised at the ardor of the singing and the lack of ranting, she was now astounded. "If Lucretia Mott had suddenly arisen, flung down her Quaker bonnet and announced herself an inveterate drunkard I could not have been more profoundly amazed."

Men and women from the congregation now gave their testimonies. Mrs. Campbell listened and felt that a "strange, invisible presence was at work." McAuley invited those who wanted to be saved to come forward to pray for themselves. They did, one by one.

"Oh Jesus," said a man, weeping, "You know all about it. I'm sick of my sins. I want to be decent. You can help me. Don't let me get into the mud again."

"I can't pray," said the next. "I'm too bad. I'm afraid to."

"You can't be too bad," McAuley replied. "Just say, 'God be merciful to me a sinner.'" The man repeated the words.

As each finished his prayer he stood and faced the congregation. When they were all finished McAuley

63

Yours sincerely,
Helen Campbell.

stood facing them. He prayed that God might give them strength. For the first time Mrs. Campbell had a chance to look directly at his face.

"I had seen the wild excitement of camp meetings in years gone by but there was a hush, a power deeper than anything I had ever known. One by one trembling voices made their first petition; seven men straight from the slums. Then they took their places before the bench and for the first time I saw McAuley's full face. No tenderer soul ever looked upon human pain than that which now shone in his eyes and glorified his coarse features; a look more convincing of the power at work there than years of argument could have been."

It was nine o'clock. The congregation rose and sang "Praise God from Whom All Blessings Flow." Maria went down the aisle and stood at the door to shake hands, with a word of greeting or a message of support for everyone. The old converts stood talking to the men who had come to the bench, offering whatever help and guidance was needed, seeing that they had a place to eat and sleep. As Mrs. Campbell left she said she would come again. She did the next night and for many years thereafter.

That meeting was a turning point of her career. She came so often she learned to look at the poor not as types or characters but as living beings with human and social problems. Her later books contained some of the earliest factual accounts of the horrors of tenement life. She anticipated the "muckrakers"—that generation of writers who exposed the evils of *laissez faire* economics. She could go on for her many remaining years to propagandize for social reform because her own faith was now firm.

"As months went on every question answered itself. With my own eyes I saw men who had come into the mission sodden with drink turn into quiet, steady workers. Now and then one fell—in one case permanently—but the prodigals commonly returned confessing their weakness and laboring earnestly to prove their penitence. I saw foul homes, where dirty bundles of straw had been the only bed, gradually become clean and respectable; hard faces grow patient and gentle, oaths and foul words give place to quiet speech. Whatever the liberal thinkers might feel as to the limitations of their faith, the fact remained that absolute reformation in bodily and mental habits had taken place and was working powerfully toward a change in all about them."

The "strange invisible presence" which Mrs. Campbell felt worked its wonders for John Calvin Knox in January 1879. He came from a comfortable home. His name itself indicated the hopes his parents had in him from the day he was born. They wanted him to be a preacher. He was raised by a loving mother on the Bible and the Psalms.

But their hopes were blighted. Knox left home at the age of sixteen and grew up to be a confirmed atheist. He had many jobs and often lived as a professional gambler.

On the afternoon of the first Sunday of 1879 a friend invited him to go down for the afternoon meeting at the McAuley mission. He went along out of curiosity and to pass time. After the services they returned to their hotel. As evening approached his friend said he wanted to go back to the mission. He had been drinking heavily for several months and wanted to take the pledge.

"You know I never go to church," Knox replied. "I have passed all that kind of thing. If you want to stop drinking, why not stop?" He went along anyhow. The invitation was given to come forward for prayer. His friend said he wanted to go up.

"Well, why don't you?" Knox asked.

"I haven't the nerve," his friend replied.

Knox laughed and with a feeling of bravado said, "I'll go up with you." He knelt at the bench but told himself it was just courtesy. Alfrederic Hatch was conducting the services that night. Knox's turn came and Hatch asked him to pray.

"No, I don't want to pray," Knox said. McAuley came and asked him if he wanted to be a different man. Knox said he did not and explained he had only come forward to support his friend.

As they were leaving, Maria shook hands at the

John Calvin Knox

door. "Goodnight. Come tomorrow night," she said.

"No, I won't come," Knox replied.

"Please come again," she pleaded.

"Well, if I promise, I will come. But I've no desire for this kind of life." He gave his promise to return. Obviously the spirit was working within him. He came the next night and felt himself touched. He went forward willingly to the bench and prayed. He came again and again to pray but continued to live his old life, drinking and gambling.

One night Jerry spoke to him. "You're not acting with common sense. You kneel here and pray and then you go out again to deliberate sin."

"Put me out," Knox replied. "Then I'll never come back. But I can't stay away of myself."

On another night Jerry stood over him praying. He looked up and one of McAuley's tears dropped down on his own cheek. "Don't you want to be good?" McAuley asked.

The meeting ended and he walked out the door and up Roosevelt Street. "Why did Brother Jerry weep over me?" he asked himself. "What could he expect to make out of me? If this man cares enough for me to weep over me, surely God must love me." But still he was in despair.

On February 11th he went to Greenpoint in Brooklyn for a gambling session. Everything went wrong and he lost all his money. He thought his life was finished. He decided not to go to the mission. But he crossed the river on the ferry and walked toward the mission door.

He paused a few steps away. "Aren't you coming in?" Frank, the janitor, called out. Knox replied that he could not make up his mind. The singing began. He went and took a seat near the penitents' bench. The testimonies ended and there was a final hymn.

Oh bliss of the purified, bliss of the free,
I plunge in the crimson tide opened for me;
O'er sin and uncleanness exulting I stand,
And point to the print of the nails in His hand.

> *Oh bliss of His mighty love,*
> *Sing of His mighty love,*
> *Sing of His mighty love,*
> *Mighty to save!*

With the song his vision came. He stood and said, "Jesus has saved me." He was enraptured with bliss. At the end of the meeting McAuley came to him and asked if he needed any help.

"I did not come here for money," he replied. He went out and walked the streets all night singing to himself, "Oh Bliss of the Purified." He walked the streets all day, this time looking for work. He returned to the mission at night and repeated that he was saved. Then, for the second night, he walked the cold streets.

Dawn came and the bliss left him. He suddenly felt weary, cold, and desperately hungry. For the first time in his life he knew what hunger was. He wanted a drink too. The old life, the old friends, were calling him back. As he walked he put his hand into a pocket and found a tract McAuley had given him the night before. It contained a quotation from Romans 14:8: "For whether we live, we live unto the Lord and whether we die, we die unto the Lord; whether we live therefore, or die, we are the Lord's."

He told himself that salvation did not mean eating or sleeping. It simply meant doing right and serving God and that if God wanted him to go hungry he would die in the streets. With that his inward peace and joy returned. He walked the streets the rest of the day. Late in the afternoon he was going down the Bowery when he met an old friend from New Orleans who invited him to dinner. As they left the restaurant they stopped to talk to the cashier, another old acquaintance.

"I understand you've been down to the Water Street mission," the cashier said. When Knox confirmed this the cashier asked if he had work. Knox said no and was given a job, to start right away. He had to work from seven in the evening until seven in the morning for board and lodging and fifty cents a week.

He later became an itinerant missionary in the streets, then a worker for the Water Street mission. At the urging of friends he entered a seminary, studied Greek and Latin, and became a preacher and ordained minister. The wishes of his parents had at last been realized.

He became a handsome, eloquent man, of aristocratic bearing. People were astonished if they learned that the Reverend John Calvin Knox knew all about the sins of the Bowery and Water Street. But he never forgot how he had been saved. Whenever he felt discouraged he would take out a picture of Jerry and another of Maria and kneel down and look at them and feel inspired anew.

For the last twelve years of his life he was pastor of a Presbyterian church in Luzerne, New York. He was killed, at the age of sixty, in an automobile accident in May 1918.

13 An Afternoon on Water Street

BY 1879 IT WAS CLEAR that Jerry McAuley's days were numbered. The tuberculosis which he contracted in the dank, diseased air of Sing Sing was eating away at his life. The doctors said one lung was completely gone and the other partly infected. But he looked death calmly in the face and kept on working.

Helen Campbell found him alone one day on the second floor of the mission. Ivy had been planted near the windows and two mockingbirds fluttered in separate cages. Like others before him who had experienced conversion and had been born anew, McAuley had discovered the fresh world of nature. The birds recognized him and chirped as his tall figure passed near their cages. He opened one of the doors and the bird hopped out onto his hand and dived into his pocket looking for something to eat. McAuley produced a live meal worm he had been hiding in his other hand. The bird dashed for it, ate it, emitted a long whistle and then a burst of clear song.

"There's heaps of satisfaction in the creatures," McAuley said. "Many's the time I come up here almost gone from tiredness in the meetings and they rest me and so I can go right at it again. I never knew I had a knack for them and could learn them anything till one was given me and I began of myself. It's the same way with flowers. They're good friends of mine now but it's strange to myself to think of the years I hardly knew there was such a thing in the world. I can look back now and think how things were in Ireland but I'd no sense of them then. It was a pretty country but me and mine had small business in it but to break the laws and then curse the makers of them."

He played silently with the birds for a while. "My life is going from me," he continued, "but living or dying, it's the Lord's. All these years He has held me and I don't know how but I'd have fallen again if I hadn't been so busy holding on to others. And that's the way to keep men. Start them to pull in somebody else. When your soul is just on fire, longing to get hold of every poor wretch you see, there's no time for your old tricks nor any wanting to try them again."

Mrs. Campbell came again on a Sunday afternoon in spring to accompany Maria on her routine visits around the neighborhood. She found Maria waiting with Dr. Amelia Barnett, a gentle-looking woman a little beyond middle age. Dr. Barnett often volunteered her services to help the poor of the mission.

"If you want to know how some of the poor souls have to live and die you can come with us," the doctor said, "but you must be prepared for everything that is dreadful. Can you stand foul smells?"

"I will stand them for I want to see," Mrs. Campbell replied. "I ought to be able to if you can."

"Ah, but I have had long training," the doctor said, "and even now, often, I have to go out to the landing two or three times in the course of a call I grow so faint. They live in them and must lose all sense of smell in the end for they do not seem to mind."

They walked to Cherry Street, passing a row of tall tenements and entering a much older one, with rickety stair rails and uneven stairs and a horrible odor in the dark passages. They went up to the top of the house and entered a narrow room under the eaves. A thin woman with bandaged face lay inert on a bed pushed as far as it would go against the sloping wall. A man, who had been stirring something in a saucepan on a tiny cooking stove, came forward.

"She's a grain easier, but only a grain," he said. "She's been praying to be released if it's the Lord's will. Look at her."

The doctor removed the bandages and exposed a face eaten away by cancer. Yet the woman managed a faint smile. "I'm most through, ain't I?" she whispered. "Oh I hope so, but I'm willing to wait."

"Yes, you are almost through," the doctor answered. "You have only a day or two longer." The man knelt down by the bed, shaking with sobs. Mrs. McAuley knelt by him and prayed for patience and strength to bear whatever pain must still be borne.

"That does me good," the dying woman whispered. "Come tomorrow and every day till I'm gone. It won't take you much longer and though it's a trouble you won't mind."

"We'll go to the next place and let the doctor come when she's through," Maria said. She hurried

Mrs. Campbell down the stairs.

"I thought you would faint," she said when they reached the street and felt the breeze from the river. "Stand still a minute, you're trembling."

"Why doesn't such a case go to the hospital?" Mrs. Campbell asked. "She could have decent comfort there."

"We wanted her to but her husband wouldn't hear of it. He wanted to be near the mission and so did she, and she said she'd got to die anyway so that there was no use in going away. They were both converted there and he's been tender as a woman with her. He's tended her all night, sleeping when he could after working all day on the dock, and it breaks his heart to think she's going."

The next stop was a six-story tenement opposite the mission. It was much newer than the one they had just left but it smelled as foul. They went up to the fourth floor and entered a room where four little children sat on the floor eating bread and molasses. Their father sat in a corner smoking. He nodded curtly as they entered but said nothing. They entered an inner room with a dense, oppressive smell. A woman in the last stages of tuberculosis sat propped up in a bed. There was a deep red spot on each cheek. Her body was wasted to a mere skeleton.

"I've been looking for you," she said. "Ain't the doctor coming too?"

"Right away," Maria replied. The doctor hurried in almost at that moment and Mrs. Campbell retreated to the outer room. The man eyed her suspiciously and so they sat silent until Maria came out.

"I'll come round tomorrow, Dennis, and straighten up a bit," she said to the man "It's pretty hard on you, trying to do all yourself." The man grunted and left the room.

"Come here, you poor, sticky little things and have your faces washed," she called to the children. "You can't see out of your eyes for dirt." She talked to Mrs. Campbell as she exposed, beneath the dirt and grime, the lovely faces of the children, with their fair skins, clear blue eyes, and long dark hair. "Their mother was up till a month ago but she can't help herself a stroke now. She's one of our people but her husband's a Romanist and there was a time he wanted to kill Jerry and me for making a turncoat of her. He don't feel so mad now because he sees we do what we can."

The oldest of the children, a girl of about five, wanted to explain how she was trying to take her mother's place. "I washed yesterday. I borryed a tub and I let Molly rub her own apron. It ain't dry yet. An' tomorry I'm going to scrub mother's floor with Mrs. O'Rafferty's brush."

"I'll be here," Maria replied. "You ought to wash them more, Bridget. You're old enough."

"They doesn't like it," Bridget said. "They hollers and that plagues mother. I can't make 'em be still for it, saving sometimes."

The doctor had finished her work and they left the flat. They went down past what seemed to be dozens of children playing in the halls and on the stairs. A little cripple sat on the step with his crutches beside him, playing toss up with another child, a hunchback. As they stopped for a minute to talk to the children, the door of the saloon down at the corner was flung open and three or four men rushed out, shouting and waving their arms.

The women retreated to the safety of the mission door. The barkeeper was throwing out a drunk. He pushed him so hard that the drunk fell and struck his head on the curbstone. Blood began to flow on the street.

"Now see if you'll hang round and beg any longer," the barkeeper shouted. A policeman ran up with his club ready. He began beating the man in the gutter.

"That can't go on," Dr. Barnett exclaimed. She rushed over to the policeman. "Arrest the man if that's your duty but stop beating him. Punishment is for the court and not for you."

"Who are you?" the policeman shouted, still using his club. The man tried to stagger up but fell back down.

"Let him alone," Dr. Barnett shouted back. She tried to stand between the drunk and the policeman.

"Get away, you old fool. I know my duty," the policeman replied and raised his club. Jerry had heard the row and appeared with his deputy sheriff badge fastened to his coat.

"It's the old story," he said, pausing at the door. "The man has been kicked out because his money is all gone." He went to restore peace while Maria explained the badge to Mrs. Campbell.

"Mr. William Dodge got him that deputy sheriff's shield because he was always going into these places and always being arrested for interfering with the law. He takes good care now to find out if there's reason for arresting a man but, you see, the policemen get brutal. They see such sights all the time and many of them are well paid by the keepers for holding their tongues. We've had these dens cleared out one day and the shutters up and the next day they'd be down and the keepers laughing and jeering at us. They're all against the law but the law winks at it all."

Jerry had returned and heard the end of Maria's remarks.

"Yes," he said, "I know the inside of this police system and it's a mass of rottenness. I ought to know. I've bought off many a detective and this corner man has bought off many another. And sometimes a man'll let his place be hauled, just as a blind, and the papers come out, 'See what admirable police.' Mind you, he's been paid to be a scapegoat and starts fresh the next day. I don't say there ain't good men in the service. I know there are. But down here too many of them is the devil's own aides.

"There's a law against disturbing the public peace, ain't there? Well, my wife and me can't sleep for the screams and howls and foul words in the street. We got crazy for want of sleep one time and one night we just got up and dressed and went to the station. 'Captain,' says I, 'we have worked as well as we know how for the people in this ward but we're being killed by the doings your men don't stop. We've as much right to our rest as the people uptown and we want the noise stopped.' He swore at us for meddling fools but he did stop it for a night or two. It began again though. There's times when you'd think hell has broke loose."

The drunk had staggered off to his house. Dr. Barnett wanted to go after him to treat his cuts. Jerry knew where he lived. It was called Slaughter Alley. Maria returned to the mission and Jerry led the way to a narrow alley running between a pair of five-story tenements on Roosevelt Street.

"Look out for your footing," he said. "It's dreadful dirty here. The time wasn't long ago that they'd pitch dirt out on you. I've gone home covered many a time. They're mostly Romanists and very bitter against a turncoat and the city missionaries has a hard time in these places. I'd a kicked one downstairs myself years ago."

They walked over the slimy stones to a basement at the end of the alley and stooped down into a narrow room lighted by a single dirt-covered window. The man lay across the foot of a soiled bed. He sat up and looked about vacantly as the door opened. A woman sat on a broken chair. She was crying. The skin was scraped from her cheek and a black-and-blue bruise was beginning to show near her eye. An underfed baby was in her lap and five children huddled around her. An old woman stood near the man. This meant that nine people lived in that one small, black room.

As the doctor treated the man, the woman spilled

Back Yard in Fourth Ward Tenement

out her story: "I wouldn't have you see the eye on me if I could help it, for Mike's as kind a creature when the drink's not in him as you'd want to see. But he came in madlike and the first thing was up with his fist and a-hitting me. He'd worked nights the whole week and there was good wages coming to him but the minute he'd his pocket full he went to Jim's.

"I knew he'd be there and I was on the watch but he'd had some as he come along and was just full enough not to mind. I says, 'Mike, give me a dollar for the children. We've none of us ate since morning.' He swore and pushed me to one side. Then I begged and the saloonkeeper pushed me out and said he wouldn't have no sniveling women around. The baker wouldn't trust me but one of me neighbors give me a quart of meal and let me cook it on her stove and so they went to sleep with something in their stomachs.

"Then I went round today and I says, 'For the love of God, don't let your children starve.' But he couldn't attend being full of drink. I don't know what we'll be doing. I've got one day's washing come

Wednesday but that won't keep us and what he hasn't swallowed they've took from him in the night. Oh, me heart's sick in me."

"She done what she could," said the old woman. "Sorry that ever I give birth to a man that won't care for his own."

When they left the cellar they found the alley blocked by a swarm of children, large and small, with stones and bricks in their hands.

"There's McAuley the turncoat," they shouted. "Hi! McAuley and his band. Give it to them. Hey."

"Are you afraid?" the doctor asked quietly.

"No," Mrs. Campbell replied, trying to bring her cowardly instincts into line and quell her terror. "Not if you're not."

McAuley stood for a moment to consider the situation. He opened his coat to show the sheriff's badge, grasped his cane firmly, and charged into the crowd with an Irish whoop. The children scattered and the women plunged through the breach. Two or three stones flew by but a policeman appeared and they returned safe to the mission.

"Do you wonder I want to clean them rumholes out?" McAuley asked as they sat in his parlor to get back their breath. "Here's temptation right before the face and eyes of everyone that comes in here and the grace of God Himself can hardly make headway against such devil's doings. It's awful odds to work against and there's minutes when I'm clean discouraged and wonder what the Lord means letting such wickedness go on."

McAuley was weakening with every passing month but he tried to hide his weakness from all except close friends. Mrs. Campbell was at a meeting about a year later. The third floor was finally finished as living quarters. They walked slowly upstairs. Three or four people sat waiting for McAuley on the second floor but he passed them by.

"I love them, every one," he explained, "but I'm hoarse with talking and singing. I can't but just peep. Of course, they don't think nor know but what I can keep right on when I want two pairs of lungs instead of part of a bad one to do the work that's called for. It's talk from the minute I'm out of bed to the minute I'm in. If my words meant a cent apiece I'd be the richest man in New York and you'd see a mission at every corner."

Yet night after night he was back on the platform, seemingly full of health and vigor. His closing address hardly varied. He was the witness of the truth that he offered.

"We're going to have prayers now. Don't you want to be saved tonight? Who'll stand up for prayers? There's one, there's two, three, there's another. Don't be afraid to stand up. It don't make any difference what kind of clothes you've got on. The devil tells some of you not to do it. He holds you back. I tell you the devil ain't much of a friend. He goes round putting up all sorts of jobs on sinners and he makes it pretty hot sometimes. You can't get the best of him, nohow.

"You've got to cry to God for help if you want to get rid of your bad habits and keep crying till He gives it. He won't be long about it. 'Ask and you shall receive,' is what He says. We need His help, every soul of us, great and small. When I see people who think themselves smart and cunning, dabbling in sin and forgetting God, I wonder they ain't suddenly snapped off, squelched just where they are. They all need help. Put 'em in a bag— rich sinners and poor sinners—and shake 'em up, do you think there'd be any difference in 'em when they come out?

"You hear some people say the Bible is a sham and religion is all a hoax. Well it may be to them, but it's God's own power to me. Yes. Look at me, friends. Once I was a loafer and a rough. Never knew what it was to be contented and happy. Head on me like a mop, big scar across my nose all the time. I had an old red shirt and a hat that looked as if it had been hauled up out of a tarpot. If I had a coat it was one of the kind with cuffs up here to the elbows, split open in the back. Latest style, d'you see?

"There ain't a drunken rowdy round the corner worse-looking than I was. I cursed God. I held up my hands and cursed Him for giving me life. Why had He put me in a hell on earth? Why had He made me a thief and a rascal while He gave other

Water Street Saloon

69

people money and fun? And then it came across me that He hadn't done one of those things. It was me that brought myself to what I was. Yes, I did it myself. I made myself a drunkard and a thief and then blamed Him for it. Where was my common sense? If you want some—and who don't—ask Him for it.

"Some say, 'Ah, I'm too bad. God wouldn't give me a show.' That's all a mistake. He can save the vilest sinner. God will take what the devil would almost refuse. The very worst people are welcome to Him. Didn't He save the thief on the cross? I knew a man who came here into this place to lick another for saying 'Jesus saves me.' Well, Jesus saved that very man himself. He came looking for a fight here but the starch was knocked out of him. God did it. He went away like a cur in a sack trembling all over and now he is a good man. That's the way it is. Jesus is willing to save every one who asks Him honestly to do it.

"My friends, I want to tell you that it pays to serve Jesus. He's a good friend. I used to hang round that rumshop on the corner and they were glad enough to have me there as long as my money lasted. But when that was gone—'Jerry, take a walk. Take a walk round the block and cool off.' I felt the insult down in my heart. It stung me. But I couldn't help it. I was such a slave of my appetite. I hadn't a friend in the world. But I can tell you it's not so now. I have friends and everything I need since I began to love and serve Jesus.

"Just look at me. Do I look like a fraud now? I'm a new creature, inside and out. I'm honest, I'm clean and respected and happy. Why those rich rumsellers over there respect me now. They call me Mr. McAuley. 'Good morning, Mister McAuley.' They are very polite, d'you see? I can go into a bank now and the president will ask me into his private office, while the big guns have to stand outside. 'Sit down, sir. What can I do for you?' And then he'll take me round and introduce me to the cashier. Ha! Twelve years ago if he'd seen me coming into his bank he'd set the dogs on me or send for a policeman to run me out. 'Fraid I'd steal all the money.

"Can't you see what the religion of Jesus has done for me? I've got friends and a good home and a good wife and I've got money in my pocket, besides a clean heart full of joy and peace. The blessed Jesus has done it all. Do you want to know how to get those things? The Bible says how: 'Seek first the kingdom of God and His righteousness and all these things shall be added unto you.'

"There was a time when I'd cut a man's throat for a five-dollar bill and kick him overboard. Do you suppose I'd do it now? Eh? Why not? 'Cause I've got the grace of God in my heart. Jesus saved me and He can save any man. There's not a poor fellow here tonight that isn't welcome to salvation. Jesus says, 'He that cometh unto Me I will in no wise cast out.' Jesus died for every poor fellow that hasn't got any home or friends tonight. Won't you come to Him and let Him save you? Won't you come now?"

Everyone stands for a hymn while converts move through the congregation urging penitents to come forward. Fifteen or twenty walk and kneel at the bench or at either side. The congregation kneels and prays for the penitents. Jerry walks down the line and asks each man to pray for himself.

One by one they do. Some are Caucasians, some are African-Americans. Some are thieves, some are drunks. Men or women, young or old, each prays in any words he can utter. Some pray in foreign languages. Some have long prayers. Some merely sob, "Oh God, save me."

One man gropes back into the dim mists of his childhood and recites:

> *Now I lay me down to sleep,*
> *I pray the Lord my soul to keep,*
> *If I should die before I wake,*
> *I pray the Lord my soul to take.*

70

Sailors' Lodging House
Water Street

14 The First Halfway House

PART OF MCAULEY'S VISION was work with former convicts. He once said he wanted to rent a building and fit it out for men who had just come out of prison. He knew what had happened to himself when he got out of Sing Sing, how he had tried to avoid his old haunts and old friends, how he had looked for help and advice but did not find it. His problem was as basic as finding a place to sleep. He wrote in *Transformed:* "I must say it does not seem to be right to turn men out of prison and make no provision for their future well-being."

With all the progress of our society since then the problem still exists. Many states and welfare institutions are seeking the answer in halfway houses. These are places where convicts can be sent to serve part or all of their parole; where they can eat and sleep, be taught an occupation if they are unskilled, be cared for while they begin new jobs in the outside world, and only then, when they are adjusted, be sent out on their own.

McAuley was so swamped by men and women of all sorts and conditions that he could do nothing separately for ex-convicts. But the vision did not fail. The first American experiment with a halfway house was begun as a result of the McAuley Water Street Mission. McAuley did not do it himself. He and his friends and supporters—particularly Alfrederic Hatch—helped someone else to take up the work.

His name was Michael Dunn. He led a fantastic life. He had been a criminal and convict on three continents. Yet he could stand up at a meeting at the McAuley mission in 1879 and call for a crusade:

"I know now if I can be happy and hard at work making up for all the deviltry I was up to in the old days there ain't a man that can't do the same. And so I lay for every one of you boys and I'm going to lay for you as long as I live. You do the same, boys, and between us we'll make over this ward and get things all our own way. There won't be any saloons when we're through and not a tenement house anywheres in sight to breed more of the sort we were. And that's a big enough job for as long as there's strength for work or thinking how to get even with the devil. And that's Michael Dunn's first wish and his last."

Dunn was born in Manchester, England, in 1826. He was never sent to school or church; in fact, never learned to read or write until he was twenty-five, and then in jail. He was raised by his parents as a criminal and by the time he was twelve he had been arrested five times and served five sentences in prison.

His first arrest was when he was eight, for robbing a till. He was sentenced to two months in Old Bailey Prison, Manchester. His mother and his aunt were in the same prison at the same time.

It was customary in those days to flog a boy before he was discharged from jail; two, four, or eight dozen lashes with the cat-o'-nine-tails until the blood ran down his back. It would be three or four weeks before a boy could put on a jacket. Mike received his flogging one night and was discharged the next morning. The keeper put his jacket over his shoulders, buttoned the top button in front, and said, "Now Mickey, do right." A crowd gathered around him after he passed through the gates. They wanted to see his back.

His parents, when not in jail, lived in a cellar on Garden Street, Shutehill, one of the worst streets in Manchester. He went home and found his father half drunk. His father asked him if he had seen his mother in Old Bailey and then asked if he had any money. Mike gave him the ninepence he had received on his discharge from prison. His father took the money and went out to buy beer. He returned, got even more drunk, and turned the boy out of the house.

Thrown into the street, he went back to thieving and was arrested again for stealing a silk dress. He was sentenced to three months even before his back was healed from the flogging. He served the last month of this sentence in solitary confinement on bread and water—still only eight years old. Once again the flogging and out the gate, to be met by his mother, who brought him a change of clothes and took him to a public house and gave him a glass of ale.

The next sentence—for stealing a pocketbook—was for six months, with flogging at the end of three months and another flogging before his discharge. He met an older crowd of criminals in jail this time. After his release he was taken up by a pair of counterfeiters, named Kelly and Harris. They used him to spend the false money, figuring his youth would make him less suspicious. They traveled throughout England and Ireland and then Mike was caught and sentenced to six months.

On his discharge Kelly and Harris met him at the gate with a new scheme; they would break into a store by passing him up through the fanlight over the door. This went on for a while, then he was arrested, served a short sentence, came out, and took up with Kelly and Harris again. For more than a year they made good money and spent it on clothes, gambling, and liquor. Then the three of them were captured. Mike was twelve. He used the alias, "Peter Featherstone." Kelly and Harris were sentenced to transportation for life; Mike to transportation for seven years. The judge intoned: "I transport you beyond the high seas, to wherever her Majesty, Queen Victoria, pleases to send you, as you are three notorious, traveling thieves."

Three hundred sixty-two boys, including Mike, were crammed between the decks of a ship which sailed for ninety-four days to Tasmania, off the coast of Australia. They were allowed on deck for an hour or two a day and fed a gill of lime juice every day to keep away the scurvy. The older boys amused themselves by hazing the younger ones. If caught they were flogged or put in the sweatbox.

The ship dropped anchor at Hobart Town on the Derwent River in Tasmania. The governor was Sir John Franklin, the Arctic explorer. He came on board four days later, looked the boys over, and tried to give them kindly advice.

"You cannot steal here for we put thieves to watch thieves," he said. He pointed to a large hotel near the dock. "Do you see that hotel?"

The boys shouted, "Yes."

"Well," he continued, "some years ago two boys came out here, each under sentence of fourteen years. One of them became honest and feared God and God took care of him. That hotel belongs to him and everyone respects him. The other one was a bad boy. He was always in trouble and did not care about or fear God and where do you think he is today? He is now working in double irons in the coal mines. So you see it is better to be good and honest."

The boys were then taken to the small island of Point Pure where they joined another thirteen hundred boys who had preceded them. The oldest was

fifteen. Many of them were so young that older boys had to be appointed to take care of them.

There was a school but no one was compelled to attend. Work, however, was compulsory: shoemaking, boatbuilding, bookbinding, brickmaking, tailoring, clearing land, and farming. Mike began as a shoe repairer and then as a stevedore.

One day he took pity on a dirty and bedraggled little boy named Hookey Walker. An inspection was coming up. Mickey took Hookey down to the sea and scrubbed him and then mended his clothes and made him presentable. The inspector saw him and said, "Why Hookey, who's been fixing you up so nice?"

"Peter Featherstone," Hookey replied. Mike was given Hookey to care for after that and, as a reward, was made captain of one of the boats.

The years passed and were not too hard. Mike grew to be a strong lad of seventeen. He then joined the fifty thousand adult convicts on Tasmania. He was put to clearing the land near Port Arthur. Any minor infraction led to terrible punishment. The convicts hardly cared whether they lived or died. Two men threw up a button "shank or blank"—like heads or tails—to see which one would kill their keeper. Twenty minutes after the tossing, the keeper was dead; a month later the man who did it was hanged.

Mike was sent to another station for road building. He escaped into the bush, was captured and flogged. He escaped again, was captured, and sent to the coal mines. A leather harness was put around him, as if he were a horse, and he had to pull a cart in tunnels so low he could not stand erect. To compound his misery he was kept in chains for the entire eighteen months that he worked in the mines.

Then he was sent to Hobart Town to be hired out to a master. Such masters might have thirty or forty men working for them as virtual slaves. If a master was displeased with a man for whatever reason he could take him to the nearest police station to be flogged and then returned to work.

After a few months the wife of his master sent him into town to buy a bottle of gin. His master found out, discharged him, and told him to report to Hobart Town barracks. On the way a magistrate nicknamed "Bully" Price saw him and asked if he was working. Mike replied that he was not. "Bully" Price said he would give him something to do. He was arrested and sentenced to walk the treadmill for three months.

His term of transportation ended shortly before

his twentieth birthday. He shipped out from Tasmania aboard a whaling vessel. After roaming the Pacific as far north as the Arctic, he signed off in New Bedford, Massachusetts. He wandered through most of the east of the United States as a criminal. Then he served for a while in the United States Cavalry in Ohio. He took to crime again, returned east, and enlisted in the Navy in New York.

But the Navy did not suit him and he tried to desert. He was captured and flogged. While the blood flowed down his back he looked up at his tormenter and sneered, "My mother gave me a worse licking with a dishcloth."

He was successful on his next attempt at desertion. He returned to crime, was arrested, and escaped from Blackwell's Island in New York. He then had a successful period of crime. He married a woman who turned out to be an alcoholic. In 1851 he sailed back to England with his wife, a Newfoundland dog, and six hundred fifty dollars in his pocket.

Mike tried to go straight and opened a restaurant in Manchester. But his wife squandered the receipts on drink for herself and her friends. He shipped her back to America, where she soon died, and he returned to a life of crime, ending, as always, in prison.

He was sentenced to ten years in the Model Jail at Northhampton, with fifteen months' solitary confinement at the start. Apparently it was not rigorous, since it was here, through the kindness of the warden, that he learned to read and write. But he was then sent to work in some rock quarries and, as punishment for bad temper, was transported to Western Australia.

He served part of his sentence, was given "ticket of leave" to remain free in Australia, wandered through the back bush living with the aborigines and learning their language, stowed away on a ship, found service with the cavalry in India, sailed again, was put ashore almost dead on the coast of West Africa, and eventually returned to England in 1861. There he stole a dozen gold rings, was captured and sentenced to Walton Prison outside Liverpool, with the first eleven months of a five-year sentence to be served in solitary confinement. The remainder of the sentence was to be served in the prison colony at Gibraltar.

There were about eight hundred convicts on Gibraltar. The governor was James Blair, who strutted with two revolvers and a large dagger in his belt and kept order with the lash. The scarred and brutalized men, however, had learned to accept the lash as part of their lives. Governor Blair would assemble the most ill-tempered men every Wednesday to watch the floggings. Instead of being awed the men would bet among themselves on how many lashes a man could take before he would cry out.

A keeper stood on each side of the man to be punished. The first would give twenty-four lashes. The other, left-handed, would then give twenty-four, and thus they would take turns so both sides would be torn to ribbons. With the first few blows the pain was intense but then the shock passed and the back grew numb.

Once a sickly looking man named John Brown was sentenced to forty-eight lashes for striking his keeper with a shovel. The keepers were eager to get revenge and bet among themselves that they could make him cry out. Brown was stripped and strapped down. As the first blow fell he began to sing, "I am sitting on the stile, Mary." The blows fell, harder and harder, but he continued to sing until the last had fallen. A rough towel, soaked with salt brine, was put on his back and they began to take him to the hospital. But he stood up defiant. He went straight back to his work pushing a wheelbarrow heavy with stones. Brown was flogged again five times in the next three years but never once cried out.

Dunn survived his sentence. The British were then still happy to dump their outcasts on American shores. They offered Mike free passage and he accepted. He landed in New York the day before Lincoln was assassinated. He took to crime again and, while at it, got to know Jerry McAuley, who had returned to the life of a river pirate after his release from Sing Sing.

In 1866 Dunn married for a second time. His wife was also a criminal. They were together only a short time when he was arrested and sentenced to Sing Sing for two years and four months. He was released, returned to stealing, was arrested in Philadelphia, and sentenced to three years' solitary confinement. He survived this ordeal too, although when he was released from his solitary cell he staggered like a drunken man and had to learn to walk anew.

His next arrest was in Canada. He served six months in a Montreal jail in 1871. He returned to the United States and was soon arrested in Boston and sentenced to two years and nine months in jail in South Boston. He was almost starved to death. When he objected he was put in a pitch-black solitary cell to sleep on the flagstones without a mattress or blanket. He was fed an ounce of bread and three tablespoons of water once a day.

He left the South Boston jail a walking skeleton. He drifted to New York, lived high on the proceeds of his robberies for six months, was arrested, and sentenced to Sing Sing for four years. By now most of the fight had been beaten, starved, and tortured out of him. He served his time quietly and was released early in 1878. He was then about fifty-two years old. Thirty-five of these years had been spent behind bars or in a penal settlement. His hair was gray and his deep-set eyes were cold and dull. As he was about to leave, the head keeper said, "Mike, I'll keep your cell for six weeks. I know you'll be back in that time." He said they would never see him again in prison but no one believed him.

During the previous twelve years Dunn had kept in touch with his second wife. They had been together a total of thirteen months during all this time. When he would be out of jail and in New York she would be in jail, and when she was out he might be in. They met again when he came out of Sing Sing for the second time. They lived in a house on East 24th Street. It was a hand-to-mouth existence for about a month. Then Dunn heard of his old friend, Jerry McAuley, now set up in a mission on Water Street. On the afternoon of March 18, 1878—a date burned into his memory—he went down to see Jerry.

"You're about at the end of your tether, Michael Dunn," McAuley said. "Yes, you are. You've got brains and you've used them for naught since God gave them to you but to do rascality and teach the same to others. It's time now to turn round and see if you can't undo some of your wicked work. Do you like it? Do you want to keep on serving terms till you go up to your last Judge? I believe you can be an honest man and a happy one if you will."

Dunn laughed at the thought of himself being honest and happy but it was not a cheerful laugh. McAuley continued: "It's your last chance, Michael Dunn. Come here tonight and see what you think of what goes on in this place."

Dunn returned that night. As he opened the door he heard the words of a hymn: "For weary feet remains a street, of wondrous pave and golden." He told himself he would like to walk a road like that. He came back every night for a week to listen to the testimonies and then was converted.

He went home and told his wife he had prayed to God for forgiveness and had promised never to steal again. She told him he was crazy; that his parents were Catholics and he would never have a day's luck for the rest of his life. He replied that his parents had never gone to church and that he could not have any worse luck than he had had all his life. They separated and she died soon thereafter.

Dunn was given a recommendation to the Prison Association of New York, a charitable organization partially subsidized by New York State, which tried to help discharged prisoners. Stephen Cutter of the association gave him a job, at fifteen dollars a month plus room and board, to try to find work for other ex-convicts. It was while at this work that Dunn was inspired to start the first halfway house in America. He once, briefly and simply, wrote the story:

"While working for the Prison Association I often wished I only had a home to take the men to that came out of prison and that had no place to go to; someplace where they could work for their daily bread—men whom I knew did not want to steal and who were sick of such a life. Then again, if I was living with these men I could find out whether they intended to lead a new life. Night and day this subject was uppermost in my thoughts. How often did I dream of it in my sleep, and then again strive to forget all about it, but I could not. God kept it in my heart and I firmly believe no human being could have turned my thoughts from it.

"At the end of December 1878 the funds of the association were exhausted. Mr. Cutter told me I would not be wanted any longer as they had no more money. All the money I had at that time was about ten dollars. I had no work to go to.

"On January 13, 1879 I was reduced to the small sum of two dollars. I went and pawned my watch and some clothing and by that means raised fifteen dollars. I then rented the premises at 311 Water Street and got a receipt for one month's rent. The next day I called on three Christian gentlemen and told them of my intentions. They each gave me a five-dollar bill. It was the first time I told anyone of my intentions. I went to Cowperwaite's in Chrystie Street and gave them five dollars for a few things to furnish the house with and agreed to pay one dollar per week for the remainder. I then lit my fire and bought bread, tea, sugar, and some skins of meat and made a pot of soup. I went out and brought in six poor men. I spread my homely meal before them. We then offered thanks to God and asked Him to bless our new home and He did so.

"I did not know what work to put the men to, for work they must. I made a vow to God that no

74

man should eat the second meal in the home unless he worked for it. We made a six-foot frame and I bought some white Berlin wool and we commenced to make women's shawls. One young lady came in and gave me thirty-one dollars and fifty cents for two of them. We also made pants, jumpers and overalls, and watch fobs from horsehair. I went peddling these articles, also pencils and books. I often had to pawn articles and we many a time went to bed hungry.

"A great many people began to think we were a band of ex-convicts come together to live on the charity of Christian people and many of them would talk hard of us and laugh at each other when we passed them or they passed us. But we let them see we were not and I can say we gained the friendship of all the people in the neighborhood."

The cellar where Dunn started his home was across the street from the mission, in a wooden tenement that was caving in at the roof and bulging in most places. He had no trouble finding ex-convicts who wanted help. They became a little band of brothers. One after another, as they learned to steady themselves in the outside world and then found regular work, they would bring back some of their wages to help others. While the home would care for their material needs, the McAuley mission would try to care for their spiritual needs.

The trustees and friends of the mission did all they could to help, especially Alfrederic Hatch. Later Dunn wrote a brief biography which he dedicated to Hatch: "To the man who first took me by the hand, who helped me when I was down, who inspired hope in my breast, who pointed out the way of life—my earliest, my true and faithful friend."

The cellar soon proved too small. Another house was rented at 305 Water Street. It was called The House of Industry and Home for Discharged Convicts. Every now and then Stephen Cutter would send someone down for help. Cutter mentioned a few of these cases in the annual reports of the Prison Association. In the report for 1879, the year Dunn started his home, Cutter wrote:

"A young man came from Blackwell's Island penitentiary on October 27th having served two months for petit larceny; parents both dead, no home, no friends, and very poorly clad. We sent him to Mr. Dunn's House of Industry with orders to care for him till we could obtain a place for him. He proved to be industrious and tried to make himself useful, thus laying the foundation of a recommendation. After several weeks a good Christian lady from an

A Resident Mending His Clothes

adjoining state wanted such a lad on a farm and took him home with her, paying his passage. So the orphan was provided for. We have heard from him since; he is giving satisfaction."

This from the report for 1880:

"An Englishman by birth, forty-two years of age, committed to the Tombs for intoxication, acknowledged he had been in prison seven times but he wanted to reform and made many promises if he could be helped, as he was now entirely friendless and homeless. We told him we would be that friend and would provide him a home for a short time. By the consent of the judge we took him from prison and sent him to The House of Industry in Water Street where Mr. Dunn kindly advised and sympa-

Mike Dunn Interviewing an Ex-Convict

Making a Shawl

thized with him and took him to the McAuley mission where he became deeply interested if not converted."

Later that year the Englishman wrote to Cutter to report on his further progress: "I have not drank anything since I have been spiritually blessed. I am sure I don't know where I should have drifted had not this place been open to me." The man said he had booked passage to return to his wife and child in England, whom he had not seen for two years.

Cutter also sent a well-educated German down to Water Street. The man had just served a year in jail for attempted larceny. In February 1880 he wrote to Cutter: "Notwithstanding my efforts in all directions I have as yet obtained no employment but I trust in God and pray to Him. Since I saw you I have taken a step, the most serious I ever made, which has already made a different being of me. From the time I came here to Mr. Dunn's I have attended McAuley's prayer meetings and three nights ago I made up my mind to serve God who gave His Son to die for me."

A few months later the German wrote that he had found work and was strong in his faith.

In May 1881 Dunn established a new home at 37 Bleecker Street with room to feed and lodge twenty-seven men at a time. In return for their room and board the men were put to work making brooms or at other industries. If any man had special skills or could work faster and thus earn more than the expenses of his keep, he was paid the difference in cash. They were encouraged, but not obliged, to spend their evenings in the reading room and to attend religious meetings held three nights a week.

In February 1882 the home was incorporated. Its trustees included Alfrederic Hatch, James Talcott, R. Fulton Cutting, and several others who simultaneously were trustees of the McAuley mission. By that time Dunn had cared for more than eight hundred men.

Dunn married again, had a son, and went on to establish similar homes in Detroit, San Francisco, Philadelphia, and Brooklyn. After Dunn left New York he was succeeded as superintendent by Charles Stewart, an ex-convict who had been converted at the McAuley Water Street Mission in 1876. The Home of Industry was then located at 224 West 63rd Street. Stewart continued as superintendent until his death in 1906.

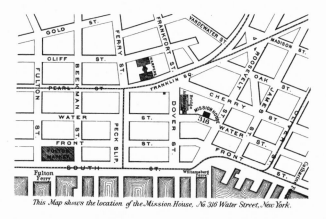

This Map shows the location of the Mission House, No. 316 Water Street, New York.

15 The Growth and Spread of Rescue Missions

BY 1880 THE MISSION was well established and well known. Visitors from uptown were instructed to take the Third Avenue Steam Cars—as the early Third Avenue elevated train was known—or the Second Avenue horsecars to Franklin Square, walk one block down Dover Street, and then turn left on Water

Street to the mission. Visitors from Brooklyn could come by either the Fulton, Williamsburg, or Catherine ferries.

Operating expenses were still about two thousand five hundred dollars a year. The salary of the McAuleys had been raised to six hundred dollars a year and a janitor was paid two hundred and forty dollars.

The trustees were now Alfrederic Hatch, R. Fulton Cutting, James Talcott, Sidney Whittemore, John D. Phyfe, John H. Boswell, Samuel Hiscox, and Major General Clinton Bowen Fisk.

Fisk had been a friend of both Lincoln and Grant, an official of the Freedmen's Bureau, and founder of Fisk University in Tennessee, one of the pioneer schools for African-Americans in the south. He was also an ardent prohibitionist. In 1888 he would be a candidate for president on the Prohibition Party ticket, running against Cleveland and Blaine.

McAuley too, of course, was a prohibitionist. But he kept his views to himself and his own circle and took no part in the prohibition movement. There was enough work for him in the Fourth Ward. Moreover, the longer he worked in the slums the more he realized that alcohol was only part of the problem. There was also poverty, unemployment, disease, and the horror of tenement living. Drink was as much the escape from misery as the cause of it.

At about this time another friend and helper appeared—a young architect named Bradford Lee Gilbert. He was born in 1853 and traced his ancestry to Sir Humphrey Gilbert, the half brother of Sir Walter Raleigh. Gilbert came to New York as a student in 1872. In 1888 he was to earn an enduring page in the history of architecture as the builder of the first modern skyscraper in New York. By using a steel framework he was able to cram a building thirteen stories high into a space about twenty-one feet wide at 50 Broadway. Skeptics were certain the steel skeleton would collapse at the first strong wind. It did not and the New York skyline ever since has testified to Gilbert's imagination.

Early in his career Gilbert became a friend of the McAuley Water Street Mission. He also taught Sunday school at a chapel near the Bowery. After Sunday services he would visit the homes of children who had been absent. He grew fond of three children, Katie and Gertie Jaeger and their younger brother Julius. They seemed to come from a sturdy German family. When they did not show up for their lessons on a scorching Sunday in July 1881 he decided to visit them for the first time at their house on Eldridge Street. As he walked along looking for the number he heard the children shout. They led him to a high stoop where a tall German stood. He had black hair and a long black beard. His arm was in a sling and he was half drunk.

He spoke little English. The children interpreted and explained that here was their Sunday school teacher. They trooped upstairs to talk with their mother. When Gilbert asked how Jaeger had broken his arm he was informed, still through the children, that Papa had been drunk and had fallen off his wagon. Remorse was apparently at work as they talked. The children informed Gilbert that Papa wanted to be taken to a place where he could pledge to give up drink.

Gilbert returned that evening and found Jaeger so drunk he could hardly walk. Gilbert steered him to the horsecars and they went down to the McAuley mission. Jaeger did not seem to understand much of what was happening but when the call came for those who wanted to pray for themselves he walked forward and knelt at the bench. McAuley stood over him and asked him to pray.

Many years later Jaeger recalled that day, July 9, 1881: "I was sitting on Eldridge Street on a sidewalk loaded with rum and beer and the Lord sent a messenger even around on Eldridge Street. I did not understand what salvation meant. I did not understand what church or religion meant. I did not understand so much as a mule from Texas. But by kind words I was invited to go down to the Water Street mission.

"I said, 'Yes, I will go,' but I can't tell you today how they got me down there. But one thing I remember—when they got me in and put me on the

*Tower Building
50 Broadway*

second bench and I heard the witnesses speaking of Jesus. I did not understand many words, only Jesus. I came forward and got down on my knees. He put his hand on my shoulder and said, 'German man, pray.' I said, *'Nicht verstehe'*—I don't understand. There was another German there and Jerry McAuley said, 'Cross over and pray with this brother.' I opened my mouth and said, *'Jesu,* help me. *Jesu,* help me.' In the twinkling of an eye I saw the Son of God face to face. I began to cry like a baby. I went home that night and opened the door and said, 'Wife, forgive me the way I have treated you so long. I have got Jesus.' My wife said, 'Oh John, you are a bum. I wouldn't trust you five minutes.' "

She was wrong. Jaeger never drank again in his life. He first became a missionary among the Germans and then sexton of the Dewitt Memorial Church, one of the most famous and most active churches of New York's Lower East Side. In 1889, with the help of the now prosperous and well-known Bradford Lee Gilbert, he established a mission of his own—the Mission of the Living Waters—in a former saloon on Chrystie Street. In 1902 he was still going strong, with meetings every night of the week and twice on Sundays, when he celebrated the "coming of age" twenty-first anniversary of his spiritual rebirth. By then his mission had moved to new and larger quarters at 23 Delancy Street. Jaeger lived the last few years of his life at the McAuley mission and died in June 1908.

The ease with which Mike Dunn began his homes for ex-convicts and John Jaeger later established his mission are illustrations of how quickly McAuley's inspiration was accepted and elaborated.

Previously, the attitude of religious people toward drunks and ex-convicts was one of scorn and condemnation. At best the sinner was prayed for but he was expected to work out his own regeneration.

When McAuley opened his mission in 1872 the idea of extending positive help to drunkards, exconvicts and prostitutes was like a ripe fruit ready to fall from a tree. McAuley's inspiration was original. He was the first to act. But soon he was not alone.

As a direct result of the religious enthusiasm generated by the Moody and Sankey meetings in the Hippodrome in 1876, the New York Christian Home for Intemperate Men was started on June 7, 1877. The two most generous contributors to the home were William E. Dodge and James Talcott. Dodge and Talcott, along with John Noble Stearns, were also on the board of trustees. All three had been active supporters of Jerry McAuley for several years and fre-

quently attended his meetings, where they saw proof that the alcoholic was worthy of help and could be helped.

The Home for Intemperate Men, first located at 48 East 78th Street, tried to catch men before they sank to the depths of the Bowery and the Fourth Ward. As such, it was not a rescue mission. It later moved to Westchester County, New York, under the name Chester Crest.

A few months later there was an even more significant development. On September 15, 1877 Colonel and Mrs. George Clarke opened the Pacific Garden Mission in Chicago. This was the second rescue mission in the United States. How much the Clarkes knew of the work on Water Street is not known. There is no record of any direct connection. The Pacific Garden Mission is also still in existence. It is one of the foremost institutions in the United States for the rehabilitation of skid row derelicts.

At about the same time, McAuley inspired the spread of the idea abroad, beginning halfway around the world in New Zealand. Although early records of the McAuley mission are scanty, it appears that William H. Smith became a convert in about 1872 or 1873. He was associated with the work on Water Street for about four years. Then he returned to Auckland, New Zealand, where he formed the Helping Hand Mission, using the original name of the McAuley mission. About ten years later he founded a second mission in Auckland and continued in the work until his death in August 1912.

In November 1877 John Gough, the most famous temperance speaker of his time, took a noted English worker down to Water Street. His name was William Noble. Like Gough he made his living by giving lectures on the evil of drink. Noble had been a drunkard as a young man. He swore off drinking, made a small fortune in business, and then took to drinking again and lost everything. He swore off again and became a temperance lecturer, urging his listeners to sign the pledge. Both Gough and Noble were secular speakers. They did not preach any particular religious belief.

John Jaeger

Noble listened to McAuley and was not particularly moved. Then he heard the testimonies. In his own words his life was "revolutionized." He realized that drunkards could be reached with a religious message and that men could not only be reformed, they could be transformed. From then on he became a preacher, urging his audiences to become Christians as well as abstainers.

When he returned to London he was determined to repeat McAuley's work. The Hoxton Music Hall in the East End had lost its license for staging what were considered immoral performances. Noble raised funds to rent the hall for three months as an experiment to see if a mission designed specifically to bring the gospel to drunks and derelicts would work in England.

His meetings began on March 29, 1878. Night after night and three times on Sunday he drew audiences ranging as high as fifteen hundred men and women. He told them: "We only want the ragged and the wretched." Once a man had been fed and clothed and inspired to lead a new life he was urged to break off from Hoxton Hall and join an established church. The experiment was such a huge success that Noble had no difficulty in raising three thousand pounds to buy Hoxton Hall and continue the meetings.

The third rescue mission to be opened in the United States was directly inspired by McAuley. He had long hoped that a mission could be opened on the Bowery. He met Reverend and Mrs. A. J. Rauliffson, who were engaged in missionary work on the Lower East Side of New York. They often discussed the project. On November 7, 1879, "after much prayer and earnest thought," the Rauliffsons opened a mission in a small, dimly lit room at 14 Bowery. They were soon overcrowded and moved to larger rooms at 36 Bowery. The mission had various names in its early days but came to be known simply as the Bowery Mission. Its fame spread around the world wherever derelicts gathered. Year after year it fed tens of thousands of homeless men and rescued many of them from their misery.

Thus, by 1880, McAuley's vision was taking shape, either through his own initiative or through the inspiration of others. There were places for drunks and places for ex-convicts. But there was another group of outcasts still largely uncared for—the prostitutes. He continually worried and fretted about their condition and eventually opened a new mission—the fourth to be founded in the United States—in an effort to help them.

McAuley had been brooding about the extent of vice in New York since 1878. In that year the Reverend T. DeWitt Talmadge, a famous preacher of the Brooklyn Tabernacle, spent a night touring the brothels, saloons, and dance halls which lined Sixth Avenue from 24th Street to 40th Street. He delivered a series of sermons describing some of the vice he had seen and demanding that the police enforce the laws against prostitution.

Religious leaders had been trying to stir action for years. In 1866 Bishop Simpson of the Methodist Episcopal Church startled an audience at Cooper Union by declaring there were as many prostitutes in New York as Methodists. He later estimated the number at 20,000.

At the time the Reverend Talmadge delivered his sermons the number of prostitutes was estimated at about 25,000 and vice, once confined to the Fourth and Fifth Wards, had spread far uptown. Talmadge was a voice in the wilderness. A concerted effort to reform the police department and then move against the brothels, dance halls, and gambling houses did not begin until the early 1890's when the Reverend Charles H. Parkhurst became head of the New York Society for the Prevention of Crime.

McAuley acted in his own fashion. If he could not help the unfortunate women he could at least try to cut at the root of the trouble. He opened the Cremorne Mission on West 32nd Street—a beachhead in a vast jungle of vice and debauchery known as the Tenderloin. It was so named by Police Captain Alexander Williams, who was transferred to the area in 1876 and remarked to a friend, "I've had nothing but chuck steak for a long time and now I'm going to get a little of the tenderloin." The area extended from 14th Street to 42nd Street and from Fourth Avenue to Seventh Avenue, with Sixth Avenue as its main street. In 1885 it was estimated that half of the buildings in the Tenderloin were devoted to some form of entertainment or dissipation.

Some years after the Cremorne was started, McAuley recalled how he had been inspired to act: "Dr. Talmadge was the first one that started me to thinking about it. Dr. Talmadge had been round the dives and seen what was going on and preached about it. I had been round New York some and I thought I knew the worst places in it but I was mistaken. I'd never seen anything so bad as this neighborhood. The first time I found out what it was really like happened this way: There was a fellow they called 'Happy Joe' came up one night and got a little full and began to sing a hymn he'd heard down at our Water Street place. At last he said, 'Let's have a Jerry McAuley prayer meeting right here.' Well, the girls jumped at the idea and he took me off and made fun of the whole thing. Well sir, that blaspheming rascal was the cause of my coming here.

"Those girls were so interested from his description that two of them came down to Water Street in a carriage to our meetings and then often came. One of them came to me afterwards and she was afraid. Mrs. McAuley and I got interested and we came up to look for the girl's sister. We started in at Bleecker Street, took in The Allen's, Harry Hill's, Wes Allen's, and all the rest there, and came up and went to nearly all the Sixth Avenue dives. Before we got through I made up my mind that this was a worse place than Water Street and resolved, if the Lord would help me, to start a mission up here. I finally fixed on this place because it was the worst I could find."

The Allen's real name was Theodore Allen. He had three brothers who were burglars and another who ran a gambling house. Allen never drank and seldom spoke. He seemed to be made of ice. His place on Bleecker Street, one of several he owned, had a dance hall in the basement and a concert saloon on the ground floor.

Harry Hill's was on West Houston Street, east of Broadway. It was a large, two-story house with a dance hall in the rear of the ground floor. Hill was a small, stocky man who went to church twice a week, wrote poetry, and tried to keep a semblance of order in the main hall, confining his more disrespectable customers to the basement or other parts of the building.

The most famous resort in New York was the Haymarket on Sixth Avenue just south of 30th Street. It had once been a theater. The boxes and galleries along three sides of the building were retained and small cubicles built off of them. Nude dancing and peep shows were some of the mildest of the perversions practiced in these booths. The most abandoned dive of all, in the estimation of the police, was the Cremorne Garden on West 32nd Street, presided over by a huge man with a large mustache and beard nicknamed "Don Whiskerandos."

Jerry and Maria found a vacant building right next to the Cremorne Garden and it was there they decided to establish their mission. They prayed for guidance and received what they felt was a specific answer.

"We felt that our work on Water Street was done,"

80

Maria recalled, "and the time had come when we ought to make a change. After that visit it seemed to us that the cry went up to Heaven for a mission here so that some of the hundreds of men and women frequenting these dens and dives might be saved. We went home and asked God if he wanted us up here, and if he didn't want us here to put up a barrier so high we couldn't climb over."

McAuley encountered immediate opposition. His friends wondered whether he was strong enough to take on a new burden.

"When he felt that his work on Water Street was done," Alfrederic Hatch recalled, "and that he was called to labor uptown, I did not think it was wise for him to leave, broken in health as he was, and assume the responsibilities and labors of a new enterprise. I was afterwards glad to see and acknowledge that Jerry's divinely guided impulses were right and that what I thought my coolheaded judgment was wrong."

McAuley had learned to follow his inspiration.

"I never undertook anything," he told a meeting at the Cremorne, "but what the prophets said, 'Jerry, you've made a mistake.' When I started the Water Street mission none of these wise fellows would come near me for a while. One man said, 'Well, if it's a success, I'll give you twenty-five dollars.' 'Yes,' I thought, 'if—and if they were all like you it could not be a success.' When I came uptown they said again, 'Now Jerry has made the mistake of his life.' Even some of the trustees objected and said, 'Water Street mission will go down if Jerry leaves,' as if

*The Cremorne Mission
104 West 32d Street*

Jerry McAuley was anything or that God couldn't do without me. Not so. This mission would just run on the same if I should die tomorrow morning."

The months went on with planning and prayer. Once they knelt and asked God that if He meant for them to move uptown He should send the means that day. The means did begin to come. Later, William Dodge agreed to pay ten per cent of whatever the cost. They soon raised nine thousand dollars and were able to start anew.

16 The Conversion of Samuel Hadley

ON JANUARY 8, 1882 Jerry McAuley opened the doors of the Cremorne Mission at 104 West 32nd Street. McAuley deliberately located his mission next door to the Cremorne Garden and deliberately chose a similar name. He wanted to encourage drunks to wander into his mission in the mistaken belief that they were entering a song-and-dance place. He knew many lives had been changed because of similar mistakes down on Water Street.

The opening of the Cremorne aroused the excitement and adventure of a new beginning. It attracted new interest and new workers. It created the opportunity to train new leaders. McAuley knew he had not long to live. However, for a twice-born man, death holds no terrors. The worry, if it exists at all, is that so much needs to be done and time is running short. Life is to be lived to the full and death comes as a welcome rest.

The origin of the name Cremorne is not known, although it is assumed that the Cremorne Garden was named after a saloon or dance hall in London. Some books dealing with the wickedness of New York in the 1880's have charged that McAuley would lock the doors of the Cremorne Mission and preach to the befuddled roisterers before permitting them to resume their rounds. One book calls him a "tricky evangelist." McAuley was well known and did not have to preach to captive audiences. The doors were always open and the meetings were crowded from the start.

On the night of Sunday, April 23, 1882, a man came to the mission weak from the aftereffects of a severe attack of delirium tremens. He could not push through the crowd. A tramp saw how anxious he was and asked, "Do you want to go in?"

"Yes," said the man.

"Then hang on to my coat." The tramp forced his way through the crowd and dragged the man up toward the front. He listened to the testimonies, prayed, and was born anew. The man was Samuel Hopkins Hadley. Almost every moment of his adult life before that night had been compounded of self-gratification, pleasure, fraud, and deceit. Almost every moment after, until his death in 1906, was compounded of self-sacrifice, sympathy, and love.

Some details of his conversion are included in William James' *The Varieties of Religious Experience.* It followed the classic outline. First there is the paralyzing sense of guilt, or sin, to use the theological term. Then there is the heartbreaking struggle away from sin; the sick man is totally absorbed in what he wants to get away from and has almost no sense of what he wants to move toward. Then comes surrender and release; the sick man feels a sense of mystery, a sense of higher control, a sense of being a passive spectator in a process that is shaped from above. Finally there is the experience of being reborn. The guilt that had crushed him is lifted away. He is able to face up to his past lies and deceit. He is happy and the world is fresh with dew.

Hadley was born in Ohio on August 27, 1842. His father had gone west as a pioneer from New Hampshire. His mother was a direct descendent of Jonathan Edwards. Her great-grandfather had founded Hopkins Academy in Massachusetts. Her father and brother were both clergymen. Samuel Hadley was the youngest of four children, two boys and two girls. In 1845 the Hadleys moved to Salt Lick Township, Perry County, Ohio, where the children were raised in a log cabin with snow sifting through the cracks in winter. It was a life of piety and hard work. The children were educated mainly by their mother and whisky and tobacco were never permitted inside the house.

Hadley promised his mother he would never drink. But one night, when he was eighteen, an older friend coaxed him into taking a sample swig from a crock with a corncob stopper. Within a week he could drink a half pint of whisky straight down. His initiation into drinking coincided with a number of personal tragedies and disappointments. His mother died soon thereafter, not knowing that her son had broken his promise. His father died six months later.

When the Civil War began his older brother, Henry Harrison Hadley, went off to serve with gallantry. He eventually rose to the rank of colonel. But Samuel Hadley had accidentally cut his knee with an ax when he was sixteen. He walked with a limp and had to remain behind. He went to study medicine with a doctor in a nearby village. The doctor was a drunkard and Hadley kept him company. His studies ended when he got into some sort of trouble and had to leave town as fast as his horse would carry him. He became a professional gambler.

Through the years Hadley rarely went to bed sober. He got into a series of scrapes and in 1870 had to come to New York, where his brother had become a lawyer, politician, and insurance agent. Colonel Hadley found him a good job with a liberal expense account. Then the company failed and Sam Hadley began to go to pieces. His wife died in 1875. He was married again in 1879 to a young southern girl. She did not know he was, by then, a confirmed alcoholic. He drifted from job to job and supplemented his meager earnings by embezzlement and forging checks. Then the attacks of delirium tremens began and his wife left him. He often spent hours by a window of his rooming house trying to get courage to jump out.

On Tuesday evening, April 18, 1882 Hadley sat in Kirker's saloon at Third Avenue and 125th Street. He had pawned and sold everything he owned. His forgeries were discovered and it was only a matter of time before he would be sent to prison. He had not eaten for days. For four nights he had not dared to close his eyes in sleep because he knew an attack of delirium tremens would begin. He had always told himself he would never become a tramp. Now he was a tramp. For two hours he sat on a whisky barrel in Kirker's saloon and brooded. Something seemed to come into his mind. It was a sort of presence, then a kind of spectacle. All his sins were being written on the wall in letters of fire. He looked another way and there were the letters again. He thought he was about to die. Then he thought a saloon was an awful place to die in and he stood up, walked to the bar and pounded on it with his fist.

"Boys, listen to me," he shouted. "I'm dying but

Samuel Hadley

I'll die in the street before I'll take another drink." When he later thought of those moments, Hadley was convinced that God had begun to guide him with the first vision of doom. He walked into the street thinking only of death but a voice inside him reminded him that he had actually made a promise. The voice said, "If you want to keep that promise go and have yourself locked up."

Up to that moment he had lived in fear of arrest. But he walked to the station house on East 126th Street near Lexington Avenue and explained that he wanted to be forced to sober up. They put him in a narrow cell which later became a holy place for him. For the next twenty-four years he would begin the observance of the anniversary of his rebirth by visiting cell number ten for a few moments of prayer. Even when the delirium tremens began and all the demons of hell seemed to crowd around him, he still felt a higher presence. A voice told him to pray and he got on his knees and said, "God be merciful to me a sinner."

He was released from the police cell on Saturday and went to his brother's house, where he was cared for and put to bed. The next day he felt the higher presence was still with him. Someone suggested he go to a new mission, the Cremorne. He went and the tramp helped him find a place. Until that moment he never knew that religion could cure a drunkard but he listened to the testimonies and went forward for prayers. He began to tremble as McAuley came down the row, placing his hand on the head of each man, and saying, "Brother, pray. Tell the Lord what you want Him to do for you."

Hadley wanted to withdraw. He felt a devil was kneeling beside him, whispering his crimes. He had forged the name of a single man one hundred and twenty-five times. He could actually hear the devil talking. "What are you going to do about this if you are going to be a Christian? You can't afford to make a mistake. Don't you think you should fix these matters up and get out of some of these troubles and then make a start? How can you go to Sing Sing and be a Christian?"

He felt McAuley's hand on his head and heard the words, "Brother, pray."

"I can't pray," Hadley replied. "Won't you pray for me?"

"All the prayers in the world won't save you unless you pray for yourself," McAuley replied.

Hadley paused. Then something inside him broke. "Dear Jesus, can You help me?" he asked. With that a light seemed to flood within him and he rose from his knees and said he was saved. He began to babble about himself and his crimes, telling the truth for the first time in many years. People crowded around him to shake his hand. Later he walked out to the street and looked up at the sky. As a drunkard he had always looked down and this was the first time he could remember looking up in ten years. He went to his brother's house and knelt by his bed to pray. He kept saying over and over again, "Dear Jesus, I want You to so fill me with love that I'll never never fall, never never fall. You can do it, Jesus. I'll stay here until You do." He could never remember how long he spent on his knees this way. Suddenly it seemed the room was lightened by a great halo and he cried and shouted. He got into bed and fell into his first deep sleep since his youth.

His first thought when he awoke the next morning was that it had been a dream. But he knew it was real when he opened the blinds and saw that the whole world was new. Yet he still did not feel sure of himself. At eight o'clock he prayed, "Lord, keep me from drinking until nine o'clock." At nine o'clock he prayed for strength until ten o'clock, and so on through the day. After a while he felt strong enough to begin the process of making amends. He went to Vesey Street in lower Manhattan to see the man whose name he had forged one hundred and twenty-five times. He knew they were collecting evidence to send him to prison. The man was out when Hadley got there and he sat and waited. Then the man came in. He was astounded.

"Hadley! You here?" he exclaimed.

"Please sit down," Hadley replied. "I have some-thing to tell you." But instead of simply confessing the forgeries and promising to make good he began to tell of his conversion. After a few minutes he began to cry.

"Mr. Hadley," the man interrupted. "I don't know anything about the kind of religion you've got. But I would give all I am worth if I had what you have. Now go ahead and do all the good you can and I will never trouble you."

This was just the beginning. All alcoholics are liars. They lie to themselves and others.

Hadley had one lie that was part of his life. Toward the end of the Civil War he had gone to Nashville, Tennessee, to bring home his brother, who had been wounded. He had to stay for some time. People kept asking how he became lame and one day he said he had been wounded in the war. Everyone looked at him differently and there was a competition to buy him drinks. He saw that he had struck it rich. If someone asked him where he had suffered his wound, he said at the battle of Stone River, Tennessee. But he found he had to answer many other questions too. What division was he with? What regiment? Who was the commander? What part of the field had his regiment been on? He had to buy a history of the battle with a map of the field and study it carefully so his lie would not be discovered. He later became enmeshed in a series of lies to his second wife explaining why he did not draw a disability pension.

After leaving Vesey Street, Hadley was so full of religious enthusiasm he found a drunk on the street and brought him to the Cremorne Mission that night. He became friendly with Sam Irwin, a former prizefighter who acted as a roving missionary for the publisher, Joseph Mackey. There is a curious similarity between the name of this man, Sam Irwin, and the Samuel Irving who gave his testimony at the time of the John Allen excitement in 1868 but it is not possible to discover if they are the same person. In any case, this Irwin was the first man to shake Hadley's hand after he was converted. He sought Hadley out the next day to see if he needed help or advice. A few days later, as they were parting at the mission, Irwin asked, "By the way, Brother Hadley, how did you get your lameness?"

"I was wounded in the army," Hadley replied without a second thought.

"Is that so?" Irwin said. "I'm glad to hear it. I'm an old soldier myself." Then he ran to catch a trolley car going downtown. He was gone in a moment.

A voice came into Hadley's mind. "You're a

Christian, are you? But you can lie as easy as ever."

Then another voice came in. "If you are not a Christian how is it you don't swear or want a drink? Go after him and tell the truth."

Hadley jumped on the next car. He knew Irwin would go to Mackey's office at 3 Beech Street. Hadley went into the office and asked the clerk if he could see Mr. Irwin. The clerk, knowing that Irwin acted as a missionary and thinking that Hadley had come for a handout, replied, "No, you can't see him."

"I must see him. I will see him," Hadley insisted. He felt his entire future was in the balance. The emotion must have showed since the clerk went into the private office and soon returned.

"Well, go in," he said. "But be in a hurry."

Irwin and Mackey were in the middle of some business and appeared annoyed at the interruption. "Mr. Irwin," Hadley blurted out, "I lied to you about being in the army and I want you to forgive me. I was never in the army in my life. I cut my knee with an ax as a boy. Can you forgive me?"

Now they were both interested.

"So you thought you had to come and tell me, did you Brother Hadley?" Irwin asked. But before he could say more, Hadley abruptly said good-by, turned, and walked out. He did not want them to see the tears running down his cheeks. As he walked by the clerk, out into the hall, and down the steps to the street a voice was scolding inside. "You are a fool to give yourself away like this. Why didn't you keep still? No one would ever have known and now you have lost the only friend you had."

But as he stood on the sidewalk another voice came in. "Just think of it. See what you have done. You will never have to tell another lie all through your life." With this his crisis passed. Hadley felt as if he were walking without touching the ground.

Within six months he had found work and saved enough money to furnish an apartment and ask his wife to come back to him. She agreed and he brought her to her new home. As they entered the room— even before taking off his hat—he began the confession he had been preparing so long. He told her the truth about his leg. It was the first of many shocks she was to receive as she learned to live in her husband's strange new world. But she was a patient, self-effacing woman and they lived the rest of their lives in love and harmony.

17 McAuley's Death

JERRY McAULEY'S LAST YEARS are obscure. Early records of the Cremorne Mission have disappeared and there are almost no subsidiary reports. Apparently, as he grew weaker, he virtually retired from his evangelical work. He appears to have spent a great deal of his time resting in his quarters over the mission or at a cottage on the New Jersey shore. Hadley seems to have carried on the work of the Cremorne.

In April 1883, the *Christian Herald* printed a short biography of McAuley, drawing heavily on *Transformed.* In passing, it noted, "Within the past few days Mr. McAuley, exhausted by continuous labor and needing rest and change of air, went to Jacksonville, Florida, and his hand was grasped to his amazement by Christian men, respected by their fellow citizens, who owed all that they are to his efforts on Water Street."

This was the strange fact of McAuley's influence. Even he did not know how many lives he had changed. Men came to Water Street or the Cremorne, heard him preach, listened to the testimonies, and left, never to be heard of again. But they moved on to start new lives in new cities, even new countries.

There is no mention of McAuley in newspaper accounts of a meeting on March 30, 1884 which drew a great deal of attention because Alfrederic Hatch presided. His firm had long since recovered from its near failure in the panic of 1873. Hatch was now president of the Stock Exchange. The newspapers, unaware of his long association with McAuley, thought it strange that the head of the Stock Exchange would kneel in prayer with drunks and girls from the Tenderloin. The *Herald* described the meeting:

". . . After the assemblage had sung several hymns and a clergyman had prayed, Mr. Hatch preached a simple but forcible little sermon depicting the peacefulness, rest, and happiness of the Christian life; explaining how easy it was, by the grace of God,

THE ORIGINAL McAULEY FOUNTAIN
The people in the picture cannot be identified.
The policeman is holding a brass cup on a chain.
On the opposite side of the fountain,
not shown in the picture,
was a watering trough for horses.

no longer active in the mission's affairs. He died in 1903.

McAuley died in September 1884. The crowds which came to his funeral were the first public indication of the extent of his influence.

In 1885 a memorial was erected to his memory on 32nd Street, just south of Sixth Avenue, not far from the Cremorne Mission. It was an elaborate cast-iron fountain designed by Bradford Lee Gilbert, with a water tap and metal cup attached to a chain, and a water trough for horses. The fountain disappeared along with the horses it was designed to serve. It was replaced by the small drinking fountain which now stands virtually unnoticed at the south end of Greeley Square.

Maria McAuley was appointed superintendent of the Cremorne and the meetings continued every night of the week and twice on Sundays. She retired in March 1892 and married Bradford Lee Gilbert who, by then, had become a specialist in railway architecture. The Gilberts were associated with the Cremorne and Water Street missions for the remainder of the long lives that stretched before them and occasionally led an evening service. Gilbert died in 1911 and Maria lived on until 1919. The McAuley Cremorne Mission was later moved to 434 West 42nd Street in New York. It closed in 1972.

At one point in his career, the Reverend John Calvin Knox was pastor of the Second Rotterdam Reformed Church in Schenectady, New York. He built a new church, from a design by Gilbert, with a bell and clock tower. He called it the Maria Gilbert Tower. Knox added a bronze tablet to the honor of the woman who had grasped his hand so many years before and helped to lead him from darkness. The tablet is still there.

for those who willed it to step from among the lost over the line into the ranks of the saved. He exhorted all who were in sin or unhappy from any cause to cast their burden upon the Saviour.

"When it was requested that those present who had been converted at the mission to bear witness, a dozen or more persons related their experience. Most of them related that they had strayed into one meeting or another without serious intention, had been moved by what they heard, and had been converted. Most of them testified that their besetting sin had been drunkenness and that they had been entirely cured. The experiences of one or two of the women were especially remarkable and they seemed to be thoroughly earnest and sincere."

This was the peak of Hatch's career. He was president of the Stock Exchange for one year and almost immediately thereafter his business failed in one of the sudden upheavals which swept Wall Street. Hatch tried a number of businesses after that. For some years he was an executive of Lord & Taylor's, then located on Grand Street in lower Manhattan. He continued as a trustee of the McAuley Water Street Mission until 1899 but apparently was

Maria McAuley after her marriage
to Bradford Lee Gilbert

85

18 His Works Do Follow Him

WHEN MCAULEY LEFT WATER STREET to go uptown he was succeeded by John O'Neill, an ex-convict who was converted at the mission and served with McAuley for several years. In 1883 the trustees appointed John Fogg Shorey as superintendent. Shorey was an Englishman of good family background who had skidded to the bottom. For a while he was a bartender in New Orleans. At the age of fifty-five he drifted—drunken and bloated—to New York and was converted by Dwight Moody at the Hippodrome in 1876. Moody took a personal interest in him and guided him as he learned to walk in his new life. Shorey served as superintendent until 1886, when he returned to England to work with John Noble at Hoxton Hall.

He was succeeded by Samuel Hadley who built a permanent structure on McAuley's foundations. Following his conversion in 1882 Hadley had dedicated the remainder of his life to helping others. He acted as McAuley's assistant at the Cremorne and also preached in the saloons of the Tenderloin and the Bowery. After a few months he found work and was able to re-establish his home. In his eagerness to help others he brought drunks to his three small rooms, sobered them up, dressed them in his own clothes, and took them to the New York Christian Home for Intemperate Men, which had moved to a large new building on East 86th Street.

By 1886 Hadley had a good job and was earning two thousand six hundred dollars a year, a substantial salary in those days. When Shorey came to him and asked him to become superintendent of the McAuley Water Street Mission there was every earthly reason why he should refuse. He could continue to help others and at the same time enjoy a comfortable life. Why should he sentence his wife

to the life of Water Street? The Hadleys searched for guidance. They opened a Bible and saw verses in Isaiah about feeding the hungry and clothing the naked. They took this as a sign and went down to Water Street.

The annual report for 1886 was the first prepared by Hadley. He wrote: "The style of service adopted by our dear departed brother Jerry McAuley when he began here fourteen years ago is still followed with very little variation. It has never grown monotonous and there are no signs it ever will. There is good singing and plenty of it, a short lesson from the Scriptures, with a few remarks, short earnest prayers scattered all through the meeting, and then comes the best part of all—testimonies from redeemed men. These are short and to the point. They have no uncertain sound. If there is anything that our converts know in this wide world it is that they are saved. We have no preaching; no long tiresome discourses. Generally from twenty to thirty men speak in a half hour and it is amazing how much can be said in one minute. After this comes the solemn part of our service, which we have been trying to lead up to all the evening. Often in a congregation of fifty men there are ten or twelve who will come forward for prayers."

Apparently attendance had fallen off after McAuley left but under Hadley the numbers became greater than ever. Attendance was 27,688 in 1887, 30,505 in 1891, 40,940 in 1893, and about 50,000 in 1904. Charity also increased. Homeless men were given tickets which entitled them to a night's lodging at a flophouse. About 5,000 lodgings were supplied in 1892, about 12,000 in 1898, and about 60,000 in 1904. Approximately the same number of meals were supplied. The cost was amazingly low. The mission's budget was about $4,500 in 1886 and about $6,000 in 1900.

Hunger and misery were everywhere. Once a week—first on Saturday nights, then on Thursday nights—the mission gave a free supper of coffee and sandwiches. Even though the meal was not served until seven o'clock, the men would start drifting in at three in the afternoon and within a half hour the room would be crowded and the doors would have to be closed. There was a similar crowd at every mission

John Fogg Shorey

which gave out food. Equally large numbers came seeking a place to sleep. But the rich and contented closed their eyes. City officials were similarly callous. New York did not open a municipal lodging house until 1896—and then it merely used an old barge on the East River as a flophouse.

The McAuley Water Street Mission could not close its eyes. The distribution of food and clothing was an elemental act of Christian charity. But this was only a start. For some men it was enough. Many were simply down on their luck, without work, and too hungry and dirty to look for work. Food and clothing, a chance to clean up, and perhaps a few dollars in cash to catch a train back home might be the limit of their need.

However many others were not down on Water Street simply because of bad luck. They were bleeding from some inward wound. Something had happened to them which had broken their will or otherwise shaken them from the ways of normal society. They needed a helping hand. They also needed a new way of life, a new set of beliefs, a new set of standards.

Once a man came forward for prayers, and thus evidenced a desire to reform, he was made part of the family. If he was too weak or too old to work room might be found for him at the mission. Otherwise he was helped to live and eat until he could find work. He was encouraged to attend the meet-

ings every night and strengthen his resolve with prayer and testimony. The mission was a place where, when he was lonely, he could find clean surroundings, kind friends, and a family meal with the Hadleys and other converts.

For many years the mission printed an advertisement in the Saturday newspapers among the listings of the church services for the next day. It said, "Everybody welcome, drunkards especially." Hadley often claimed that more drunks and thieves crossed his threshold than any other place in New York except the Tombs.

If they did not come to him, he went to them. He would go to a saloon or flophouse and sing the hymn, "Do you know why I love Jesus?" Then he would deliver a simple message: "Boys, I was once a drunkard myself and Jesus saved me. If you ever want a friend, come to Water Street." He would go to Sing Sing and other prisons with the same message, telling the convicts to come to Water Street as soon as they were free, before they drifted back to their old haunts and old friends.

His concern for the poor and helpless extended to their final days. Then, as now, a large percentage of those who died and lay unclaimed in New York City's hospitals were Bowery derelicts. Hadley often visited hospitals, such as Bellevue, which treated many of the poor. If he came across someone who was near death, and was without friend or family, he would

MISSION INTERIOR (*circa 1890*)
The airshaft led up to the roof, providing necessary ventilation for a roomful of some of the most unwashed men in New York. McAuley kept some of his plants and birds around the shaft, which passed through the rooms on the second and third floors. The white marble plaque on the center of the left wall, installed by Samuel Hadley in 1886 in McAuley's memory, is now in the vestibule of the present mission.

promise him a decent burial. He would leave instructions to be notified if the man died. The mission would claim the body and conduct a funeral such as the man would have had if he had died among his family.

He especially grieved for young prostitutes who cut short their misery with suicide. Once there was a double tragedy. In December 1894 he read a small item in a newspaper telling of the suicide of a girl of the Tenderloin named Tillie Lorrison. The story said she would be buried in potter's field. He visited the place where she had lived and found she had a friend, Trixey Cooper. Hadley arranged for Tillie's funeral at the mission. He also pleaded with Trixey to reform. Others went to her too but she postponed any change in her life, saying she had to care for her mother. Six weeks later Trixey Cooper killed herself and, when no mother or other relative claimed her body, she too was taken to the mission. The body was dressed in black and lay in a rosewood coffin for the funeral services, and a line of women who had known her came to say a last farewell.

Outwardly the mission seemed to be a welfare organization. It fed the hungry, clothed the ragged, lodged the homeless, helped find work for the unemployed, and buried the abandoned dead. But Hadley insisted that this was done for a definite religious purpose.

"In answer to many inquiries," he once wrote, "we wish to say that the McAuley mission is not a university settlement, a labor bureau, or any of the newfangled plans to simply better the condition of the human race. It is a real low-down rescue work and consequently it is the highest work in the city."

"It cannot be too clearly stated," he wrote on another occasion, "that the McAuley mission recognizes and teaches that it is only through a belief in Jesus Christ and His atoning sacrifice that souls can be restored to favor with God. There is no other way to salvation but by way of the Cross."

All religious beliefs are mere dogma until brought to life by example. Christianity on Water Street became an extraordinary concern for each individual who entered the mission. Although theologically the concern was for a man's soul, attention was focused on a man's physical welfare here and now on this earth. In fact, it was difficult to distinguish whether the word *salvation* was being used in the sense of saving a man's soul or giving him a bath and a new suit. It meant both.

Workers at the mission could never know whether a man came simply because he wanted a handout or whether, consciously or subconsciously, he was looking for a solution to his spiritual turmoil. A man making a nuisance of himself might be a simple drunk or he might, in a convoluted way, be trying to call attention to himself. His drunken rantings might, in fact, be cries for help.

The workers also believed that a sufferer might not be aware of who or what was the ultimate cause of his own actions. They devoutly believed—and offered the evidence of their own experiences as proof—that God could control a man without his knowledge.

There was one man who came to the mission with no purpose other than to beg a handout. He had no intention of attending a service, to say nothing of pretending to be converted. His name was John H. Wyburn. He was destined to succeed Hadley as superintendent and remain at his post until his own death in 1921.

Wyburn was an Englishman. He came to the United States when he was about nineteen years old to help his brother, who owned a chain of bakery shops. Upon his brother's death in 1882 Wyburn inherited a large share of the business plus cash and real estate. He ran the business so well he had an income of ten thousand dollars a year. Then he became a drunkard. He tried every known cure, including the Christian Home for Intemperate Men, but managed to sneak drinks while there. Finally his relatives had him declared legally incompetent and his business was taken away from him.

Wyburn spent his days drinking and going from friend to friend to borrow money. He had many friends plus a large number of business associates and for a while easily managed to raise five or ten dollars a day. One day someone gave him a letter of introduction to Mr. S. H. Hadley of 316 Water Street, without explaining who Hadley was or that this was the address of a rescue mission. Wyburn decided

Hadley would be good for a loan of ten dollars and went to Water Street. Hadley was not there and Wyburn spent the rest of the day looking for someone else to get money from. He searched all afternoon for a man who had once been his foreman. When he finally found him the man explained he had just started his own bakery business and had paid out all his cash. He gave Wyburn twenty-five cents. Wyburn had been drinking during his search and his mind was in a fog. He used the money to buy what turned out to be the last drink of his life and took the trolley across the Brooklyn Bridge to search again for Hadley.

Looking back at that day—September 25, 1888—Wyburn was convinced he had been in the hands of God. He did not know the neighborhood and could not remember how he found his way to the mission. He woke from a daze to find himself seated on a bench telling someone he wanted to see Mr. Hadley.

Hadley came toward him, limping slowly. Wyburn handed him the letter. Hadley read it and asked, "Well, what can I do for you?"

Wyburn explained how he had lost his business because of drink. He wanted to become sober and get his business back. Hadley seemed to be indifferent. He asked, "Is that all you want?"

Wyburn thought Hadley simply could not understand. If he knew how difficult it was to give up drink he would not treat it so lightly. But then Hadley continued: "What you need, my dear brother,

Hadley at Wesley Hall 291–293 Bowery He is standing in a characteristic pose, leaning on a cane to favor his injured leg— an injury which, for many years, he claimed was the result of a Civil War wound. After his death the name of the mission was changed to Hadley Hall. In a previous metamorphosis, the building had been McGuirk's "Suicide" Hall, one of the most notorious of Bowery dives.

is Jesus Christ as your Saviour. He will sober you up and you will never want another drink of whisky."

Wyburn thought he was talking nonsense. But when Hadley asked him to remain where he was for the night's service, Wyburn agreed.

The meeting began. After a while a man stood up. Wyburn knew him. This man had waited on him while he was a patient in a hospital for alcoholics in Fort Hamilton, Brooklyn. He knew this man was as big a drunkard as himself. Now the man was saying he had been cured. Wyburn saw the man was sober and saw that he looked different. He decided he wanted the same cure. He went forward when the invitation was given for prayers and knelt at the bench.

Then the inward struggle began, familiar to so many others who had knelt at the same spot. The inward voice said, "What's the use of praying? You don't believe in prayer." Wyburn began to get up. Someone gently urged him to kneel down again. This was repeated several times. In his daze, Wyburn felt he had an old umbrella in his hand and was pounding on the floor and saying, "I will, I will, I will test this thing." With the words "I will" release came to him.

Wyburn was given a free ticket to a cheap flop-house. It was his first experience with this sort of hell. He was gripped by an attack of delirium tremens and spent the night in agony. He thought it was the powers of good and evil fighting inside of him. Throughout the night he was confident the good would win.

He found a job as a clerk in a lodginghouse at six dollars a week—a sharp contrast to his previous ten thousand dollars a year. He helped on Water Street in his off hours. In 1892 he became assistant superintendent of the Grand Army Mission, a newly opened mission on Canal Street. In 1896 he was named superintendent of the Bowery Mission, which had moved to 55 Bowery. He served there three years. He met and married a young girl, a volunteer from a nearby church. The girl was eighteen and he was forty. He had once been a man of considerable business success. He thought he could now resume his private life and affairs. He resigned from the Bowery Mission and moved to Cincinnati, Ohio, where he began a small business.

In 1900 Hadley asked him to return to Water Street as assistant superintendent. Just as Hadley gave up a life of potential ease for the slums of New York, Wyburn too came back.

Late in his life Hadley became an ordained

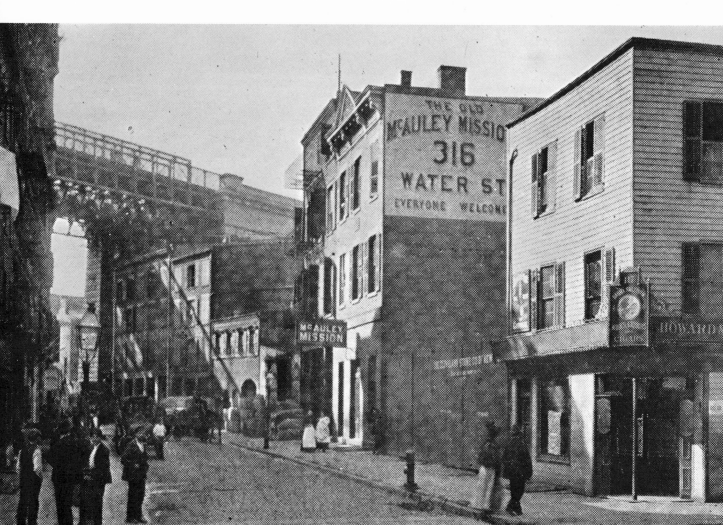

John Wyburn

Methodist minister. In May 1904 he opened a new rescue mission at 291–293 Bowery under Methodist sponsorship. One of the most notorious of Bowery dives—McGuirk's "Suicide" Hall—had once been located at this address. The mission was originally named Wesley Hall but after Hadley's death the name was changed to Hadley Hall.

Samuel Hadley died on February 9, 1906 soon after completing the annual report for 1905. In it he wrote: "This is the twentieth report that I have published for this mission. It is not a very inviting place to live in. The Brooklyn Bridge thunders over our heads with a ceaseless rumble of trains the whole day and night through. A great boarding stable is next door to us. From early morning until late at night a constant tramp of weary feet comes up the stairway into my office bringing tales of sorrow and despair and they are never turned away. . . . We have a kitchen downstairs where those who are not fit to come upstairs can get something to eat, for it is hunger that brings people into our mission. During the past year I am not aware that I have turned away a living soul without assistance of some kind. Everything has to be done for the men and women after they come here. We do not find work for them, or seldom do, but we stand by them and help them to find it for themselves. When they fall we pick them up and encourage them to try again and we keep picking them up as long as we can reach them."

One of Hadley's closest friends was the Reverend J. Wilbur Chapman, the famous evangelist. He was a successor to Dwight Moody and preached to audiences of thousands in many parts of the world. In an introduction to Hadley's autobiography, *Down in Water Street,* Chapman wrote: "I do not believe it is sacrilegious for me to say that if Jesus were here upon earth in the flesh He would do first the work which the superintendent of this mission and his colaborers are striving to do with eminent success for the outcast and downtrodden members of society. Neither can I be misunderstood when I say that if Jesus were here I could quite imagine Him walking the streets of New York by day and by night going down into the subcellars and climbing rickety stairs into high attics, making His way into dens of iniquity, and reaching down into the depths to save the lost, such as Samuel Hadley goes about our city streets."

Hadley traveled for most of the year giving lectures during the last years of his life. He also had the responsibility of Wesley Hall. Thus Wyburn had been, in effect, acting superintendent since he was called back to Water Street in 1900. He became superintendent upon Hadley's death and served until his own death in March 1921. Except for that one year in Cincinnati, Wyburn spent the last thirty-three years of his life in helping others.

His superintendency was a new beginning—but the story remained unchanged. Skyscrapers were growing in New York and subways were burrowing under the streets. Electricity and telephones were becoming commonplace and men were learning to fly. But the lines of homeless, hopeless men remained as long as ever down on Water Street.

Previous to 1906 the Wyburns lived in Brooklyn, far from the mission. They had a baby daughter and Mrs. Wyburn could not often make the trip to New York. May Wyburn was still in her middle twenties when they moved to the rooms over the mission. It was her first sustained contact with the misery of these homeless men. Many years later she recalled a story about her husband. It could just as well have been told about Hadley or McAuley.

She could not understand why her husband tolerated drunks to such great lengths. Whenever he felt someone had gone too far and had to be removed, he acted with the greatest gentleness. He was a quiet, reserved Englishman in any case. He would come down from the platform, take up the man's hat, if he had one, and beckon him to follow up the aisle and out the door. His very gentleness disarmed the burliest of tramps. They would become quiet and meekly follow him out.

But even this action was a last resort. There was once a big fellow—they never learned his name—

who came to the meetings often. Previously he had been quiet but this night he was roaring drunk and talked loudly as the meeting began. He joined the singing as if he were part of a barroom quartet but without the harmony. When he interrupted the testimonies the doorkeeper told him to be quiet. He continued to talk and Wyburn finally came down from the platform, took his hat, and led him out through the main doors. They stood for a while in a small antechamber, built outside to stop the cold winter air from coming directly into the hall. Then they returned and the man took his seat again.

He soon began talking loudly again and once more Wyburn showed him the door, only to stand with him for a while in the outer chamber and then bring him back. This was repeated several times through the period for testimonies. Wyburn finally brought the man back when it was time to extend the invitation for prayers. The man was placed with those who asked to be prayed for but gave no sign he knew what was happening.

Mrs. Wyburn watched him leave with the others, giving no indication that the prayers had done him any good. When they went up to their apartment she asked her husband, "Darling, do you think you were justified in allowing that man to disturb the meeting as he did?"

"I could not put him out," he replied.

"But he disturbed everyone there," she argued. "The men could hardly testify and I do not believe anything was accomplished in his life."

"That is something we do not know," he corrected gently. "At least we had the privilege of praying for him and the result rests with God. I wonder what would have happened to me if I had been put out of Water Street the first night I came here. I talked all through the meeting."

Mrs. Wyburn said no more but she was not convinced. Then the same man returned for the evening service two weeks later. This time he was sober and when the time came for testimonies he stood and recalled the nuisance he had made of himself. He explained that shame had made him remain away but now he felt he had to come to tell what had happened. Although no one was aware of it he had gained an experience of God that night and had not had a drink since. He said he did not know what would have happened to him if he had been thrown out.

All institutions face the problem of leadership and continuity. Men, by nature, become bored if they are confined to the same place and the same job for long.

They want to move on to other challenges and other opportunities. This is especially true for public institutions, including churches—despite a pastor's sense of vocation. A person who seeks to serve the public finds the hours long, the criticism sharp and often ill-founded, and the pay poor. Men feel they should do more for themselves and their families. They tend to seek a change or, if they remain, they work with diminishing enthusiasm.

Yet the McAuley Water Street Mission had just three superintendents for an almost unbroken period from 1886 to 1943. They all were men who could have led more comfortable and more pleasant lives elsewhere but they served to the day they died amid the squalor of Water Street, trying to help others as they themselves had been helped.

The third man in this succession was Alexander L. Jones. He was born in Richmond, Virginia, in October 1873. He was well educated, became an executive for various railroad and shipping concerns, and then lost everything—job, home, and family—through drinking and gambling. He drifted to New York dependent on relatives to keep him supplied with handouts. After a seven-week binge he sent a letter to his brother-in-law, a man who had always helped in the past. His letter came back with just two words written on it, "Nothing doing." The next day, October 31, 1915, he came to the McAuley Water Street Mission and was converted.

He was given a job as a porter with the Huyler candy factory, then found a better job, and soon had reunited with his wife and re-established his home. All the while he helped in the mission. After three years he went to Washington where he entered government service as an official of the United States Shipping Board. He bought a home and settled down to a quiet life.

When Wyburn died his wife, May, became superintendent. After two years she realized the work was too much for her. Moreover she wanted to remarry. She asked Jones if he was willing to return to

Alexander Jones

Water Street. He agreed, sold his house, and became superintendent of the mission in March 1923 and served until his death in June 1943.

It was not only drunks and criminals whom the McAuley Water Street Mission gathered to a life of service. Franklin Smith, in whose house McAuley had reunited with God, was a missionary to the poor in general and had no special concern for derelicts. But he became closely associated with the work on Water Street in 1884 and served until his death in December 1896.

There were also several women, the most remarkable of whom was Mrs. Sarah Sherwood. She was born in Connecticut in 1832. Her father was Nathan Lounsbury. One of her brothers was a state senator and the other a bank president. Both served as governors of Connecticut.

Sarah Sherwood

She came to the mission in 1882, when McAuley left for the Cremorne. Mother Sherwood, as she was called for the fourteen years that she spent on Water Street, was known to every old-time drunk and saloonkeeper for miles around. She would go into the saloons and dance halls to preach a short sermon and be listened to with respectful silence. She would also go to the merchants of the neighborhood and raise considerable funds for the support of the mission. She shook hands with the derelicts as they left the meetings and she knelt with the converts as they passed through the trial of surrender. Like so many others, she served until her death in October 1896.

There were also men like John R. Huyler who, in many ways, was a friend and supporter of Samuel Hadley in the same way that Alfrederic Hatch was the friend of Jerry McAuley. Huyler was a wealthy candy manufacturer. He was invited to the mission one night by a convert of Water Street. He had never been to a mission before. When the invitation for prayer was given twenty-six men came forward. Huyler was sitting next to Hadley.

"What are you going to do now?" he asked.

"We are going to pray," Hadley replied. "Brother Huyler, pray for these fellows." There was silence. Hadley thought he had made a mistake and had embarrassed his visitor. Then he noticed Huyler was crying.

"Oh Lord," Huyler prayed, "Brother Hadley says 'Pray for these poor fellows.' Dear Lord, I need praying for as badly as they do. Oh Jesus, help me and save us all." From then on he became closely associated with the mission. He became a trustee in 1890 and served as president from 1894 until his death in October 1910. In addition to these executive responsibilities he regularly presided at meetings, made large annual contributions, paid for the weekly dinners of coffee and sandwiches, and found work for converts in his factory and shops.

Several of the trustees set records for service that could be equaled by few large corporations. Robert Fulton Cutting was elected as a trustee in September 1878, when McAuley was in his prime. He became treasurer in March 1884 and served in this position until his death in September 1914. He told close friends he had been converted at the mission while listening to the testimonies. He was a man of great wealth and elegance. Sometimes he would attend an evening service in a dinner jacket.

James Talcott served as trustee from 1878 to 1889, when he resigned and was replaced by his son, J. Frederick Talcott, who served until his death in March 1944. In turn, his son, Hooker Talcott, became a trustee in 1928, served as president from 1949 to 1959, and continued as a trustee to 1968.

Thomas Savage Clay, the descendent of a colonial American family of Savannah, Georgia, served as trustee from November 1906 until his death in July 1938.

On November 22, 1922, the fiftieth anniversary of the mission was celebrated at a packed meeting in New York's large Carnegie Hall. Chauncey Depew

(left to right)
John R. Huyler
Robert Fulton Cutting

The People of the State of New-York,

To all to whom these Presents shall Come:

Whereas, At a Court held in and for our County of *New York* in the month of *January 1857*, *Jeremiah McCauley* was convicted of *Robbery* and was thereupon sentenced to be imprisoned in the State Prison at *Sing Sing* at hard labor for *the term of fifteen years and six months* under which conviction and sentence thereupon, the said Convict now lies imprisoned; and *he* being represented unto us as a fit object of our mercy, therefore KNOW YE, that WE have pardoned, remised and released, and by these Presents DO PARDON, remise and release the said Convict, of and from the offense whereof, in our said Court, *he* stands convicted, as aforesaid, and of and from all Sentences, Judgments and Executions thereon.

In Testimony Whereof, We have caused these our Letters to be made Patent, and the Great Seal of our said State to be hereunto affixed.

Witness, *Horatio Seymour* Governor of our said State, at our city of Albany, the *eighth* day of *March* in the year of our Lord one thousand eight hundred and *sixty four*.

Horatio Seymour

PASSED THE SECRETARY'S OFFICE, THE *8th* DAY OF *March*, 1864.

Chauncey M. Depew SECRETARY OF STATE.

was the honorary chairman. He was one of the celebrated men of New York politics, a wit and a famous after-dinner speaker. He was then an old man. Early in his career, in 1864, he had been secretary of state for New York. In this position he had added his name to Jerry McAuley's pardon. He could not attend the celebrations but he sent a letter:

"I remember when pardons came from the Governor to me as Secretary of State to countersign I always wondered what would be the future of these unfortunate men who were thus returned to citizenship. They entered upon a new life with almost insurmountable obstacles before them. There was the difficulty of obtaining employment because of their past; old associates were both tempting and threatening them; and the world was cold and inhospitable."

It had been all of that for Jerry McAuley. But he triumphed. In April 1887 Hadley was ordering a white marble memorial tablet to be installed at the old mission in McAuley's memory. He thought for a while and then wrote, "He resteth from his labours and his works do follow him."

19 A Harvest of Men

THE MCAULEY MISSION helped thousands of men and women in their daily misery. It turned outcasts into productive citizens, restored broken homes, and gave children back their fathers. It also brought a few, out of the thousands who came through the doors, to a lifetime of service. These, in turn, set about sowing the seeds of love and compassion, creating a number of useful citizens, and reaping the harvest of a selected few.

On November 6, 1884 Shorey approached an old tramp named Frank Lawrence. He was cold and ragged and wet to the skin. Once he had been a member of the Stock Exchange, rich and happily married, with a son and daughter. He lost everything through drink and became a familiar hanger-on at the mission. Sometimes he would fall asleep and snore away. The workers at the mission had often tried to convert him, but with no success. On this night Shorey decided to try again.

"Frank," he said, "how much longer are you going to sit night after night and hear these testimonies when you know that these men are living new and saved lives and you can have the same blessing, be restored to your family, and again have all the comforts of a home by accepting Jesus Christ as your Saviour?"

"Not another moment," Lawrence exclaimed. He jumped to his feet, went forward, and surrendered himself to God. He was reunited with his family and became one of the leading workers on Water Street.

At about this time the mission began a practice which, in effect, made it a seminary for the instruction of rescue workers. The seven evening meetings and the one on Sunday afternoon were divided among the converts who lived at the mission or who were able to attend on a regular basis. One or two converts, depending on how many were available, would conduct the services for a given night. It was a practice which had several benefits. It helped build a feeling of self-confidence and self-respect among men who were just learning to live new lives. It gave them an opportunity to fulfill their newly awakened desire to serve others. It introduced an element of variety in a service which, in many ways, was starkly repetitious. Finally, although this was not planned, it became a training ground for mission leaders.

94

Frank Lawrence was an early graduate. In 1891 he became the first superintendent of the newly opened Wilson Memorial Mission, established by the Presbyterian Church on West 42nd Street in New York. He retired after many years of service but remained active in church affairs until his death in 1913.

Another early graduate was a tramp known as "Ash Barrel John." His real name was John R. McConica. He was a man of college education who came to New York, established a prosperous printing business, married, and began to raise a family. Then he became an alcoholic and lost everything. He was reduced to picking crusts of bread and other bits of food from trash cans, hence his nickname.

He came to the mission on October 12, 1885. Winter had come early that year. McConica had snow and sleet packed in the cracks of his shoes and was shivering under an old linen duster. He was converted and reunited with his family. He went on to become an ordained minister and was named superintendent of the Old Brewery Mission in Montreal, Canada. He later had charge of a mission in Fall River, Massachusetts. In 1903 he took charge of a large mission in Savannah, Georgia. Finally the Reverend McConica, alias "Ash Barrel John," moved to Norfolk, Virginia, where he was superintendent of the Union Mission until his death in 1912.

The most remarkable convert of 1890 was John M. Wood. He was born in Kentucky, found his way to the sea, served for thirteen years in the United States Navy, was drunk in almost every port in the world, and then was given four hundred dollars and a discharge across which was written, in red ink, "Discharged for chronic alcoholism." He went on a wild binge and four months later found himself with no money and on the verge of delirium tremens. He thought he heard an inner voice saying, "John, you're no good. You will never be any good. Go to the river and drown yourself." On October 21, 1890 he started toward the river but when he came to the corner of Water Street and Roosevelt Street he heard some music and stopped to listen. It was the hymn, "There Is a Fountain Filled with Blood." It was a song his mother had sung to him. He went into the mission and was converted.

As with so many converts, he wanted to rescue his friends from the hell he had been through. The Navy was suspicious when he asked permission to tell his story at the Brooklyn Navy Yard. Finally the captain of the warship *Chicago* allowed him to hold shipboard services one Sunday afternoon. He went with

Frank Lawrence   *John McConica*

Hadley and eight or ten converts from Water Street. At the end of the service he asked those who wanted to lead a better life to stand up and nearly two hundred men rose to their feet.

Navy officials were so impressed that, although not an ordained clergyman, Wood was later named chaplain of the Navy Yard. He died suddenly in 1898. At the funeral services, the coffin of this man, who had been thrown out of the Navy in disgrace, was draped with the flag of the United States Navy, carried on the shoulders of six sailors, and followed by a detachment of men from the Navy Yard.

John Wood   *Harry Prentice*

It is surprising how many Englishmen have been associated with the McAuley mission. Two years after John Shorey resigned as superintendent, John Wyburn was converted and soon became Hadley's assistant superintendent. Then, on December 7, 1891, another Englishman, Harry Prentice, was converted. Prentice succeeded Wyburn as assistant superintendent and served under Hadley for five years. He then left rescue work and moved to Philadelphia. He returned to New York in about 1912 to become superintendent of the Open Door Mission on the Lower East Side. He later became superintendent of the James Slip Mission in lower Manhattan where he served until his death in 1919.

In 1897 a man was converted who was to serve the last thirty-two years of his life as leader of the Sunday night service on Water Street. He was John Mergenthaler. Three times he had started a low-price restaurant, become rich, and then gambled away all of his earnings. He had a wife and seven children and for seventeen years his wife prayed that the gambling mania would leave him. On the night of June 12, 1897 he sat in his shirt sleeves during services at the Mariners' Temple at Oliver and Henry Streets. A visiting evangelist was preaching and when the invitation was given for prayers, Mergenthaler came forward and uttered one of those strange prayers that come from a man in distress. He did not call himself a sinner nor did he beg forgiveness or mercy. He cried, "Oh God, give to my wife a new husband and to my children a father." From that moment he never had the desire to gamble again. He later began a successful business manufacturing buttons, braids, and trimmings. He never forgot how he was saved. He became a friend of John Wyburn and in 1900 was appointed leader of the Sunday night service. He continued to serve on Water Street until his death in 1932 at the age of eighty-three.

John Mergenthaler

William Anderson

On April 1, 1899, William Anderson staggered into the mission. He had been a heavy drinker since he celebrated his twenty-first birthday by going on a week's spree. Almost inevitably he became a derelict and for three years lived in the backroom of a saloon. The horror of such a place is beyond imagination; night after night with men lying in their own filth and vomit, breathing stale, foul air and listening to the groans and shrieks of nightmares and delirium tremens. It was fairly common for a man to wake in the morning and find that the man who was sprawled on the floor or table next to him was dead.

Anderson never had the slightest desire for church or religion. On that Saturday night he hitched a ride on a wagon and was jolting along the uneven streets,

sodden and stupid. By chance—or so he thought—he saw the mission. Something made him hop off the cart and go in. He was converted. In July 1901 he was appointed leader of the Friday night service and served for more than thirty years. He died in 1942.

Among the men who were converted in 1904, three can serve as examples of how impossible it is to generalize about a "typical drunk" or a "born criminal."

Thomas J. Farmer was born in the Fifth Ward, which vied with the Fourth Ward in squalor and depravity. His father was a saloonkeeper. Young Tom never went to school and was an accomplished thief by the age of twelve. When his father died he left Tom a sizable inheritance, which the young man promptly used to go to California to live high. When the money ran out he turned to crime. He was arrested for highway robbery and was sentenced to San Quentin for eighteen months. He was released, went to Montana, was arrested, and spent five years in Deer Lode Penitentiary. Upon his release he went to Washington State and was arrested in Tacoma for robbery and burglary.

By now, if he knew how to get into prisons, he also knew how to get out of them. He organized an escape from the Tacoma jail and turned all the other inmates loose with him. He was arrested in Olympia, the state capital, and again escaped and took several inmates with him. Then he was arrested in Seattle, escaped while awaiting trial, but was caught, tried, and sentenced to seven years in Walla Walla prison. He almost managed another escape. He got into the prison yard and captured the warden. Two companions seized a railway engine, which had come into the yard to pick up bricks. One of them pulled the lever the wrong way and the engine backed up instead of going forward. In the confusion the warden was rescued and Farmer's two mates were shot dead. Farmer himself was punished with eighteen months' solitary confinement. For most of the time he was given only bread and water to eat. On some days he did not get even this. Obviously the officials preferred him dead. But he survived it all. Upon completion of his sentence he walked out of Walla Walla alive—but just barely.

He returned to New York. He had spent fifteen and a half years inside prisons. His health was broken and if he did not reform he would soon be dead. His mother, brother, and sister were still alive. He knew where they lived and had not seen them for twenty years.

Crime was the only life he knew. On the night of

Thomas Farmer

Edward Mercer

March 22, 1904 he stood in the shadows of a doorway on Water Street, plotting a burglary. He saw the mission and something prompted him to go in. He listened to the testimonies and when the call was given he went forward. He said, "Mr. Hadley, I want help if God will help me." He was converted that night and served for three years as janitor of the mission. He then moved to Philadelphia where he was employed as a missionary by the Christian Association of the University of Pennsylvania. He visited prisons, hospitals, and slum homes giving advice and comfort and distributing aid where needed. For a while, in about 1916, he also became associated with Edward Mercer, another Water Street convert of 1904.

Some readers can probably recall Ted Mercer. He was raised in a mansion in Savannah, Georgia. His great-great-grandfather was General Hugh Mercer, hero of the Battle of Princeton in the Revolutionary War. His father, Colonel George Anderson Mercer, was a noted lawyer. His mother was related to the wife of President Chester A. Arthur. Mercer could recall when President Arthur visited his parents in Savannah and his own visit to the White House with his mother.

In 1898 he graduated from college, where he had learned to be a heavy drinker. He married and found a good job but in four short years he was separated from his wife and fired from his job. He became an absinthe addict and sank down and down. He moved to Philadelphia in the hope of finding work where he was not known but soon was again thrown out on the street.

It occurred to him that not far away was Trenton, which is in Mercer County, New Jersey. There is a statue of Hugh Mercer just outside Trenton. He went there but even the Mercer name could not get him

work. Someone who knew him from Philadelphia saw him standing in the street, dirty and tired. He had slept in a park for two days and was thinking of suicide. The friend bought him a railway ticket to New York, where he had a relative he thought he could touch for a loan.

The relative turned out to be Thomas Savage Clay, who promptly brought him down to Water Street. It was the night of August 6, 1904. When he heard the testimonies he gained the hope there might still be a chance for him. He was converted that evening and soon found work checking freight on an East River pier.

The testimony of converts often leaves the impression of instantaneous reformation. It appears that every one loses the urge for drink at the moment of conversion. This is because the testimony is generally highly compressed and the stories concentrate on the moment of release, while skipping over the agony which may precede it or the struggle which may follow.

For Mercer, the struggle continued for another eight months. He never drank again but he was often tempted and would lock himself in his room to help overcome the urge. Finally the appetite was totally destroyed. In 1907 he became assistant superintendent of the McAuley mission but then resigned in 1908 to begin what was to be his life's work.

He became a lecturer to university and high school students under the sponsorship of the International Committee of the YMCA. In the first five years he spoke to about 200,000 young men and women. The lectures were generally concerned with drinking and religious regeneration. For this reason he teamed with Tom Farmer. Mercer also branched out to a wide range of topics and was a pioneer in sex education. He resigned from the YMCA in 1908 and continued as a private lecturer, speaking mainly to high school students. By 1928 he had spoken to millions of students. There was hardly a city in the United States where, if he appeared for a lecture, someone would not come up to him and mention how his life had been changed by a talk Mercer had given years pre-

Thomas Savage Clay

viously. He retired sometime in the thirties and died in March 1943.

The third noteworthy man converted in 1904 was Matthew Gallagher. If there was ever a young man who should not have ended on the Bowery it was Matt Gallagher. He was born near there and as a youth was president of the Young Men's Society of his church. For ten years he taught Sunday school. From the age of sixteen he was a volunteer for a charitable organization which helped the sick and needy of New York's Lower East Side. He knew from daily experience how some men's lives were destroyed by excessive drinking yet he himself became a drunkard, sleeping in the back room of saloons and on park benches. He was disowned by his family and relatives and was a regular patient in Bellevue's alcoholic ward.

Just as Mercer's story demonstrates that there can be a long period of struggle after conversion, Gallagher's story shows there can be—and generally is—a long preliminary struggle too.

In May 1904 Gallagher realized he was near the end. He was walking down the Bowery when he passed Wesley Hall, where a man was handing out cards saying, "Drunkards Especially Welcome." He went in and prayed for help but it did no good. He continued drinking. He tried again a few months later and then a third time. Prayers still did not kill his appetite for drink. On October 23rd he went to Water Street just for warmth and food. Wyburn asked him to come forward for prayers. He refused. But Wyburn was persistent and just to end the nuisance he went and prayed, "My dear Jesus. I leave myself in Thy hands. Thy will be done." He stopped drinking from that moment. Delirium tremens began the next day and he was taken to Bellevue.

He surmounted the crisis and served for a year as janitor of Wesley Hall while learning to walk again in his new life. He later got other work, married, and had children and grandchildren. He was leader of the Sunday afternoon service at the McAuley mission from 1907 to 1934 and continued to attend the meetings until his death in 1942.

On October 9, 1906, Louis J. Bernhardt was released from prison. At the age of forty-eight he was a hardened criminal, brutalized by twenty-two years in various prisons. Most of these years had been served in southern prisons, which seemed never to have heard of the reforms that were gradually easing the lot of prisoners in the north. He experienced the lash, the shackles, the water cure, the club, and solitary confinement. He had been raised in a cultured home in Georgia and had gone through college. He committed

Matthew Gallagher   *Louis J. Bernhardt*

a crime and was sentenced to prison. When he was released his family would have nothing more to do with him and former friends rejected his appeals for help. He felt there was nothing left but crime and he paid the penalty in prison after prison.

On October 10th, the day after his release, Bernhardt came to New York. He was a marked man, an habitual criminal. Detectives spotted him and ordered him to leave town. He spent the next three days dodging the police. Then, on a Saturday night, he decided he could not go on any longer. He began a walk others had taken before him, the walk to the East River. And, like many others, he heard songs coming from the McAuley mission which reminded him of the distant days of his youth. He entered the mission and listened to the testimonies. Many of them were drunkards and had nothing to say which interested him. But one man stood up and began telling of his long years in prison, of his many attempts to escape, of the horrors he suffered in solitary confinement. It was Tom Farmer. Bernhardt knew then that there was hope for him too. He went forward and surrendered himself.

From then on his life echoed that of McAuley, Hadley, Mike Dunn, and scores of others. After sufficient wretchedness and futility for an entire lifetime he was reborn and lived a second life of service and love. Since he did not have to undergo the alcoholic's period of mental and physical rehabilitation he could begin almost immediately. Within a few months after that night of October 13, 1906 he was named superintendent of the Yale Hope Mission. The contrast was astounding. In one year he was marked as an habitual criminal, a hunted, friendless, starving man on the verge of suicide. In the next year he was well clothed, well fed, with troops of friends and the respect of the officials of New Haven and the authorities of one of the great universities of the United States.

He spent four years in New Haven and was married there. Bernhardt then went back to his native state to be field secretary of the Prison Board of Georgia. He helped initiate such reforms as an adult probation law and the establishment of the state prison farm. From there he went to Tennessee where he helped the Southern Howard Association in its prison reform work. He also became an ordained Presbyterian minister.

The Reverend Louis Bernhardt returned to New York in about 1914 to work for the City Mission and Tract Society of Brooklyn. He was put in charge of the Good Will Home, a large institution on Clinton Avenue, which had once been a school. It had quarters for about sixty men plus a number of workshops. Converts of various Brooklyn missions were sent there to live and work until they could stand on their own feet. In 1915 he had two new blessings. A daughter was born and President Woodrow Wilson signed a decree which restored to him the full rights of citizenship. In about 1917 he became director of the Church House in Providence, Rhode Island. It was there that he lived out his life and, in the fullness of ninety-one years, died in 1949.

Alexander Russell was a Scotsman who drank himself out of a comfortable existence and left a wife and three children to come to the United States to seek reform in new surroundings. He discovered the mission, would profess conversion, lead a sober life for a few months, and then start drinking again. It happened several times over a period of about four years. The Wyburns often felt discouraged but never gave up hope. Russell barely managed to keep his job. Sometimes he would be beaten in a brawl and would sleep in an old boiler near the mission. He would go to the mission to be cleaned up and then had to hide in a corner from his employer so his bruises would not be seen. He finally surrendered himself for good on March 30, 1909.

Russell had not completed his high school education but as a Scotsman of his generation he had a thorough grounding in the Bible. The Home Mission Society learned of his conversion and his intense desire to serve others. He was selected as a licentiate of the Congregational church and sent as a missionary to the pioneer settlement of Carter, South Dakota, to establish churches and Sunday schools. His work was cut out for him. There were about a dozen buildings in the town and five of them were saloons. He did so well that most of the saloons had to close within a year. The governor of South Dakota, G. S. Vesey, wrote a testimonial calling Russell's work "the greatest ever done by any man out in that part of the country."

In May 1910, the McAuley mission paid for the passage of his wife and children so that they might join Russell in the hard life of the frontier. On a Sunday he had to ride about thirty-five miles in a horse and buggy to preach at four churches and look after three Sunday schools. He was ordained as a Congregational minister in 1914. He later was the pastor of several small churches in Iowa. When he retired at the age of seventy-seven, he had served forty-five years in the ministry.

Alexander Russell   *Carlton Park*

The horror of the Bowery or some other skid row lies before every alcoholic. The horror is compounded because he realizes he is slipping down to the ultimate of disgrace and misery. It is this pit of hell which makes many think of suicide.

Carlton Park reached this point. He was a glass blower and an ardent trade-union man. He was so well liked that he became an executive in the national office of his union. He also became an alcoholic. He reformed for a while but fell again. His wife left him and his home was broken. He sat in a dingy room at the Gerber House in Easton, Pennsylvania, and realized he had reached the end. He burned his papers and stuffed the bedspread up the chimney. Then he turned on the gas jets and lay down on the bed to die. The manager smelled gas, broke open the door, and saved his life.

Park had been raised in a religious family. Eight years earlier he had heard of the McAuley mission. He came to New York and thought he would try this solution. He came to the mission on March 23, 1910, three days after his suicide attempt, and was converted. A year later he became the founder and first superintendent of the Williamsburg Rescue Mission in Brooklyn. In 1915, while continuing in charge of the mission, he was ordained as a Presbyterian

Line for Noon Gospel Service and Lunch, 1932

minister and became pastor of a small church. He later started the Greenpoint Mission in Brooklyn and then became head of the Brooklyn Goodwill Industries.

The aftermath of World War I brought many changes to the United States, including a change in religious attitudes. This revolution in American manners, morals, and customs would have its effect on the McAuley Water Street Mission, although none of the workers realized it at the time. They were too busy. The mission began its period of greatest expansion and service.

In 1912 the old building erected by McAuley in 1878 was torn down and replaced by a four-story structure with separate rooms for about ten men.

The architect was Bradford Lee Gilbert, who did not live to see it completed.

In 1926 the trustees purchased the old stable next door and made plans for an elaborate campaign to raise funds for a separate dormitory. At about that time John Markle, who had made a fortune in the coal mining business, became interested in the mission. He first contributed small sums and then spent several weekends studying the work. He was invited to the luncheon at the Union League Club which was to inaugurate the campaign. Before anyone could make a pledge, Markle announced he would give the entire amount, which eventually came to more than one hundred thousand dollars. The John Markle dormitory was dedicated in 1927.

This was the period of prohibition but the work of the mission never changed. There were saloons nearby with wide-open swinging doors and as many drunks and derelicts as ever.

The work went on through the depression. In 1932 attendance was almost 84,000. More than 79,000 meals were served, and more than 17,000 free beds supplied in the dormitory. The daily task of caring for the long lines of men, which stretched from the mission doors, continued to the start of World War II.

But this was accompanied by a growing sense of frustration. The primary function of the mission was to bring men to God and not merely to feed their stomachs. With the passage of years, the mission did not seem to be fulfilling this function.

There are several possible reasons for this. One is a change in attitude toward the conversion experience.

*Third Mission
and Markle Hall*

There are styles in religion as there are styles in politics, war, and fashions. As the years passed, conversion went out of style among many American Protestants. The fervent emotional approach to God, which had shaped religious life of most of the English-speaking world since the days of John Wesley, had largely evaporated by the interwar period.

Comparatively few people believed that God could—and would—guide a man's daily footsteps. The emphasis of religion changed. Instead of probing the depths of spiritual turmoil and then seeking, through an heroic "leap of faith," to come to a direct knowledge of God, the focus shifted to regular church attendance and formal worship ceremonies.

Previously, a man who acknowledged both his failings and his redemption, was considered part of the mainstream of religion. He was not ashamed to tell what had happened to him. But then this frankness became strange and old-fashioned. As a result, when conversions did take place, fewer men were willing to share their experiences with others.

Conversions themselves became fewer. The reason for this can also be traced to the change in religious practices. It is probably true that up until World War I most Americans who called themselves Christians followed religious practices in their homes. The child hearing the Bible at his mother's knee was so common it became a literary cliché. But when Protestantism in America became more formal and more church-centered, religious instruction largely disappeared from the home. The Sunday school was an extension not of the church but of the home.

Many of the conversions which occurred at the McAuley Water Street Mission resulted from this practice. A hymn filtered through the noise of Water Street could remind a drunk or ex-convict of a peaceful home and loving mother. A few words heard at a meeting or a phrase from a hymn was sufficient to recall the lessons he had learned in Sunday school and the Bible he had read at home. It was possible to rebuild a man's life on foundations laid in his youth. By the thirties this was seldom true.

Finally, it appears that the mission—even with its expanded facilities—was overwhelmed by the hungry and homeless who came to its doors during the many years of the depression. The men who came saw the mission as another welfare institution and were seldom interested in its religious message. Yet some undoubtedly were touched.

In 1937 a minister wrote to tell of a convert he discovered in the Philippines: "When we first came to Pagsanjan I found the station in possession of a

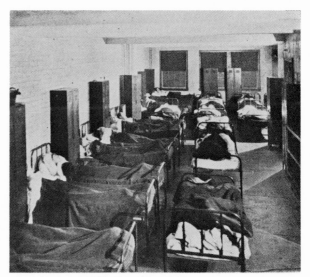
Interior, Markle Hall

fine little gasoline launch used for itineration around the lake. . . . The engineer of the launch was Macario Cabaney, a sailor who had seen service on the seven seas, had got into the worst of sailors' ways, had abandoned his wife and child, and had become perfectly reckless. But one night in New York he wandered into the old Jerry McAuley mission and there found Christ and Christ found him. He went back to the Philippines, hunted up his wife and little girl, and reestablished his home. . . . When the launch was in port and there was no particular duty calling him, he got out his Bible and read it. Often I found him surrounded by a group of interested listeners to whom he was giving the message of the evangel and telling how Christ had rescued him."

Line for
Thanksgiving Day Lunch
1941

20 The Rise and Fall of Skid Row

WHEN JERRY MCAULEY started his mission, Water Street and its saloons were surrounded by tenements with hard-working families, many of them new immigrants. There was no such place as skid row but urban America was changing swiftly. With sudden demobilization at the end of the Civil War, tens of thousands of men from farm families, unwilling to return to the isolated lives of their farms, migrated to the cities. Simultaneously, immigration was rising to flood proportions. Then the economic collapse of 1873 put perhaps a quarter of the work force out of jobs.

If anyone could be called the father of skid row it was the Reverend John Dooley. When he opened his first dormitory on the Bowery in 1873 his only thought was to provide inexpensive lodgings for some of the men looking for work. Commercial operators copied the idea and similar dormitory streets for single men grew in every major city.

Then the older commercial areas of large cities decayed. Residential areas were replaced by warehouses, small manufacturing plants, and entertainment facilities patronized by the middle classes. Only the cheap and tawdry were left. Skid row became a segregated area of flophouses for unskilled men depending on temporary work as dock and railroad laborers, construction "stiffs," contract laborers paving streets and digging sewers, and seasonal workers for resort hotels or harvesting commercial crops. It was also a refuge for the elderly poor and the mentally retarded and a zone of toleration for chronic alcoholics.

Every skid row had its symbiotic institutions of saloons, restaurants derided as hash houses, pawn shops, cheap clothing stores, employment agencies seeking temporary laborers, barber colleges, and brothels. There might also be a municipal welfare institution but it was mainly the missions that tried to meet the spiritual and physical needs of a population injured by alcohol and victimization.

The period between the two World Wars brought demobilization, the peak tide of immigration, and then the most severe depression since the 1870s. As skid rows flourished and seemed a permanent part of American urban culture, a minor literature developed romanticizing the hobo way of life with its argot and code of hard drinking masculinity: This man was not a bum; he was merely a tramp unwilling to conform. The myth mocked the reality of loneliness, poverty, wracking ailments, unset fractures, and badly healed wounds.

After World War II the increasing use of machinery in the lumbering and construction industries and on railroads and farms reduced the need for unskilled labor. Young men remained in school for longer periods and could get better paying jobs. As factories became unionized, workers stayed in one place to enjoy the benefits of rising wages and seniority. The cyclical depressions that followed previous wars became recessions cushioned by unemployment benefits.

It took a generation for the effects to trickle down. In 1955, when the old elevated tracks were torn down, a shabby Bowery lined with taverns and twenty-five-cents-a-night flop houses came into full sunlight for the first time since 1878. One estimate put the number of derelict men along the sixteen blocks from Chinatown to Astor Place at eighteen thousand. Ten years later stores along the southern end of the Bowery from Canal street south to a rapidly expanding Chinatown had been refurbished into shops for diamond and gold dealers and boutiques for expensive lamps.

Simultaneously, the decriminalization of public drunkenness in 1966 ended the legal segregation of troublesome alcoholics. Previously, the police cleansed "respectable" areas of unsightly drunks by forcing them to move to a skid row zone of tolerance. Those who were stubborn were put in jail until they sobered up. More than twenty-five percent of the arrests in New York City, and upwards of fifty percent in other large cities, were for this and related offenses.

Debilitating alcoholism affected only from twenty to thirty-five percent of skid row populations but all attention focused on this minority. They were mainly "plateau" drinkers who sought a steady, even level of numbness. When they chose, they could circulate in outside society, working in menial jobs such as kitchen or laundry help at resort hotels that sought men who could be as easily fired as they were easily hired.

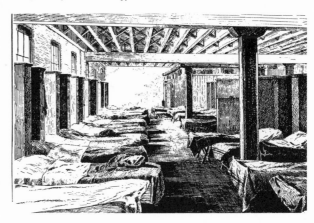

The emphasis on alcoholism and the sociological discussion of skid row men as "disaffiliated" abstractions added to the feeling that little could be done for the skid row man. Casual references in social studies to the "failures" of religious missions appeared to confirm that these men were hopeless. The literature served as an excuse for society to close its eyes to all residents of skid row, as if bad character brought them there and not bad luck or the lack of a safety net for those with little education, almost no skills, and weak family ties.

The first significant portent of the end of skid row as a way of life came when decriminalization allowed the plateau drinkers to circulate in the richer business and entertainment areas of cities where passersby were easy targets for deliberately aggressive panhandlers or where motorists were willing to part with money just to stop someone from swabbing a windshield.

By the late 1970s, as cities rebuilt their core areas and real estate developers gentrified unprofitable slums, social scientists and urban administrators realized homelessness had taken a new form. It now included entire families, including children, without shelter of any kind. Moreover, following the emptying of large psychiatric hospitals in favor of promised community care that was never delivered, the streets also filled with schizophrenics and others with severe mental illness. In the early 1980s, television broadcasters dwelt on the incongruity of men and women sleeping on heating grates or in cardboard boxes amid modern buildings and sleek, well-shod office workers and executives.

It became apparent that modern homelessness was different from the previous skid row configuration of poorly housed single men. It was now typified by a complete lack of shelter combined with three social factors: extreme poverty because of low earnings and low benefit levels, disability through age, alcoholism, or physical or mental illness, and tenuous or absent ties to family and kin and few or no friends. Most people with family, friends, and property have the financial and psychological reserves to survive months of sickness or unemployment. But even a few days of sickness or unemployment can push someone who is extremely poor over the edge to homelessness. Then clawing back to a minimal level of respectable poverty is difficult.

Alexander Jones died in 1943 and was succeeded as superintendent by his wife. In turn, she was succeeded by Ludwig Armerding in 1946. Armerding, then fifty-three, was a former businessman who had been converted in May 1907. The mission at 316 Water Street was razed in 1949 to make way for a housing project but the compensation paid by the city was not enough to build equivalent facilities. A small building was purchased at 124–126 Water Street—around the corner from Wall Street—with only enough space to hold gospel services and to feed the men coffee and sandwiches.

When Armerding retired in 1962 at the age of seventy, there was a serious question whether the mission should be continued. However, spurred on by its president, Dr. James H. Humphries, the board of trustees investigated the work of other mis-

sions, sought the recommendations of secular welfare officials, and decided not only to continue the mission but to expand its work.

Armerding was succeeded as superintendent in December 1962 by Ernest Woodhouse, an Englishman following in the footsteps of John Shorey and John Wyburn. Woodhouse had been an evangelist since the age of seventeen. He came to the United States in 1948 and preached throughout the country, coming to believe that few in his audiences had studied the Bible deeply enough to appreciate the spiritual promises it offered. He was just the man needed to give new vigor to the McAuley Water Street Mission.

The city offered, at a low cost, an ideal building at 90 Lafayette Street that had been built during World War II to provide cafeteria and other facilities for workers in neighborhood factories who were making the secret Norden bombsite. It was bought and Woodhouse supervised the renovation. The adjacent blocks to the south and east form New York's civic center, containing all the major courts and federal, state, and municipal office buildings, including

the Tombs with its grim, looming, narrow-windowed walls. Although the name is the same and the building still houses minor courts and police detention pens, the old Egyptian-inspired building of McAuley's day has long since disappeared.

The building is newer than many of its immediate neighbors. Except for the sign, "McAuley Water Street Mission," it could be a business office. A receptionist sits behind a high desk in the wood-paneled lobby and there are fresh flowers on bookcases along the walls.

Woodhouse served until July 1965, when the extensive renovations were completed. He then resumed his life as a traveling evangelist while remaining as a member of the mission staff. He was succeeded by Earl Vautin who, for the previous six years, had been a superintendent of several rescue missions in neighboring New Jersey. Like Woodhouse, Vautin brought a new sense of purpose to the work. "With the depression in the thirties, you had an enormous growth of city, state and even federal welfare activities," he said. "You might have a bread line or a free meal at a mission and also at some

Mrs. Alexander Jones Leading Noon Bible Class, 1940

104

Ludwig Armerding at Thanksgiving Day Lunch, Fourth Mission, 124–126 Water Street

Evening Service at the Fourth Mission, 1954

105

municipal center. The public became confused about the purpose of a mission, especially since many missions, in their sincere desire to help the hungry and homeless, allowed their welfare activities to be publicized at the expense of their spiritual activities. Rescue missions were seen as just another welfare program. They were not understood for what they really are. The Christian church does this work out of love for the individual and out of a desire to bring him to the gospel. But this does not mean we will neglect our other responsibilities. It says in Galatians 6:10: 'Do good unto all men.' *Good* implies more than simply telling a man how to pray."

In 1972, Victor Jacobson, who had spent most of his life as an independent insurance agent in the financial district of lower Manhattan, came to the mission. Years earlier he met an alcoholic on the streets who had been an engineer for a large company in Pittsburgh. This gave him a determination to help such men. Sometimes, to the dismay of his office staff, he would take them to his office. At other times he would take them to the McAuley mission.

Finally, he volunteered as an assistant at the mission.

Later in 1972, Vautin left to take up the work of foreign missions. Charles Ross was asked to come from Chicago to lead the mission into what would become the era of homelessness. Jacobson remained as his assistant. When Ross took a leave of absence in 1976, Jacobson served as interim superintendent. After Ross returned in 1978, Jacobson remained for another two years as his assistant. Only then, when he was almost eighty, did he end his work for alcoholics.

Like Vautin, Ross believed rescue missions must not lose their way. "The experts tell us in the next decade we'll have a wave of new poor, more alcohol and drug abusers, more mentally ill and the children of the mentally ill. Ideally any mission should be a multifaceted institution to reach out to any and all of them. But if we spread ourselves too thin, the emphasis may shift from the spiritual to the social. If we leave out the spiritual, we will be offered all kinds of money from the government and foundations and business organizations that now shy away because of the constitutional separation of church and state. A subtle form of pressure could come in that could tip the scale toward welfare work at the expense of our mission to bring men to Christ.

"We have an example in Christ himself. He had a three-year ministry on earth. He healed lepers, made blind men see, restored hearing to the deaf and speech to the mutes. He touched people wherever He went. But He did not begin to touch the whole world. He did not even meet every need in the land of Palestine. We need to learn we can't meet everyone's needs. When a mission gets into everything, the director sits in his office reading computer printouts and conferring with his staff. I want a mission small enough so I can be down with the fellows. That personal touch is important."

Earl Vautin Counseling a Resident

21   The Mission Today

The predominate reason for men seeking the help of a rescue mission is not alcoholism, as popularly supposed, but the inadequacy of America's safety net for the elderly, the infirm, and those with inadequate skills or education.

THE MCAULEY MISSION is a sanctuary that does not look for a reason to say no. One winter day in 1989 a man walked in from the street and announced he had just gotten out of jail and needed a place to sleep—this in a city where newspapers and television programs are chronicles of murder, rape, and robbery and people have two or three locks on their doors and iron grates on their windows. Yet the man was told to come back at the regular admission time and if a bed was available he would get it.

"Here," said the man at the reception desk, in words that would have gladdened the hearts of Jerry McAuley and Michael Dunn, "no questions are asked and no information is volunteered. Unless the police come and ask for a specific man, we tell them nothing."

The mission's day stretches from four in the morning, with preparations for breakfast, to ten at night when lights go out in the dormitory. Charles Ross and his wife, who acts as office manager, come at about noon and remain past the evening chapel service and meal, generally leaving after 9 p.m. Work with the men earlier is the responsibility of Chaplain Ted Woodruff, who came to the mission in 1974 after ten years as a missionary in Mexico. Woodruff arrives at five-thirty in the morning and sometimes does not leave until five at night.

Housing Project on the Site of the Original Mission

The men are divided into two groups: the "line" and the "program." This last comprises about thirty residents who maintain the building, staff the reception desk, and prepare and serve about 240 meals a day.

The man who has worked the longest with the program is a gruff Irishman named John. He fought in both World War II and Korea and then fell on hard times. In 1974, he came to the mission, rediscovered God, and was reunited with his family. John was raised in a devout Roman Catholic family and still calls himself a Catholic. He found work nearby and became a valued supervisor while simultaneously watching over building maintenance for the mission. Now that his children are grown and on their own, he has taken early retirement and lives in a small room at the mission, with responsibility for the weekend activities.

"When I first came we had dirty old gray walls without one stick of presentable furniture," John said. "Color is a psychological thing. I said, 'Let's get away from the jailhouse look.' We painted everything new with a desert sand color. One day I went out to work and the Lord threw me onto this Italian fellow who owned a lot of furniture and he gave me all the beautiful desks you see in our offices. We had something that looked like sheets hanging on our windows. We put up valances and the mission's ladies auxiliary made curtains. Everything started to bubble. Mr. Ross had a friend from the midwest who came here for a vacation who installed the paneling in the lobby. We made wooden plaques of different colors and put the Living Word on the walls and we put flowers on tables and bookcases.

"Men on the program have to sign in and out if they leave the building. They are given at least one day off a week. On those days they can get an overnight pass. They're grown men and some have families. Sometimes a man might not come back for two or three days and we might need someone to fill that position. Sometimes we take a few extra if we think our spiritual program can do something for them.

"Mr. Ross says, 'Don't kick a man when he's down. Give him another shot.' One man has been on and off our program seven times. We still think he's salvageable and can go back into the mainstream of society. Another man does his job and goes to Bible class but he still drinks, although he thinks we don't know it. He's accepting God in the mission but accepting the Devil outside. We keep working with him. I want to salvage a man, not throw him out in five minutes. He's living with us. He's family. To me, I'm a small-time apostle trying to bring somebody into the fold."

The man who wakes up the kitchen staff to start the day is Bob, who is on the lobby desk from eleven at night until six in the morning. Bob once had a federal position of great responsibility and served overseas for many years.

"I've been pretty far down the tube," he said. "I've been in and out of hospitals and have tried half a dozen of the best alcoholic programs there are. Finally, I put myself entirely in the hands of the good Lord. Without His help and this mission I wouldn't be alive today. Faith and the mission work together. Here, you are in a controlled environment. In the beginning you need that. Still, a man can walk out the door anytime he wants. If you don't want to quit, any control short of a jailhouse will not work."

The mission has ninety-six, double-deck dormitory beds. Depending on fluctuations in the residency program, men on the line are allocated between sixty and sixty-eight beds on a single night basis. With rare exceptions, such as paydays or welfare or pension or Social Security check days during hot summer months, when a man can drink himself to sleep on a bench, the beds are full every night. The beds are allocated over the course of the day to meet the needs of different men at different times.

Fifteen are reserved for those who have stayed the night and say they need a bed for another night but cannot be on the line because they have jobs and cannot be present for the afternoon line-up. Chaplain Woodruff, who has a hand-written note on his door reading, "Love in any language fluently spoken here," deals with their problems.

"Each individual is different," he said. "There are those who are not interested in their triune need—body, soul, and spirit—and only see the loaves and fishes. Others may have deteriorated so far physically, emotionally, or spiritually they either cannot or will not respond. Still others develop patterns of living that can make it difficult to receive help. Their impulsive reactions prevent follow-through.

Lying, or not telling the whole truth, could become a rule of life. Discouragement may settle in due to what seems to be an impossible situation. Others don't want to follow advice. It's not what they wanted to hear or seems too difficult to achieve.

"Some of these so-called failures are apt to be like 'a brand plucked out of the fire' (Zechariah 3:1-5). Our goal is to reach the whole man: body, soul, and spirit. It says in 1 Thessalonians 5:23: 'Now may the God of peace sanctify you entirely, and may your spirit and soul and body be preserved complete and without blame at the coming of our Lord Jesus Christ.'"

Woodruff asks those who have requested a bed where they are working and what they do. He is able to sort truth from untruth. Then others waiting in the chapel for help are called in one by one. There might be a man with military service who can be steered toward a veterans' program. Some want help finding work. Woodruff will tell them of temporary employment agencies within walking distance. Another might have lost his social security card or it was stolen when he was mugged after heavy drinking. The mission keeps a record, including social security numbers, of all who have stayed there. Woodruff will write a letter attesting to this number. The man can take it with him when he applies for a new card.

The mission is also a mail drop for several hundred men. Woodruff will write a letter attesting a man has permission to receive mail at 90 Lafayette Street. Social security and other agencies require this before they will send a check. When these and other checks arrive during the first days of a month, he is busy distributing them to men and keeping a record of checks received and handed out.

Often someone phones offering a donation of food or clothing. For instance, city schools with lunch programs are not allowed to save food until the next day. A school might say it has left-over milk, bread, or salads. Bakeries, large and small, offer left-over bread, some of it fresh at the end of the day. In the morning and early afternoon, Woodruff has to find time to drive out to accept the offerings.

One afternoon an agent of the Food and Drug Administration drove up with several boxes of canned goods used as evidence in a nearby court. The trial was over and the food had to be legally disposed of. Ross prepared and signed a receipt and the FDA man left.

"Their office is nearby," he said. "This is the third lot we've had in the past four or five weeks but then a year might pass and we will get nothing. When you've been around for more than a century, people are sure to know you. At Christmas and Thanksgiving when the court officers and others have their parties, whatever is left over, which is often plenty, they bring it to us. There's also a group at one of the offices of AT&T. Every Thanksgiving, they come over with half a dozen turkeys. Every two months, we also get a certain number of items from the surplus food programs of the Department of Agriculture. But that's drying up. Now we get mainly honey, macaroni, spaghetti, and some canned meats."

A more recent source of food is an organization called City Harvest. It collects platters of cooked foods and fine cakes, pastries and bread, from some of New York's finest restaurants and left-over sandwiches and salads from corporate receptions. City Harvest will call any of dozens of voluntary agencies with food programs informing them of what has suddenly become available. If they can use the offering, a City Harvest truck will make delivery, saving time and effort for the always hard-pressed Chaplain Woodruff.

David, a young resident who is one of three cooks, estimated that 75 percent of the food served comes by way of donations. David also plays the piano and sometimes accompanies the services in the chapel.

In addition to the fifteen beds held for working men, a second block of fifteen to eighteen beds is set aside for referrals from more than sixty churches, hospitals, and agencies, including The Salvation Army and Catholic Charities that operate smaller and more selective shelters. There are also requests from city, state, and federal institutions, such as the Veterans Administration. Mrs. Ross deals with them in the afternoon.

A bed is saved through an outside agency only once: after that a man has to stand in line like everyone else. A social worker at one city agency once called for a bed and was indignant when she was asked if the man had been at the mission before. She put her supervisor on the phone and he demanded the client be given space. When the man's name was checked in the mission's files, he was found to have been there many times. Men from the street often look for an easy mark. The mission has received requests from several agencies for the same man on the same day. The trick is to wheedle an agency out of carfare and apply it toward the cost of a pint of wine.

If a man is mugged in Times Square and loses his money and identification, Travelers Aid or the city's Victims Services Agency may call the mission to see if there is a bed. Once a judge called for placement for a man he was releasing. Parole officers frequently call or, since the mission is near the courts, a parole officer might walk a man over to show him the place is clean and the faces are friendly.

Such requests are ironic. Following the publicity about homelessness and complaints of derelicts sleeping in Grand Central Station and the subways, New York City opened a dozen overnight shelters for homeless men in armories and other large buildings with underutilized space. The use of alcohol and drugs is so flagrant, and thievery, fights, and killings so frequent at these city shelters that even city officials will not recommend them. There is a small plaza with benches a block away from the mission. Men who could not get a bed at the mission have said they prefer to sleep there, even in the coldest weather, because they are afraid of the city shelters.

There is another irony. The referrals, in effect, are reversing the desegregation of the former Bowery skid row area brought about by the 1966 decriminalization of alcoholism and vagrancy. This allowed derelicts to scatter through the city. Now religious and other voluntary institutions, as well as civic institutions, are sending them back to the old skid row district.

Another block of tickets, for about twenty-six men, is distributed to men who line up for admission beginning at 12:30, after the residents have finished lunch. The men from the street can use the toilet facilities—rarely available in New York for disheveled, homeless men—and can also get clothing on Mondays, Tuesdays, Thursdays, and Fridays. All the residents have multiple responsibilities and also pitch in where needed. They know that as the mission helps them, they are in the mission to help others. The man who takes care of clothing distribution is named Roberto.

"At about five-thirty in the morning, after all the men leave the third floor, we start making beds and cleaning the floor," Roberto said. "I make twenty beds. Someone else does the rest. Then, if clothes have been donated, I take them upstairs and sort them according to size and what it is: pants, jackets, suits, shirts, underwear, socks, shoes, sweaters, ties. After lunch, I take back upstairs the sheets and pillow cases that have been laundered.

"Between thirty and forty men come for clothing. They ask you for everything, from underwear to coats and shoes. It can take a long time to get the right fit. If I don't have the merchandise, we keep a list in the lobby of other places that give clothing, but many still come here because it's close to where they hang out or work."

There is always uncertainty in dealing with a large group of men who walk in from the street. There are

Charles Ross in Lobby of Fifth Mission

rules all must obey. Arthur, who is usually posted at the lobby desk in the afternoon, explained:

"Most homeless men look forward to just sitting in the chapel. When they come in the afternoon and it's cold outside, they would like to stay all day. But we can't allow that. After a while they'll get restless. They'll try to go down to the kitchen to get something to eat or wander in other parts of the mission. Many of them are light-fingered. We had fake packages for decoration under a Christmas tree in the Chapel and someone swiped them.

"We must have simple, easy-to-understand rules —and stick to them. That's what's wrong with the city shelters. The men run amok and the staff doesn't care. They have regular hours and salaries and they can go home and forget all about the place. The residents are here twenty-four hours. We feel this is our house as much as theirs."

When Charles Ross and his wife arrive, Mrs. Ross heads up to the office to begin work on the correspondence and other chores while Mr. Ross goes to the basement dining room for a half-hour Bible class for men on the program. Only a minority are former alcoholics. The others have fallen through the gaps in America's inadequate safety net.

One is Larry, who works alone in the steaming basement laundry room washing and drying sheets and pillow cases from the dormitory plus whatever else needs to be cleaned from the resident's dorm. He has been at the mission since 1982.

"Larry has had a conversion experience since he's been here," Ross said when he was asked about the program. "He has trouble living under the stresses of outside society. He needs a structured situation. He was employed at a small variety store. The owner said he was a good worker but he could not keep him on the payroll. He called me and said Larry had no place to live and didn't know how to manage his money. I said send him over. We have another man who has been here since 1983 and will probably be with us for the rest of his life. He is the victim of a tragedy. When he first came, someone got angry at him and took a bottle of drain cleaner and threw it at him. He was in a hospital for a long time and came out so disfigured people shy away from him if he rides in the subway. This is his only home.

"Another man came in here homeless and we found out he needed dialysis treatment. Now he's a resident, has found the Lord, and is one of the most diligent men on the household staff. He has relapses sometimes and has to return to the hospital. Should we throw him out? Should we put a time limit on how long he can stay? Some missions have time limits but we don't.

"Theoretically, there are welfare services. But it's a big job for older or disabled men to get into a decent home. They have long waiting lists or are beyond the means of what our men can pay. We have a man in his middle seventies who has been with us since 1984. His name is James. He came one night and appeared to be very sick. We found he had been in prison for forty-four years and then was discharged onto the street. We took him in and sent him to several clinics. They could not find what was wrong with him. One day he toppled over during the evening service. We rushed him to the hospital and they found he had a brain tumor. Chaplain Woodruff went to see him and urged him to agree to surgery. James said no. He had read in prison that a brain operation meant death and he preferred to die without having his head cut open. Well, James had been reading the Bible and had a Bible in the hospital with him. One day Chaplain Woodruff came running back from the hospital and said James had found the Lord. He agreed to put himself in the Lord's hand and accept surgery.

"Now he walks around here every day, happier than he has been since he was a little boy. Shall we put him back on the street? He has applied for a nice home and may get a place, although there's a long waiting list. We'll keep him until that happens. This doesn't mean we encourage people to stay. I tell men at Bible class to make some goals and work toward them. But we don't make setting and achieving goals the basis for coming here. We only ask, 'Do you really want to better yourself?'

"A man says, 'I've got to get myself together and get off the streets.' He may never have been in a communal situation before. The collegiality is part of the business of getting back into society. About everything we do here, and they do, is a therapy of sorts. Just to know that every day at such-and-such a time he has to clean the floor or do the laundry or work in the kitchen is a discipline and training for a man who comes from an environment of doing what he wants to do at any time. Then we expose them in our Bible studies to the teachings of the Scriptures. From there we would like to get them out to a local church."

At about 2 p.m. lay ministers employed in nearby government or private offices conduct a short Bible class, after which Chaplain Woodruff distributes the twenty-six reservations available for that night. After

Evening Service, 1989

that, anyone who comes asking for a bed is told to return at 5:30. Theoretically, only about ten beds remain unallocated but with the indeterminate life of the homeless, some men with promised beds will not show up. The chapel fills quickly for the evening service and meal.

In recent years, the mission has been getting a more belligerent type of man. An estimated 5 percent are thought to be sociopaths or under the influence of alcohol or drugs. For that reason some of the taller and stronger residents, who have been through the tough school of the streets themselves, are assigned to security. They do not have uniforms or weapons and do not use physical force. If necessary, the nearest police precinct is only four blocks away and the police are quick to respond to a call from the mission. Real trouble is rare. A man will quiet down quickly if he is calmly approached by one of the men on security.

At about 6:30, one of the men on security recites the rules for the benefit of newcomers. One night the task was assigned to Jim, a trim, well-built man with a low, commanding voice:

"There will be no smoking, no drinking, and no drugs in the building. Anyone caught will be barred for an unspecified time. No bags of any kind are al-

lowed on the third floor. That includes packs, hand luggage, shopping bags, or whatever. They will be checked in and locked away for the night. One ticket will go on the bag and you will retain the other. After breakfast in the morning, you will go to the front desk and will be told where to pick up your bag. After chapel service, you will go down to dinner and then will proceed to the third floor, exiting through the rear of the dining room, giving your bed ticket to the man at the door. Once on the third floor, you will receive a small plastic bag for your personal items such as wallet and important papers. You will keep this with you at all times. The bag is water proof so you can take it into the shower. Razors are also given out in a limited amount. No clothes are allowed on the walls, under the beds, or under the mattress. You will put your clothes on wire hangers and then hang them on the nearest of two iron clothing racks. These clothes will be locked away for safety during the night and come out in the morning when the lights go on.

"Showers are mandatory. If you don't strip you will not stay. There is soap in the shower. When you come out you will receive a towel and a nightshirt. There is no washing of clothes in the shower but the sink areas can be used and the clothes can be hung

112

on the walls to dry. Lights are out at 10 o'clock. They come back on Mondays through Fridays at 5:10 a.m. On the weekends it's 6:10 a.m. In the morning, beds should be stripped with sheets and pillow cases put in the large cartons on the floor. Blankets should be folded and left on the beds along with the pillows. There's a line-up to come down to breakfast, usually at 5:30."

Some of the homeless carry large bags of their meager possessions. Taking their bags and locking them away for the night removes a source of bugs and also hidden alcohol, drugs, and weapons. Having the men strip and put their clothes in a separate room is another way to keep bugs out of the beds. It also ensures safety for personal possessions. Stripping allows the man who sits at the door of the shower, dispensing soap and razors when needed, to watch for open sores. If so, a senior resident will be called. If he believes the sore appears infectious, the man will not be allowed to stay. He will be told the mission has good reciprocal arrangements with neighboring hospital clinics and if he comes back in the morning to see Chaplain Woodruff, he will be referred for examination. He will be readmitted if the clinic says there is nothing contagious. With so many men sleeping barely eighteen inches apart, the need for health precautions is obvious.

Intake begins after the recitation of the rules. Sometimes it is conducted by Don, who has a lung disability and has been on the program for a dozen years. His main responsibility is the lobby reception desk in the mornings. About 85 percent of those who come have been in the mission before. Some have beds reserved from the previous night. Nevertheless, all must report for processing.

When a man first comes, a card is filled out giving his name, date and place of birth, profession or most recent occupation, social security number, military service, if any, marital status, and source of referral. The card has little boxes to note the date of each stay. The cards of men who come regularly are kept handy. If a man does not reappear after a few weeks, his card is filed with several thousand others in large drawers to be retrieved if he later shows up.

Some have two or three cards stapled together. One gray-haired man can be seen throughout lower Manhattan maneuvering one or more shopping carts loaded with his accumulation of treasures. His cards at the mission go back twenty-three years.

A man was once freed from a murder charge through these records. A social worker was killed in lower Manhattan and police asked passersby and others if they could describe the assailant, who had fled the scene. The descriptions seemed to match a known street person. He was soon arrested. He said he could not have committed the crime because he was at the McAuley mission that night. The police checked the cards and his alibi held. He was set free.

Men waiting in the chapel are sent one at a time to a small admitting office, starting with those with tickets from the previous night or who had been referred by outside agencies or received tickets during the afternoon distribution. One night, Don was seated behind the low counter. He retrieved their cards from the file, noted the new admission date, and kept a separate list of their names and the beds to which they were assigned. When they left, he commented on some of their histories:

"That was a man who came from South Carolina for a job and was mugged. He showed up with his left eye closed and is still recovering."

Don asks all men coming for the first time for identification. Some say they have none, because of muggings, and need a short stay until they get their lives back in order. "It's also possible they say this because they simply don't want to show identification," he added. "We don't press the point."

The next man had originally been referred by the city's detoxification agency, about ten blocks north of the mission. "A man has to be sober to sign himself in there," Don said. "He'll be kept for a week or two and get good food and vitamins and a clean bed

Bunk Beds in Third Floor Dormitory

in a warm building. It's like a vacation. Then he'll be put back on the street. If he wants to stay sober, we might have a bed for him and later might even have a place for him on our program, but there are too many people on the street for all to be taken on a long-term basis."

Another man was thirty-eight and had been referred by a hospital. "He's been coming for two months," Don said. "He says he's working and thinking of going back to school to become a licensed practical nurse."

One man was in his early thirties. "He'll straighten out and get a job and go back to his family or find a place to stay and then fall by the wayside again and return here," Don said. "He's not prepared to reenter society on a long-term basis."

Another had been coming since 1970. "He's a likeable guy, but an addict and an alcoholic," Don commented. "He has been in and out of our program several times. He is useful as a translator for the Hispanic men who come here. This is not like the city detoxification program, where you have to sign up for a definite program and if you break the rules you get thrown out and not taken back. Nor is it like encounter psychology where people sit around in a circle and call one another names. Rather than pointing out each other's faults we try to help and encourage one another. We are supportive. It does seem to work."

The next man was small and frail, almost seventy years old. "He's on extended social security," Don commented. "When his check comes, he disappears. Perhaps he finds a cheap room until the money runs out. Then he comes back here."

About ten percent of those who registered that night were either too old and frail to work or were partially disabled. One man had an artificial leg under his trousers. Another had a twisted limp as if from a broken hip. The most pitiful was a fifty-year-old roofer from Puerto Rico who has been on the line for six years. Some years ago he fell from a roof and was left paralyzed on his right side. He walks with a pronounced limp, his right arm is twisted up to his cheek and he can barely speak. Like so many others, he was working off the books when he was injured. There was no workmen's compensation or insurance.

Unloading trucks is a common source of emergency work. A man who strains his back on a heavy load may be unable to work for weeks or months. Still, the jobs are eagerly sought. One trick is to jump on the running board of a truck coming off the nearby

Brooklyn Bridge from factories on Long Island. On the same night that Don was registering arrivals, there was talk of a man who slipped and was killed by a car speeding to pass the truck.

Most were in apparent good health. Their desperation was mainly due to the lack of shelter. Several had polished shoes and pressed, although somewhat tatterd, suits. They were obviously trying hard to keep up appearances. Most listed their occupations as house painters, construction laborers, messengers, truck drivers or farmers (meaning migrant agricultural workers).

"My guess is there are not many who are even high school graduates," Don said, "although we have had school teachers, engineers, computer operators and once even, a man who said he was an airport architect, whatever that is."

When Don finished registering those with tickets, he found only nine of the fifteen who had asked the Chaplain to hold a bed had shown up. Some whose names were on the list of referrals from outside agencies also had not appeared. All unclaimed beds went to those who had come at 5:30 to take their chances on finding a place in from the streets.

By about 7:15 all available beds have been allocated. Often as many as a dozen men are disappointed and have to be satisfied with a meal. There are many who come just for the food. The mission is in a non-residential area but thousands of poor live within a half-mile radius. A free hot meal at night is welcome, especially toward the end of a month when pension money runs out. The chapel seats one hundred people. It is often filled to capacity.

There is a service every night except Saturday. About thirty-five churches in the greater New York area come once a month, or every two months, to lead the prayers and hymns. Their congregations also contribute regularly to the mission's funds. One small church in Brooklyn sends $25 a quarter while a large church in a wealthy Long Island suburb contributes $600 a quarter.

The mission's budget is about $195,000 a year. Seen in perspective of city salaries, the cost of providing about 33,000 bed nights and serving about 85,000 meals a year is infinitesimal. A low-ranking clerk in a nearby court earns $30,000 a year and a middle-ranking bureaucrat in a city office earns $60,000, without including pensions, extensive medical benefits, and at least six weeks of vacation and sick days.

The business and administration side of the mission is guided by a fifteen-member board of trustees, some of whom have served as long as forty years. The chairman, Dr. David Morley, a psychiatrist formerly of New York now practicing in Greenwich, Connecticut, has been on the board since 1966. Although trustees come from a variety of professions and occupations, since the days of Alfredric Hatch there has been a strong showing of men from New York's financial world. A current member is F. Russell Esty, Chairman of the Security Columbian Division of the United States Banknote Company, who has served since 1939.

"The mission is in our geographic area, so there's a feeling we should support it," he said. "Just because there's so much absolute greed for money and power, and human beings mean nothing to the culture in the financial community, it doesn't mean in many places there are not true believers. When we have to find a man for the board, we look for somebody who loves the Lord and human beings and knows the gospel should be presented to them and that they should be helped physically too. If he also happens to be a great lawyer, businessman, or investment broker, that's fine too. If he happens to have a good amount of the Lord's money, which he knows he's holding in trust for God and he wants to give some of that to the mission, that's great too. But that would be a secondary, or tertiary, or even quaternary factor.

"All trustees are evangelical Christians, although we try to keep a balance among Baptists, Presbyterians, Plymouth Brethren, and others. We support the mission because it has the foundation of the Word of God. As 1 Corinthians 3:11 says: 'For other foundation can no man lay than that is laid, which is Jesus Christ.' Romans 10:17 says, "Faith comes by hearing and hearing by the Word of God." But trusting the Lord isn't jammed down anyone's throat. Someone can put it aside and enjoy the food or lodging and could even say, 'I don't believe in your God.' He would still not be turned away."

The mission does not receive many large contributions. Most donations come from individuals, ranging from two dollars to five hundred. Some are from outside the normal range of church support. Charles Ross recalled a few:

"Several years ago a man walked in and handed us a check for $300. Now he does that every month. I only know his name. He's a retired man who once contributed regularly to a radio gospel mission but then thought it would be better to give to a mission that he knew in his home city. Lawyers and other people who work around here sometimes drop in and leave a donation. Recently, a woman from one of the city offices came and said, 'I've been telling myself for years I would come and give you a donation. Now I've decided to quit lying and do it.' Her check was for $100.

"Once a man and woman came in. They said they lived in another part of the city and had passed by and seen our place. They asked to see our operation. I showed them around and told them how it started and what we try to do. Then we went into an office to chat. They said they had come into some money and wanted to put to a good use. The woman wrote a check and folded it and gave it to me. I got up to my office and looked at it. It was for $1,000."

Ross usually greets the men at the evening service and stays for the first hymns. He also closes the meeting. The visiting churches do the rest, providing a variety from night to night: a man and wife duet, a solo trombonist, a lilting soprano, a booming tenor, whole families of children and grandchildren. To someone accustomed to sophisticated mainline churches, this may seem naive and mawkish. But in the harsh world of homeless men, with often blurred memories of wives and children and the balm of family love, this is a brief hour of sweet solace. A child reciting a Scripture portion or the soft voice of a woman is heard in rapt silence. Surprisingly, to anyone accustomed to the somber delicacy of a standard church, the men show their appreciation with cheers and clapping hands.

In 1878 Helen Campbell was surprised at the intensity and heartiness of the singing at Jerry McAu-

Don Landaas and His Sons Donnie and Kurt, 1975

ley's recently renovated mission on Water Street. The same ardor warms the chapel at 90 Lafayette Street in the final decade of the twentieth century. The men who sit idle and snicker are few. The others sing verse after verse in loud clear voices without prompting from the visitors. Words like, "Oh Bliss of the Purified," "Take It to the Lord in Prayer" and "There Is Rest for the Weary," have deep and powerful meaning. The sound fills the large room. These are no longer isolated, alienated men. They are part of a group—comrades in suffering and perhaps in hope.

When the service ends, the men file out through a door and go down to the dining room where they line up for a dinner, generally consisting of a bowl of soup with chunks of meat; bread, butter, coffee, or tea. If the City Harvest has been bountiful, there might also be salad and pie or cake. The men are hungry. Most eat quickly and go back for another full bowl of soup. They stack their empty plastic bowls and cups as they leave. Few have leftovers to scrape into the garbage. Since some in the dining room have come just for the meal, bed tickets are collected as the men leave, thus barring entry to the dorm to those without tickets.

An attempt is always made to assign lower bunks to the elderly and disabled. The men undress quickly, with a minimum of noise. They put their clothes on hangers and then on the iron racks, put their wallets and watches, if any, in the plastic bags, shower, put on nightgowns, and get into bed. In little more than an hour since the end of the service,

perhaps 110 men have been fed and sixty or more have undressed, showered, and are in bed. These are not disciplined soldiers or cowed school boys. They are the homeless, including some of the most despised and feared men in a city notorious for its disorder. How is this model of order and mutual accommodation accomplished? It can only be ascribed to the spirit of the mission.

Some weary men are soon fast asleep. Others talk until lights out at 10 p.m. The residents, who had dinner at 5 p.m., just before the men from the line were let in for the night, can now sit in the cleared-away dining room to talk and watch television. At 4 a.m. Bob, on the reception desk, wakes up five men to begin preparing breakfast. An hour later he wakes up two more to augment security. The men in the dormitory are also stirring by then. They retrieve their clothes from the racks, which have been wheeled out from the room where they were locked overnight, and file down to the basement for a breakfast of oatmeal or cold cereal, bread and butter, and coffee or tea. Some eat two full bowls of oatmeal plus several slices of bread. Others, who have been waiting outside in the cold pre-dawn, are also let in for breakfast. Between 110 and 130 men are fed each morning. By 6:30, all men from the outside, except those waiting in the chapel to see Chaplain Woodruff, have left and the residents are sweeping and mopping the halls. In the laundry room, Larry is sorting the linen to be washed and dried. Another day has started at America's oldest rescue mission.

Evening Meal, 1989

God Is the Bookkeeper

HUNDREDS OF MEN known along the Bowery as hard cases have spent months in the residency program and then were never seen again. An assumption can be made that they have straightened out or else they would be back with their old gangs. Don, who has long worked on the reception desk, recalled some who suddenly reappear briefly:

"They will just walk in through the front door and the man at the desk will remember them. They'll say, 'I just wanted to stop by and thank you for helping me when I needed it.' They're reluctant to give details of where they are now and what they're doing; they want that memory and all records to stay here. They might contribute a little money, and we'll never see them again. Or someone will come from another part of the city and say he saw a man who was once at the mission in a bank or other office job.

"We had one guy who was here twice. The first time he messed up and started drinking and had to leave. The second time here he did well. He went back to trade school and studied maintenance and got a good job and now has a place of his own."

Don recalled another man known up and down the Bowery as a spectacular, obnoxious drunk. His name was Jim: twenty-seven years old from a small town in central Pennsylvania. He was accepted on the residency program in the fall of 1981 and appeared to be doing well. One day he announced he was returning to his family. There he tried to remain sober but kept going on binges. This continued for two years until his family threw him out. He returned to New York and managed to hold a job for six months but he started to drink steadily, lost his job, and was back on the street.

He fell in with a notorious group of winos known as the Walker Street crowd. They hung out at the corner of Walker and Lafayette streets, a block north of the mission, panhandling from the drivers of cars and trucks stopped for a traffic light and pooling their money for a bottle of cheap wine. They would fight among themselves until one or more ended battered and bleeding on the sidewalk. Ambulances were called so often that paramedics got to know their names. Sometimes they came into the mission, where they were so uncontrolled during the evening service they had to be asked to leave.

One night, when a minister asked for testimonies of those who had been helped by God, a man from the Walker Street crowd stood up and said, "If it weren't for this mission most of us would be dead now." A month later that same man did die on the corner.

In May 1984, after he joined the Walker Street crowd, Jim was in and out of the mission for brief stays. His condition grew worse and during the winter of 1986 he was more often out than in, often being told to leave because of obnoxious behavior. He was then only thirty-three but he was so bruised and scarred he looked twice his age.

Finally, in the spring of 1987 he appeared sober and asked to be taken back on the residency program. There was every reason to turn him away but the McAuley mission is a place where they don't like to say no, so Jim was taken into the residency program again. In June 1987 he said the Lord had entered his life. Over the next three months he gave frequent testimonies thanking God for saving him. He then returned to his family in Pennsylvania and as far as anyone has heard, is living a peaceful, settled life.

The values and mystery of Christianity are tangible only when they are incarnated in a human life. Then the invisible presence is given flesh.

The McAuley mission tries to accomplish what is known in theology as the gospel of reconciliation. Briefly, this maintains that man is separated from God by original sin. Christ atoned for this sin by His death. Anyone who accepts this act of atonement—who accepts Christ as Saviour—can be reunited with God. He will then discover that God has always had a personal interest in his life. This belief maintains that God desires the reconciliation to take place although an individual may not be aware of His concern. God will lead a man to a point where reconciliation can take place. Then, if a man throws aside whatever doubts he may have, stops searching for his solution, recognizes that act of atonement, and accepts Christ as his Saviour, reconciliation will take place.

This is the act of conversion. A converted man often looks back and notices a number of what he once might have thought of as unrelated happenstances. Why did Jerry McAuley carefully put the cell Bible into the ventilator shaft so that he could take it out years later? Why did Orville Gardner and not someone else come to Sing Sing? Why was it that on this particular day McAuley did not have any of his usual novels so that he took out the Bible to help pass the long and boring day?

The scientific mind will look to logic and a table of mathematical probabilities. It may be said that the converted man is seeking those incidents that reinforce his new belief and that he ignores or forgets other incidents that may point to a contrary conclusion.

But the converted man will look to his present surroundings. He will see he is happier and more content than he once was. He is able to bear the frustrations of daily life. When troubled, he can find guidance through prayer. He is positive this cannot be the result of mere chance. What seems miraculous is that rebirth can come not only to the comfortable or well educated or those raised in religious surroundings but also to the lost sheep of the flock.

For instance, there is William. William came from a deeply religious family and was baptized when he was twelve. Then he dropped out of high school and soon had a $200-a-day heroin habit. He married and had a son. But his wife was an addict too and his son died. He drifted to New York and was eventually arrested and spent seven years in jail. On his release, he spent twenty-eight months in a drug rehabilitation program and then he drifted aimlessly among the homeless for six months until finding his way to the mission.

"I first came to the mission in 1986," he recalled. "I had nothing and no place to go. I stayed here just that one night and came back the next night and then after a while, I came back regularly. The people here reached out to me and gave me a feeling they cared. I just wanted to give up. At the evening prayer service, I just sat back. I just wanted to pass time. After that, things started to change. They gave me a chance to get on the residence program. I was in housekeeping, making beds. I started to lean toward the Lord and trust in Him. I didn't change completely but a lot of things I used to do I now didn't do, such as drugs and alcohol, and as time went along, I started getting stronger and stronger. I went back down south to try to reunite with my family. My mother had passed on and my father didn't know if I was coming back so he let my cousin take over the car body shop he owned. My cousin

said I could work with him but I chose to come back here and finish what I started in getting my life together."

At the mission again, William joined group Bible studies and found a part-time job. He also went back to school and earned a high school equivalency diploma.

"The Lord means a lot to me," he said. "He's the one who gave me right directions and the hope that I could get myself back together. The Lord showed me things as I went along. I had blown my credibility with other people and myself. I didn't feel people could trust me any more. I did a lot of wrong things. I went to jail and had a bad record. I was an outcast. When I look back at it, I realize it had to be the Lord as well as myself to do it. Once you accept Him, there are a lot of things you choose to do but you can't do because the Lord has His way with you. I didn't have the strength myself to do it. I knew the Lord long before I came here. I went to church every Sunday when I was a child but I didn't understand the Lord then as I do now. I drifted away from the church by coming into the streets, shooting drugs, drinking alcohol, sleeping in the streets as a homeless person.

"The Lord was always with me but I thought He had left me. When I started reading my Scriptures and putting two and two together, I saw these things are not just a coincidence. There's got to be a reason. I have never been as stable other than when I was in jail. I thank the Lord."

William now has a full-time job as a truck driver and is looking for an apartment, but a place to live for a man making $7 an hour is hard to find in New York. Sometimes, when he leaves the mission on a weekend pass, he feels the old temptations and has to return and "gas up" with spiritual fuel:

William: "The Lord was always with me, but I thought He had left me

118

"There are a lot of things I would like to do but I just can't bring myself to do. I visit friends and they might start drinking beer and doing or talking something negative. I just say, 'I got to go.' I come back because I don't trust myself enough. But I'm getting to that point. I'm working all day and I'm around people who are steady and I've gained a lot of support within myself. I pray every night, asking God to have HIS way with me and to show me the way so I can follow and trust in Him. I want to be with the Lord some day."

And yet, William's experiences are a rare exception. There are many hundreds who have stayed for a few days or weeks and then left, perhaps to return to drink or drugs or prison. Is the effort justified by the few whose rescue is known?

This is not a new question. It was asked eighty years ago by Ray Stannard Baker, one of the most respected American journalists of his time. In 1909 he wrote a series of articles on religion in New York for *American Magazine*. He did not find much that pleased him and was particularly scathing of Trinity Church in lower Manhattan, which drew a large income from slum tenements. He thought the "old" McAuley mission was an exception, calling it "one of the most extraordinary institutions in the country."

"Here in this mission of the slums, among the lowest of the low," he wrote, "is demonstrated again and again the power of a living religion to reconstruct the individual human life. And it apparently makes not the slightest difference whether the man is unlettered or a university graduate; the power of reconstruction is the same."

He examined the McAuley mission in an article titled "Lift Men from the Gutter? or Remove the Gutter? Which?" He asked, "How can such things be in an age which calls itself civilized? . . . Why should not a civilized nation provide a better school of training than the Bowery for bold and original boys like Jerry McAuley? Why, indeed, should there be any Bowery? Why should the saloonkeeper be more friendly than the church? Why all these potent agencies for tearing down and ruining men and women and why, after having ruined tens of thousands of souls, should a few feeble missions be maintained to drag away, here and there, a single man from out of the wholesale slaughter?"

While praising the mission, he pointed out how few were its successes. He estimated the proportion who were converted at perhaps 5 percent of those who came forward to ask for prayers. This, he said, did not include the hundreds who did not ask for prayers or the thousands who never visited the mission.

"How futile the church seems under such circumstances," he wrote. "Is it any wonder that the clergy should be discouraged? Is it any wonder that people should be crowding the church aside and looking to new ways of producing better results in our civilization?"

Since Baker wrote these words, Americans are better housed, fed, clothed, and educated than ever before, yet the agencies for tearing down and ruining men are as strong as ever. Perhaps the church does seem futile, and intellectuals can still look forward to the end of religion—but not among wealthy America's homeless and outcasts.

Baker called the McAuley mission an example of a living religion. That is what it is: a model society where those who believe in the atoning sacrifice of Christ demonstrate both the meaning and the results of this faith. Because of Jerry McAuley's vision, there has been an island of love and compassion for generation after generation, through peace and war, depression and prosperity. It has always been needed because the nature of man and sin remains unchanged.

How do you judge success or failure? Samuel Hadley used to say, "God is the bookkeeper." Who can tell what seed may have fallen on barren ground and what seed may have taken slow root? It is healthy to have doubts and ask questions. History and the headlines teach us to be cautious of those who would lead us in one direction or another, be they religious or secular leaders. But anyone who would wave away what is happening at the McAuley Water Street Mission should be prepared to produce an alternative.

Who can find a secular equivalent to these missionaries to the miserable? Who can find another philosophy that will motivate generations of men to devote their lives to helping the most woebegone creatures of our society? Who can find some other belief that will enable a drunkard or ex-convict to shake off his burden of guilt and live again as a normal man in a normal society.

The evangelists of Lafayette Street demonstrate their love of God by showing concern for man. They are custodians of the ark of faith. The secular world has little more to offer the Bowery man than a meal and a bed in a disorderly, dangerous, bug-ridden municipal lodging house. The evangelists offer him God and a new life.

Bibliography

HISTORIC

Asbury, Herbert. 1928. *The Gangs of New York*. New York: Knopf.

Campbell, Helen. 1882. *Darkness and Daylight: or Lights and Shadows of New York Life*. New York: Fords, Howard and Hulbert.

———. 1893. *The Problem of the Poor; A Record of Quiet Work in Unquiet Places*. Hartford CT: A. D. Worthington and Co.

Chapman, J. Wilbur. 1902. *S. H. Hadley of Water Street: A Miracle of Grace*. Old Tappan NJ: Fleming H. Revel Co.

Ervine, St. John. 1934. *God's Soldier: General William Booth*. London: Heineman.

Gough, John Bartholomew. 1882. *Sunlight and Shadow: or Gleanings from My Life Work*. London: Hodder and Stoughton.

———. 1887. *Platform Echoes: or Living Truths for Head and Heart*. Hartford CT: A. D. Worthington and Co.

Hadley, Samuel H. 1902. *Down in Water Street. A Story of Sixteen Years Life and Work in Water Street Mission*. Old Tappan NJ: Fleming H. Revell Co.

Miller, Kenneth D. and Ethel Prince Miller. 1962. *The People Are The City*. New York: Macmillan.

Offord, Robert Marshal (Ed.) 1907. *Jerry McAuley, An Apostle to the Lost*. New York: American Tract Society, Fifth edition.

Roberts, Philip Ilott. 1912. *The Dry Dock of a Thousand Wrecks*. Old Tappan NJ: FLeming H. Ravell and Co.

Sweet, William Warren. 1944. *Revivalism in America, Its Origin, Growth and Decline*. New York: Scribner.

Wyburn, S. May. 1936. *"But, Until Seventy Times Seven", Jeremiah, Samuel, John*. Neptune NJ: Loizeaux Brothers.

PAMPHLETS

Annual Reports, McAuley Water Street Mission, 1887–1955.

Annual Report, Howard Mission and Home for Little Wanderers, 1895.

Annual Report, Water Street Home for Women, 1870.

Annual Reports, Prison Association of New York, 1875–1880.

Annual Reports, New York City Mission Society, 1863–1875.

Dunn, Michael. 1884. *An interesting account of his 35 years a prisoner . . . and his . . . work in founding the Home of Industry and Refuge for discharged convicts*. San Francisco: Bacon and Company.

Bliss, William R. (Ed.). 1880. *Down in Water Street Every Evening*. New York.

Brown, Helen E (Ed.). 1876. *Transformed: or The History of a River Thief, Briefly Told*. New York.

Dyer, Oliver. 1868. *The Wickedest Man in New York*. "Truth Stranger than Fiction*. New York: Dwight and Co.

Mercer, Edward Clifford. 1928. *A Twentieth Century Miracle*. Salisbury CT: E. C. Mercer.

Stryker, Peter. 1866. *The Lower Depths of the Great American Metropolis*. New York: Bancroft & Co.

MAGAZINES AND NEWSPAPERS

American Magazine, July 1909.

Century Magazine, January 1911.

Frank Leslie's Illustrated Newspaper, 1866–1886.

Outlook, February 2, 1901.

New York Observer

New York Herald

The World

MODERN

Bahr, Howard M. 1973. *Skid Row: An Introduction to Disaffiliation*. New York: Oxford University Press, pp. 31–35.

Blumberg, Leonard U. and Thomas F. Shipley and Stephen Barsky. 1978. *Liquor and Poverty: Skid Row as a Human Condition*, Rutgers, New Jersey: Rutgers Center of Alcohol Studies, pp. 1–25, 195–205.

Bogue, Donald J. 1963. *Skid Row in American Cities*. Chicago: University of Chicago, pp. 46–77, 475–496.

Hunter, James Davison. 1987. *Evangelicalism: The Coming Generation*. Chicago: University of Chicago Press, pp. 3, 6–7.

James, William. 1929. *The Varieties of Religious Experience*. New York: Modern Library, pp. 186–189, 218–238, 340–341.

Rossi, Peter H. 1989. *Down and Out in America: The Origins of Homelessness*. Chicago: University of Chicago Press, pp. 20–44.

Stark, Rodney and William Sims Bainbridge. 1985. *The Future of Religion: Secularization, Revival, and Cult Formation*. Berkeley: University of California Press, pp. 1, 10–12.

ARTICLES

Fry, Lincoln J. and John Miller. *Responding to Skid Row Alcoholism: Self-Defeating Arrangement in an Innovative Program*. Social Problems 22:5 (June 1975), pp. 665–687.

Hopper, Kim. *More than Passing Strange: Homelessness and Mental Illness in New York City*. American Ethnologist, 15:1 (Feb. 1988), pp. 155–167.

Jones, Timothy K. *Tracking America's Souls*. Christianity Today, Nov. 17, 1989, pp. 22–25.

Lee, Barrett A. *The Disappearance of Skid Row: Some Ecological Evidence*. Urban Affairs Quarterly. 16:1 (Sept. 1980), pp. 81–107.

Mauss, Armand L. *Salvation and Survival on Skid Row: A Comment on Rooney*. Social Forces 60:3 (March 1982), pp. 898–907.

Rooney, James F. *Organizational Success through Program Failure: Skid Row Rescue Missions*. Social Forces, 58:3 (March 1980), pp. 904–24.

———. *Reply to Mauss*. Social Forces 60:3 (March 1982), pp. 905–07.

Index

121

ABOUT THE AUTHOR

Arthur Bonner was born in 1922 and has been a radio, television, and print journalist all his life. He was a foreign correspondent in India for eight years in the 1950s and later reported from Latin America and Africa before returning to the United States as a television writer and producer. When he was sixty-two, he took early retirement from WNBC-TV in New York to become a special correspondent for *The New York Times*. He traveled extensively with the mujahidin in Afghanistan and returned to the United States in 1986 to write *Among the Afghans*, published in 1987 by Duke University. He then returned to India to research the deterioration since the heady 1950's and wrote *Averting the Apocalypse: Social Movements in India Today*, published by Duke University in 1990.

JERRY MCAULEY AND HIS MISSION
© 1967 Loizeaux Brothers. All rights reserved.

Revisions and additions © 1990 Arthur Bonner.

Published by Loizeaux Brothers, Inc., a nonprofit organization devoted to the Lord's work and to the spread of his truth.

Printed in the United States of America.

Revised Edition

Library of Congress Cataloging-in-Publication Data

Bonner, Arthur.
Jerry McAuley and his mission / Arthur Bonner. — Rev. ed.
p.   cm.
Includes bibliographical references.
ISBN 0-87213-060-6
1. McAuley, Jeremiah, 1839–1884.   2. Missionaries—New York—New York—Biography.   3. City missions—New York—New York—History.
4. McAuley Water Street Mission—History.   I. Title.
BV2657.M3B6   1990
267′.1′092—dc20

[B]   90-31906
                                                              CIP

PICTURE CREDITS

Pictures not specifically credited are from the McAuley Water Street Mission.

New York Public Library: Cover, Pages 4, 16, 18, 19, 20, 25, 27, 28, 29, 31, 32, 35, 42, 43, 45, 51, 58, 63, 68, 69, 70, 75, 76 left, 77, 80, 88, 103, 104 bottom

New York Public Library, Print Division: Page 59

Metropolitan Museum of Art, Gift of Frederick H. Hatch, 1926: Page 36

Narcissa Brinkley: Pages 110, 113, 116, 118

John Farrell: Pages 107 bottom left, 112

William Hughes: Pages 8, 106, 107 top right, 108 top left

Bread Line at Third Mission, 1913